28 FUNDAMENTAL BELIEFS

Simply Put.

WHAT GOD'S BEEN SAYING ALL ALONG

Loron Wade

Published by Review and Herald® Publishing Association, Hagerstown, MD 21741-1119

Review and Herald® titles may be purchased in bulk for educational, business, fund-raising, or sales promotional use. For information, e-mail SpecialMarkets@reviewandherald.com

The Review and Herald® Publishing Association publishes biblically based materials for spiritual, physical, and mental growth and Christian discipleship.

The author assumes full responsibility for the accuracy of all facts and quotations as cited in this book.

Unless otherwise indicated, Scripture quotations are from the New American Standard Bible, copyright © 1960, 962, 1963, 1968, 1971, 1972, 1973, 1975, 1994 by The Lockman Foundation. Used by permission.

Texts credited to Clear Word are from *The Clear Word,* copyright © 1994, 2000, 2003, 2004, 2006 by Review and Herald Publishing Association. All rights reserved.
Texts credited to Message are from *The Message.* Copyright © 1993, 1994, 1995, 1996, 2000, 2001, 2002. Used by permission of NavPress Publishing Group.
Texts credited to NEB are from *The New English Bible.* © The Delegates of the Oxford University Press and the Syndics of the Cambridge University Press 1961, 1970. Reprinted by permission.
Texts credited to NIV are from the Holy Bible, *New International Version.* Copyright © 1973, 1978, 1984, International Bible Society. Used by permission of Zondervan Bible Publishers.
Texts credited to NKJV are from the New King James Version. Copyright © 1979, 1980, 1982 by Thomas Nelson, Inc. Used by permission. All rights reserved.
Scripture quotations marked NLT are taken from the *Holy Bible,* New Living Translation, copyright © 1996. Used by permission of Tyndale House Publishers, Inc., Wheaton, Illinois 60189. All rights reserved.
Bible texts credited to NRSV are from the New Revised Standard Version of the Bible, copyright © 1989 by the Division of Christian Education of the National Council of the Churches of Christ in the U.S.A. Used by permission.
Bible texts credited RSV are from the Revised Standard Version of the Bible, copyright © 1946, 1952, 1971, by the Division of Christian Education of the National Council of the Churches of Christ in the U.S.A. Used by permission.
Verses marked TLB are taken from *The Living Bible,* copyright © 1971 by Tyndale House Publishers, Wheaton, Ill. Used by permission.

This book was
Edited by Gerald Wheeler
Copyedited by James Cavil
Cover designed by Tricia Wegh/Trent Truman
Interior designed by Tina M Ivany
Cover art by ©iStockphoto.com/aldomurillo
Typeset: Bembo 11/14

PRINTED IN U.S.A.

13 12 11 10 09   5 4 3 2 1

Library of Congress Cataloging-in-Publication Data
Wade, Loron, 1938-   .
   Simply put: what God's been saying all along / Loron Wade
      p. cm.
1. Christian life—Meditations. 2. Bible—Meditations. 3. Christianity—Meditations. I. Title.
BV4501.3.W33 2009
248.4—dc22

ISBN 978-0-8280-2477-8

Also by Loron Wade:
   The Ten Commandments
To order, call 1-800-765-6955. Visit us at **www.reviewandherald.com** for information on other Review and Herald® products.

Contents

Chapter 1

Simon's Blessing

Classes had ended for the day, and I was gratefully heading for the nearest exit when the dean appeared in the doorway of his office. "Loron," he said, "I need to have a word with you."

As you probably know, some "words" take longer to pronounce than others. This one in particular required about 45 minutes. Of course, what my boss meant was that he had a message for me—a communication. He was naming me to chair an ad hoc committee, and he wanted to share his vision of what it might accomplish.

I sat down across from him, but without really settling into the chair. One hand kept a tight grip on my briefcase, and the other jangled the car keys. But then, as the dean outlined his ideas, I began to catch his enthusiasm and see the possibilities. Before long, the briefcase sat on the floor, and I was leaning over his desk, contributing and getting involved as he drew arrows and boxes on a piece of paper. "Words," it would appear, differ not only in length but also in their value and importance. It was clear that here was a visionary project that could be a great benefit to our students.

The Bible pictures God standing in the doorway of *His* office and saying: "I would like to have a word with you." In fact—you may have noticed— that's what He calls His message: "The Word of God."

It also pictures most of us rushing right on by.

We are not sure whether what He has to say is worth the time and effort it takes to listen. Too busy, too tired, too harried and hurried, we mutter, "Maybe later," and brush past Him. "Right now, I have a career to think about, a family to raise, taxes to pay . . . you know, a lot of really important things."

Here is how He describes the situation through the prophet Isaiah:

"I kept saying 'I'm here, I'm right here'
    to a nation that ignored me.
I reached out day after day
    to a people who turned their backs on me."
    —Isaiah 65:1, 2, Message

It was that way when Jesus was here too. One day He took His disciples aside and asked them, "Who do people say that I am?" (Matthew 16:13, paraphrase). What do they think about Me?

He already knew the answer, of course, but He wanted to make sure that His disciples recognized it too.

They did, but their reply was evasive—they were trying to be kind: "Well, some people think that maybe You're a reincarnation of John the Baptist. Others say You remind them of one of the prophets."

That was a polite way of saying: "People don't think You have a mission beyond what they've seen before. You're OK. While You do say some nice things, that's as far as it goes for most of them. They don't really think of You as the Messiah."

For three years He had lived and worked among them. All over the land were people whose lives He had changed, individuals who had been born blind and now could see, lepers who could go home again and embrace their loved ones. Day after day He had taught them. Whenever and wherever people were willing to open their hearts and their ears, Jesus had spoken, offering them a new vision of God and confronting them with a need for change. He had comforted, challenged, encouraged, and given them hope.

But still they shook their heads. Only a few were willing to make the commitment that conviction requires, so they backed off from conviction. Yes, they heard His voice, but they rushed right on by. When you're looking for a way to doubt, it really isn't hard to find one.

"Who is this fellow? H'mmm. I guess He's some sort of prophet? Yeah, that's it. He must be a prophet." They were willing to take the benefits He offered: Healing? Sure, that's fine. A free meal by the lake? Any time! But that was it as far as most of them were concerned.

Then, in the same quiet voice, Jesus said to His disciples: *"And how about you?"*

That was the crucial question: *Who do* you *think I am? Are you willing to stand up and be counted? Have you gotten the message that others are too busy, too careless, or too indifferent to hear? Or are you going to rush on by too?*

Like a candle in the dark, Peter's answer shines all the brighter against the general background of indifference and rejection. With profound feeling and conviction he answered:

"You are the Christ, the Son of the living God" (Matthew 16:16).

It was a critical moment in the history of faith.

"You Are Peter"

Now listen carefully to Jesus' response:

"Blessed are you, Simon Bar-jona, because flesh and blood did not reveal this to you, but My Father who is in heaven" (verse 17).

Jesus' meaning will be clearer if we think about what He did *not* say. He didn't respond, "Congratulations! You are really sharp."

What He did comment was: "You have been blessed!"

And what was Simon's blessing?

"You didn't get this from flesh and blood." This conviction you have that I am the Messiah is not from any human source. Definitely it is not a product of your own fertile brain. Nor is it something that you learned at your mother's knee, and you certainly didn't hear it from any of the leaders at the Temple.

While others had rushed on by, Simon had paused to listen. The blessing that he had received was a revelation directly from "My Father who is in heaven."

But make no mistake: Simon's blessing was not simply the fact that he had gotten a message—it was the Message itself. What the Spirit had revealed to him was "Christ, the Son of the living God." That was his blessing.

The apostle John later wrote: *The Word* [that is, the Word of God] became flesh, and dwelt among us" (John 1:14). Jesus is the Word of God (John 1:1-3; Revelation 19:13)—a communication that God has sent to the world. He is God's thoughts made audible, God's portrait placed on a pedestal with all the spotlights focused on it. When Jesus gathered children in His arms and spoke words of encouragement to their mothers; when He sat and taught His disciples beside the lake; when He calmed the storm and threw the money changers out of the Temple—in all these things He was saying:

God is like this. Christ came to highlight what God has been trying to tell us while standing in the doorway, and while most of us have been rushing right on by.

The Written Word—that is, the Bible, with its nouns and pronouns and verbs, the intelligible message of Scripture—has been recorded by human hands and preserved, transmitted, translated, and interpreted by them. It is printed with ink on paper, bound, shipped, and sold in stores. The Bible is the medium. But the medium is *not* the Message. The Message is Jesus. Jesus is the one that all of Scripture points to. And Jesus was the blessing that Simon had received.

But listen! Jesus has not finished speaking. "I also say to you that you are Peter, and upon this rock I will build My church, and the gates of Hades will not overpower it" (Matthew 16:18).

At least, that is how it comes across in translation. But, of course, Jesus didn't really say, "You are Peter." He couldn't have said that, because the name "Peter" didn't exist yet. What He said was "You are a stone."

Think what this means! Simon was not the calmest of individuals. Impulsive and impetuous, he tended to speak and afterward think about what he should have said. But here Jesus is calling him a stone, something you can count on, something solid, steady, and reliable.

What had made the difference? Simon had received the Word—He had received Jesus, and that is what made all the difference.

That's what accepting the Word into the life does for people. Peter himself explained it later: "And coming to Him [to Jesus] as to a living stone, . . . you also, as living stones, are being built up as a spiritual house" (1 Peter 2:4, 5).

Jesus, of course, is the great "living stone"—the ultimate definition of "solid." Peter is thinking of Jesus as the cornerstone, taking his cue from Psalm 118:22, which He quotes in the next line.[1] Everything else is squared and plumbed by comparing it to Jesus. He is the one who "holds all the parts together" (Ephesians 2:21, Message). But the cornerstone is not the whole building. "You also, as living stones, are being built up as a spiritual house."

The apostle is trying to tell us that the miracle that had taken place in his life was not for him alone. All who come to Jesus—everyone who receives the Word—will also become solid reliable material. And out of these "living stones" Jesus is building His church, a structure so strong and unshakable that even "the gates of Hades" cannot overthrow it (Matthew 16:18).

"The word of God is living and active and sharper than any two-edged sword" (Hebrews 4:12). The word translated "active" is related to the word for "energy." God's Word is a powerhouse, throbbing with force and energy. That power can take weak humans such as Peter—and you and me—and turn us into solid stones that God can use in building up His kingdom.

Do you remember what the angel said to the virgin Mary when He told her that she would be the mother of Jesus?

"The Holy Spirit will come upon you,
   the power of the Highest hover over you;
Therefore, the child you bring to birth
   will be called Holy, Son of God."
—Luke 1:35, Message

We cannot fully understand this text, and neither can we understand what happens when the Holy Spirit and the power of the Most High enter the life of a sinful man or woman who is then born again to become truly a child of God and begin a life of order and purpose.

Jesus spoke of it as a mystery. We can see its effects, He said, but we cannot explain it. "You hear [the wind] rustling through the trees, but you have no idea where it comes from or where it's headed next. That's the way it is with everyone who is 'born from above' by the wind of God, the Spirit of God" (John 3:8, Message).

It had happened to Peter, and that's why Jesus said He had become a living stone. Here is the Word, the Message that God has been trying to get across to us while standing at the door of His office, and while most of us have been rushing right on by.

Questions

People ask a lot of questions about the Bible today. I say "today," but with slight variations, they've been raising the same questions for centuries: How does "inspiration" work? What part of the Bible is human and what part is divine? How did the culture of its time and place shape it? What about the authors' personal agendas? How did their intellectual limitations and biases affect what they wrote? Does Scripture contain internal contradictions? Could there be errors in some historical details?

Some of these questions may help us uncover the true meaning of the text. But the danger is that we can easily mistake the trees for the forest, the medium for the message. While trying to figure out how many blind men Jesus healed at Jericho, for example, we can fail totally to get the Message, to perceive—and receive—the "Word of God" that the text seeks to bring us.

The apostle speaks of God's self-revelation as a penetrating sword. It cuts through the theobabble and breaks through our defensive shell. Debating the details does not help us to find this Word that reaches into the soul and spirit. Remember, the text says that the Word of God is alive. You cannot really dissect something while it is still alive. If you try, you will end up killing it.

The Bible is the Word of God, but the Word of God is not the Bible. That is, God's Word, His total communication with us, is not limited and bound in by the written text. Rather, the Bible is part of God's incredible effort to get His message across. Jesus is the living Word to which the Written Word leads us. Look to Jesus, study His life and character, accept His friendship, open your heart to His love, receive Him as the Word, and your doubt and confusion will fall away.

Getting the Message

In 1898 the United States prepared to send troops to Cuba in support of the Cuban struggle for independence. But before the Army could begin landing, it was imperative to establish contact with the Cuban insurgents and coordinate efforts with them.

American intelligence knew that General Calixto García, the leader of the rebel forces, was somewhere in central Cuba, but no one knew exactly where.

President McKinley sent for a young lieutenant named Andrew Rowan and commissioned him to carry a message to García. Four days after receiving his assignment, Rowan landed off the south coast of Cuba from an open boat and disappeared into the jungle. Three weeks later he came out on the opposite side of the island, having traversed the Sierra Maestra and many miles of hostile territory—and having delivered his message to García.

It is a dramatic story of valor and heroism on the part of Rowan and the Cubans who risked their lives to aid him. They were drenched by rain, and at other times soaked in sweat as they went slipping and stumbling over mountain trails. Violent death stalked them at every step and very nearly overtook them at a number of points. In the dim, tree-shadowed moonlight Rowan caught a faint glimmer and twisted off his hammock a split second before a machete came crashing down.

Nevertheless, he persevered and got his message through. The deadly nature of his mission becomes even clearer by a detail usually omitted when historians or biographers recount Rowan's heroic exploit.[2] President McKinley actually sent three messengers to contact the Cuban forces. The other two didn't make it.

We need to ask at least two questions about the story, and both are relevant to what we are discussing about the Word of God:

1. Why was Rowan willing to take such a risk, and make such an effort to get through with his message?

It was because he understood his mission's significance and importance. Did he realize that it might cost him his life? Of course he did. But he never doubted that it was worth it. He understood what was at stake and why the message had to get through.

Jesus told about a man who planted a vineyard and then went away. At harvesttime he sent a series of messengers to collect his profits. The farmhands beat up one messenger, threw stones at another, and tossed out a third. The owner dispatched still more messengers with similar results. Finally, he decided to send his own son, saying: "They will respect my son" (Matthew 21:37).

The story, of course, is a parable. The "messengers" represent the prophets that God called to try to get His message across. The "Son" is Jesus. Jesus is proof of the incredible persistence and the incomprehensible sacrifice of God. Why was He willing to take such a terrible risk, to make such a sacrifice? I leave the question for your consideration.

2. The second question we would have to ask is: *What do you think must have been García's attitude when the priceless letter reached him?*

"What is it you're bringing? Oh, a letter from the president of the United States. Sure, put it over there on the shelf. Maybe I'll take a look at it after a while. Right now I have a career to think about, a family to raise, taxes to pay . . . you know, a lot of really important things.

"What? You say two men died trying to get here with this message? Well, that's too bad, but I'm pretty busy right now. And by the time I finish with all I've got to do, I'll be so tired I won't be able to keep my eyes open. Maybe I'll take a look at it in the morning if I don't get up too late for that."

"I need to have a Word with you," Jesus says, holding out to us the Word of God. And He waits for our answer, eager to have us experience its incredible energy, its solidifying, life-transforming power.

You probably sense an appeal, an invitation, in what I am saying. But maybe it isn't really needed. If you have read this far, it is because you have already begun to respond. If not, you probably would have stopped after the first couple paragraphs.

Nevertheless, it will strengthen and focus your ideas if you will take a moment to record a thoughtful response in your own words to express your personal conviction and sense of purpose as you think about the Word of God.

_____

_____

_____

_____

---

[1] "The stone which the builders rejected has become the chief cornerstone." We know that Peter had the text in mind because he quoted it a couple lines later (verse 7).

[2] *A Message to Garcia,* by Elbert Hubbard, is one of the best-selling books of all time.

Chapter 2

When the Bell Rings, It's for You

A photo appeared in the news recently of a multimillion-dollar home that turned into a pile of kindling when it tumbled over a cliff and crashed into Lake Michigan. One or two others nearby still teetered on the edge.

The owners must have chosen the site for its spectacular view, without thinking how winter storms and pounding waves might affect the soft glacial deposits that supported their mansions.

The brief news report didn't give many details, so that leaves us free to imagine a bit . . .

It's pouring rain as we drive past one of these places. In a flash of lightning we can see a luxurious house starting to sag on the back side where the rain-soaked earth has begun giving way. Horrified, we pull over. Hesitating only a few seconds, we make a dash for the front door. To our amazement, the party of the century is going on inside. The music is cranked up to about 100 decibels, and people are flying past the windows.

We ring the bell frantically, but of course no one inside can hear. In desperation we run to the side and pound on a window. Finally someone notices. They approach and yell at us above the din, "Hey, watcha doin' out there? Come on in an' join the fun."

"No, no," we shout, pointing to the back of the house. "The bluff is giving way. There's not much time. Please, please, tell everyone."

Our jolly reveler does pass on the message. Great uproarious laughter erupts, and someone ups the music another notch.

Perhaps my illustration gives some sense of God's frustration with the human race. Now, if you think that God could never feel frustrated, please read the following text:

"The whole earth is wrapped in darkness,
   all people sunk in deep darkness."
   —Isaiah 60:2, Message
   And this one:
"God-light streamed into the world,
   but men and women everywhere
   ran for the darkness."
   —John 3:19, Message.

Incredible Effort

Do you really want to know how intent God is about getting His message across, and how great is His frustration as He rings our bell? Here is one of the least-known stories in the Bible. It's not on anybody's list of favorites, and it certainly isn't one that we read to our children at bedtime.

Israel was fighting Mesha, king of Moab. God had spoken through the prophet Elisha, promising victory to His people, and it was coming. It seemed as if nothing could stop them.

But something did. King Mesha "took his oldest son who was to reign in his place, and offered him as a burnt offering" (2 Kings 3:27). He did it in the most visible place possible—on top of the city wall, in plain sight of the besieging armies. The men of Israel stopped fighting and stared in horror and awe. Then silently and with no more will to fight, they turned and went home.

We're a long way from that time and culture, and yet their reaction is not difficult to understand. It's hard even to imagine such a sacrifice. The Moabite king gave the most precious thing he could possibly have offered, but by doing it, he saved his people.

Now listen to the most famous, the best-loved text in the Bible:
"God so loved the world,
   that He gave *His* only begotten Son,
   that whoever believes in Him
      shall not perish,
   but have eternal life."
   —John 3:16

That, my friend, is how earnest and fervent God is. And that is the price He was willing to pay.

If I were the one pounding on the window of those boozy people, if I were standing out there in the rain, freezing, while the cliff crumbles away and they were laughing at me, you know what I'd do? That's right—of course: I'd leave those crazies and run for my life.

But that's *not* what Jesus did. He came to call us to salvation, and He did it with a clear decision to stay right here and go over the cliff with us. He chose to share in our self-destruction, so that He could pull at least some people out of the wreckage—when we would finally sober up enough to listen.

Darkness on the Brain

What could possibly have made Him decide to do such a thing? Think about it for a minute: If the people in the doomed house laugh at my warning, it's because they think I'm the crazy one. They don't know me and see no reason to believe what I'm telling them about the danger. Humanity had a similar problem. They didn't know God. Even the people who claimed to be His followers had totally misunderstood Him. This was the terrifying "darkness" that covered the earth. Darkness had gotten into their brains. Because they had listened so long to the deafening stereo of evil, it was impossible to hear Him frantically ringing their bell.

That is why Jesus came. By accepting an infinite humiliation, by sharing our condition, by living as a human, and finally, by dying a horrifying death in the sight of everyone—only by such extreme measures could He break through and get His message across. At every step "God was in Christ reconciling the world to Himself" (2 Corinthians 5:19).

Do you know what this tells me? That I need to get away from the tremendous noise all around me and do some careful listening. I must open the Bible and read it, thinking as I do: This is God ringing my bell. What is He trying to say?

When I say "careful listening" I'm not talking about going into a trance, or doing something in which you have to sit cross-legged on the floor. Rather, I mean paying closer attention to His Word, asking Him for guidance, and using our brains to think about the implications of each verse or group of verses.

Here is a practical example to illustrate what I mean. In each of these passages, notice especially what Jesus is telling us about His Father.

1. "Are not five sparrows sold for two cents? Yet not one of them is forgotten before God. Indeed, the very hairs of your head are all numbered. Do not fear; you are more valuable than many sparrows" (Luke 12:6, 7).

From this we learn that God

_____.

2. "And they were bringing children to Him so that He might touch them; but the disciples rebuked them. But when Jesus saw this, He was indignant and said to them, 'Permit the children to come to Me; do not hinder them; for the kingdom of God belongs to such as these'" (Mark 10:13, 14).

From this we learn that God

_____.

3. "For God did not send the Son into the world to judge the world, but that the world might be saved through Him" (John 3:17).

From this we learn that God

_____.

4. "And He said to them, 'You are those who justify yourselves in the sight of men, but God knows your hearts'" (Luke 16:15).

From this we learn that God

_____.

5. "And He found in the temple those who were selling oxen and sheep and doves, and the money changers seated at their tables. And He made a scourge of cords, and drove them all out of the temple, with the sheep and the oxen; and He poured out the coins of the money changers and overturned their tables; and to those who were selling the doves He said, 'Take these things away; stop making My Father's house a place of business'" (John 2:14-16).

From this we learn that God

_____.

Only five verses, but they serve to illustrate my point. Each one opens a doorway to further study. You really don't have to wait for someone to lead you there. Take the Bible in your own hands and study it—especially, as I say, the Gospels. (This term refers to the books of Matthew, Mark, Luke, and John, which tell about the life and teachings of Jesus.)

Think of how the sky lights up at sunrise. It will be like that for you. You will discover a Friend. Each day will bring you new surprises as you learn to love Him more and more.

At the end of this book you will find a summary of some of the things that the Bible teaches about God and many other topics. But I want to assure you that it is only a bare-bones minimum of what you will learn as you continue to study.

Hear that sound? It's God ringing your bell.

Chapter 3

You Can't Get There From Here

A Vermont farmer is hoeing close to his rock-wall fence when a passing traveler stops to ask the way to Middlebury. The old man regards the stranger for a few solemn moments and then shakes his head. "You can't get there from here," he says, and goes back to his hoeing.

The interesting thing about such a story is how hard so many people work at proving the old man was wrong.

I grew up at the edge of the Rocky Mountains, an area known for its spectacular landscape. It has a lot of seemingly uncrossable chasms, un-climbable rocks, and peaks that reach above the clouds—and there are people who see every one of them as a challenge and a dare. "Who says I can't?"

Some friends spotted a dream site for their vacation cabin. It was on the opposite side of a gorge, but no matter. They installed a hand-operated cable car—actually not much more than a little platform suspended by two pulleys from an overhead cable. You would sit in the contraption, then reach up and pull yourself out and over the abyss by tugging on the cable. If you kept this up long enough, you would get there.

The compulsion to get there seems to be the only logical explanation for the fascination so many people have with Mount Everest. On the fiftieth anniversary of the first successful climb by Sir Edmund Hillary and Tenzing Norgay, *National Geographic* magazine noted that more than 2,200 people had made it to the top and that approximately 200 had died in the attempt, making it the most dangerous sport in the world. Undaunted by this appalling statistic, more than 200 went up in 2006, most of whom paid US$75,000 or more for the privilege. Only 12 died, so maybe it's getting "safer."

Someone asked British explorer George Mallory, who later died on Mount Everest, why he wanted to climb the mountain. His famous answer: "Because it's there."

When American president John F. Kennedy announced the intention of his government to begin the exploration of space, he recalled Mallory's words and then added: "Well, space is there, and we're going to climb it, and the moon and the planets are there, and new hopes for knowledge and peace are there. And, therefore, as we set sail we ask God's blessing on the most hazardous and dangerous and greatest adventure on which man has ever embarked."[1]

It was a great speech, but it claims something that not many people seem to have noticed. Kennedy said: "Peace [is] there," too. Everest was conquered in 1953, and the moon in 1969,[2] but peace? It still seems as elusive and far away as ever. Maybe it's peace that we really can't get to from here.

The first thing that comes to mind when we talk about finding peace is the situation in the Middle East, an unending soap opera in which the actors change but the plot never seems to vary much from one episode to the next.

But there is another kind of peace that seems to be equally elusive. I am talking about the more personal kind that touches each one of us—peace of mind and heart. Strange, isn't it, how we are bounding ahead in technology, climbing the highest mountains, and bridging all sorts of chasms, while actually sliding backward in the matter of personal peace?

The U.S. National Institutes of Health, citing numerous studies, reports that "the number of people suffering from depression has doubled in the last fifty years." Reports from Great Britain, Europe, Asia, Latin America, and the Caribbean confirm that the phenomenon is worldwide. [3]

Think of it! In many ways most people's lives have improved dramatically since the 1960s. Eating better and exercising more, most of us work fewer hours, take longer vacations, and have far more discretionary income than people did 50 years ago.[4] Why, then, do we find so much despair?

Even more strange is the fact that by far the largest increase in clinical anxiety and depression has occurred among those you would least expect—in the young.[5] The ones who have always been the brightest optimists, who seem to have it all and are living at a time of technological development and prosperity unequaled in history, are leading the pack in the matter of despondency.

"Studies and statistics [in the U.S.] show that approximately one in eight adolescents may be suffering from depression"[6] and that the suicide rate among young people has more than doubled.[7] A recent survey by Britain's Mental Health Foundation showed that 50 percent of university students in that country showed signs of clinical anxiety and more than one in 10 struggled with clinical depression.[8] A poll of more than 7,000 teenagers in China revealed that 36 percent have suicidal thoughts and one in 10 say they definitely plan to take their own lives. Dr. Mirta Roses, director of the Pan American Health Organization, reports that mental health disorders now comprise 24 percent of the burden of disease in the Americas, "with depression being the principal component of that burden."[9]

You can get to the top of Everest and journey two and a half miles down to gaze at the wreck of the Titanic. "Space tourists" pay millions of dollars to be rocketed above the stratosphere. But again I ask: What about peace? Where is the bridge to peace? Where is the rocket or cable car that can take us there? Or is it really the impossible dream?

Searching for Answers

Some curious people have noticed that the surge in despair coincided with the decay in moral values that has been going on since the sexual "revolution" that began in the 1950s, and they have wondered if there might be a relationship.

A survey of approximately 6,500 teenagers across the United States offers some answers. One of the questions in the survey was how often during the past week the teens felt depressed. Of the girls who were not sexually active, 7.7 percent said they had depression, while 25.3 percent of those sexually active reported that they were depressed all or most of the time. That is more than three times greater incidence of depression among those who were engaging in premarital sex. Fourteen percent of sexually active girls reported that they had attempted suicide at least once. The number of teenage boys suffering depression was lower, but the proportion was similar, with 2.4 times more serious depression among those sexually active.[10]

Of course, "sexually active" refers to only one aspect of behavior that has seen a radical change in recent years among young people. Drug and alcohol abuse, dishonesty, and violence have exploded, as has the number of youth growing up in broken and dysfunctional homes. No doubt these also do their share to increase depression. It seems hard to avoid the conclusion that the rise in despair is closely related to the widespread breakdown in morality.

You may have heard that the Bible speaks about a kind of peace that "surpasses all understanding." But the complete expression is "The peace *of God,* which surpasses all understanding" (Philippians 4:7, NRSV). The Greek form of the expression "of God" indicates origin or source. It means that such peace comes from God, is given by Him, and derives from Him.

In other words, this peace is not just some woozy state of calm or mental emptiness. The gospel we have through Jesus is the message of a well-integrated personality that achieves personal fulfillment, success, and self-acceptance. It is the message of individuals who are at peace with themselves and with other people because they have made their peace with God.

The Bible tells about a young man who found his way out of the deepest despair to a life of hope and fulfillment.

The story begins with him overwhelmed by depression, a darkness of soul so deep and powerful that it seemed impossible for him to believe the sun would ever shine again. Jacob had always prided himself on being the "good boy" of the family, the loyal and affectionate son. Now he had messed up so badly that he had to leave home, desperately running to escape his brother's revenge.

The record says that "he came to a certain place and camped for the night since the sun had set. He took one of the stones there, set it under his head and lay down to sleep" (Genesis 28:11, Message). Inns did exist in those days, and Jacob knew, of course, that sleeping outside was extremely dangerous. But reckless behavior is another symptom of depression.[11]

But during that dark night something happened that was totally unexpected: As Jacob slept, he dreamed. In amazement he beheld a glorious ladder of light. Its base was set on the earth, on the very stone that he had chosen as a pillow, and its top reached up to heaven. Angels of God were ascending and descending on this ladder! (see verse 12).

Jacob's gaze moved up and up, to the very top of the ladder. "And behold, the Lord stood above it and said, 'I am the Lord, the God of your father

Abraham and the God of Isaac. . . . Your descendants shall also be like the dust of the earth and you shall spread out to the west and to the east and to the north and to the south'" (verses 13, 14).

It Was Yours All Along

From earliest childhood Jacob had heard family stories about the "covenant," God's promise of friendship with his grandfather Abraham. The Lord had later renewed that same covenant with his father, Isaac. It was what had given his family their sense of identity and personal security. Now, as a fugitive, he found himself cast out from home and separated from everything he loved—but more than anything else, he felt rejected by God. He was sure that his sin had excluded him forever from the covenant promises.

That is why Jacob could hardly believe his ears—what he was hearing was the covenant, the same identical promises given to Abraham and Isaac, and this time it was for him personally. At the darkest hour of Jacob's life, when he felt overwhelmed with a sense of guilt and failure, God had come to renew His treaty of friendship and solidarity.

More than anything else Jacob had longed for the birthright—the status that he would have as leader of his clan and the double portion of inheritance. He wanted it so much that he had been willing to lie and cheat to get it. Now God was telling him that he didn't need to do this, because it was his all along. It was his by divine promise.

As he fought for the birthright Jacob may have focused on the family wealth. But God was opening his eyes to see that what was in store for him was incredibly greater than his father's sheep and cattle. The Lord told him: "Behold, I am with you and will keep you wherever you go, and will bring you back to this land; for I will not leave you until I have done what I have promised you" (verse 15, NKJV).

Now, even more aware of the foolishness and wrongheadedness of what he had done, Jacob saw that God had accepted his repentance and remorse. Although he was separated from his family, the Lord had not cast him out. This was what the ladder meant. It was Jacob's bridge to peace, his way out from despair.

Bring Back the Dream

With his eyes now fully opened, Jacob whispered in awe: "God is in this place—truly. And I didn't even know it!" (verse 16, Message).

The terrible darkness that was crushing Jacob's soul was his ignorance of God's love and mercy. That was what made it impossible for him to believe that the Lord could truly be with him.

You probably remember the Christmas carol about the "midnight clear," which says that angels were "bending near the earth" when they announced the birth of Jesus. That's a beautiful figure of speech, isn't it? Well, heaven was "bending near" before Jesus was born, too, but gross darkness (see Isaiah 60:2) had blinded people's eyes to His presence. It was time for a repetition of Jacob's dream, and Jesus came as its reenactment and fulfillment.

Jesus' very first description of His mission alluded to this: He said to Nathanael, "You will see the heavens opened and the angels of God ascending and descending on the Son of Man" (John 1:51). Referring, of course, to Jacob's dream, He was saying: "I am that ladder." His mission was to make the reconnection.

"God was in Christ reconciling the world to Himself" (2 Corinthians 5:19). By sending His Son to bridge the gap, God declared that Jacob's dream is for everyone. He was telling us: "I wasn't angry at Jacob, and I'm not angry at you, either. My mercy and love are not as limited as you seem to think. The covenant—the promises that I renewed to Jacob that night—are for you, also. See, I have reached down to earth and given you a bridge to hope, a way out from despair. You really can get there from here."

When Jacob woke up after his dream, he said, "God is in this place—truly. . . . This is God's House. This is the Gate of Heaven" (Genesis 28:17, Message).

Look around you, my friend—right there, where you are now. You can say it too: "This is God's House. This is the Gate of Heaven." Why? Because God is with you. That is the message Jesus came to bring. You don't need to climb some far-off mountain or travel to some exotic place to connect with God. That is why the very first name given to Jesus in the Gospels is "Emmanuel," which means "God with us."

He is here, and He is eager to get in touch. In fact, He has been ringing our doorbell for quite a while.

"But the [message of] salvation that comes through faith says,
 'You don't need to search the heavens
    to find Christ and bring him down to help you,'

[because He is already here,] and,

'You don't need to go among the dead
  to bring Christ back to life again
  [, because He is alive].'

"For salvation that comes from trusting Christ—which is what we preach—is already within easy reach of each of us;

  in fact, it is as near as our own hearts and mouths.

  For if you tell others with your own mouth
    that Jesus Christ is your Lord, and
  believe in your own heart
    that God has raised him from the dead,
      you will be saved."

—Romans 10:6-9, TLB

Yes, it really is as simple as that.

It is inward: You have to "believe in your own heart," for that is where truth becomes true for you.

And it is outward: You need to live the life and walk the walk. Jesus said: "If you love me, show it by doing what I've told you" (John 14:15, Message). You also need to talk the talk—to "confess" Jesus by publicly declaring your belief and decision to follow Him. This is because our inner conviction receives confirmation and reinforcement as we acknowledge it before others.

Jesus also said that the beginning of the new life in God is like the start of our natural life: it is accomplished by being born. "Unless one is born of water and the Spirit, he cannot enter the Kingdom of God" (John 3:5, TLB). Being "born of water"—that is, baptism—is a public and visible act. Birth "of the Spirit" refers to the change in our values and attitudes that comes from the work of the Holy Spirit in our hearts.

Praise God for the simplicity of the gospel! We can begin here and now to live the life of faith and enjoy the peace that He has made available to all of us. And as we do this, old habits and destructive thought patterns disappear, and things that we thought would never change begin to fall away.

There really is a land of new beginnings. It is found anywhere and anytime we walk with Jesus in the sunshine of His love. As He transforms our minds, hope and peace come creeping in, and our hearts find joy at last.

A way out from despair really does exist. Jesus has bridged the gap between us and God. He has come over to our side and brought heaven near. By His perfect example and sacrifice he offers us forgiveness and a life of purpose and order.

The following are Jesus' own words about His mission. I encourage you to look at them thoughtfully:

"Come to me, you who are tired and worried, and I will give you rest. Take up my work and learn from me, for I am gentle and kind, and you will discover an abiding peace in your soul. My requirements are easy and the load you carry will be light" (Matthew 11:28-30, Clear Word).

This is an invitation, and it's marked "RSVP." Jesus is asking for a specific response. It will strengthen and reinforce your purpose, if you will take a minute to record a few words expressing your decision and resolve.

_____

_____

_____

---

[1] John F. Kennedy, speech in Rice Stadium, Sept. 12, 1962.

[2] I refer here to the year when humans first walked on the moon. Some will say that humanity conquered space on October 4, 1957, when the Soviet Union sent into orbit *Sputnik I*, the first artificial satellite in history, or in 1961, when Yuri Gagarin became the first human to orbit the earth in a spaceship.

[3] According to the WHO, 15 percent of the population of most developed countries suffers severe depression (WHO report quoted in BBC-Online Jan. 9, 2001). Record numbers of Germans are suffering depression (BBC News Online, Apr. 18, 2005). The Pan American Health Organization projects a 35 percent increase in depression and other mental health problems in Latin America and the Caribbean during the 20-year period ending in 2010 (http://www.medicalnewstoday.com/printerfriendlynews.php?newsid=34832).

[4] http://www.apollolight.com/new_content/circadian%20rhythms_disorders/depression/depression_increase.html

[5] "Puberty Blues," *Reader's Digest*, February 2004, http://www2.youthbeyondthe blue.com/ybblue/index.aspx?link_id=77.356; Leon Cytryn and Donald Mcknew, *Growing Up Sad: Childhood Depression and Its Treatment* (New York: Norton, 1996).

[6] http://www.familyfirstaid.org/depression.html.

[7] http://www.cancer.gov/cancertopics/pdq/supportivecare/depression/Patient/page8.

[8] http://news.bbc.co.uk/1/hi/education/1165429.stm.

[9] From "Medical News Today," http://www.medicalnewstoday.com/printerfriend-lynews.php?newsid=34832.

[10] Data collected in the National Longitudinal Survey of Adolescent Health, Wave II. Funded by the National Institute of Child Health and Human Development (NICHD) and 17 other federal agencies. The study, led by Dr. Denise Hallfors of the Pacific Institute for Research and Evaluation in Chapel Hill, North Carolina, was published in the October 2005 issue of the *American Journal of Preventive Medicine*. A fuller report and analysis of this data is available at http://www.health-futures.org/does/TeenSexandSuicide.pdf.

[11] He may have reasoned that an inn would be the first place his brother might look for him.

Chapter 4

When He Comes, He Takes Over

Lisa has not always lived in Minneapolis. Two years ago she arrived from New York City. Now she says that in Minnesota she has found it all. The state offers family-therapy and parenting programs, and she attends state-sponsored college classes. "I kind of look on the state of Minnesota as my parents," says Lisa. "I've always gotten my needs met here. That is very spiritual."[1]

At Aspen, Colorado, Tom Hicks pauses at the bottom of the slope long enough to tell us that "skiing might be the true definition of being in the eternal present. It's definitely a spiritual experience."[2]

Over at Steubenville, Ohio, the annual National Charismatic Conference for Priests and Deacons is under way, and one of the deacons is in trouble. The people nearby discover this when he falls to the floor and begins groveling like a dog. Immediately several individuals get down beside him and urge him to confess the sin that is reigning in his life so that they can cast out the specific demon troubling him. Later the incident appears in a book on modern spirituality.[3]

A popular catalog urges people to purchase a "stick-on" that shows a raccoon singing carols. This will make it possible to "share the true spirituality of Christmas."

As such examples illustrate, spirituality seems to be bursting out all over these days. Nor is the current fascination with the subject limited to New Agers and writers of commercial hype. A review of academic books reveals dozens of titles on spirituality. They range from fairly traditional approaches, such as evangelical spirituality, spirituality of the Gospels, and spirituality for ministry,[4] to a wide range of esoteric subjects. Numerous books deal with feminist spirituality,[5] others discuss sexual spirituality,[6] eco-spirituality (for defenders of the ecology),[7] and spirituality of African native religions, as well as Hindu and voodoo spirituality and that of many other world religions.

All of this puzzles and confuses some Christians. Are there really a variety of ways to express true spirituality? We want to find out what Scripture says about the subject. It will allow us to compare the various spiritual movements with the Bible's urgent call to spiritual living.

Definitions

The word "spirituality," as such, does not occur in the Bible, but the word "spiritual" is common, especially in the writings of the apostle Paul, and as we see how he uses it, we can discover the biblical concept of spirituality.

We recall, of course, that Paul speaks of spiritual gifts (Romans 1:11; 12:6-8; 1 Corinthians 1:7; 12:1; 14:1-12). He also refers to spiritual words (1 Corinthians 2:13), spiritual songs (Ephesians 5:19), and spiritual blessings (Romans 15:27; Ephesians. 1:3; Colossians 3:16). Then he also discusses spiritual food and drink (1 Corinthians 10:3, 4) and spiritual worship (Romans 2:1), which should be done with spiritual fervor (Romans 12:11). God's people receive spiritual wisdom and understanding (Colossians 1:9). And the law itself is spiritual (Romans 7:14). Paul also notes that there are spiritual people (1 Corinthians 2:15), as well as some who are unspiritual (1 Corinthians 3:1; Galatians 6:1).

So what does the word mean? What is "spiritual" about spiritual gifts? Or what is "spiritual" about love, gentleness, meekness, etc.?

Such gifts are "spiritual" in that they are Spirit-given. That is, they are qualities or characteristics prompted, given, or inspired by the Holy Spirit.

Here is the key that opens our understanding to the meaning of the rest of the terms. Spiritual words are not just talk about God or conversations about moral issues. They are words that are inspired—breathed—and prompted by the Spirit. And so it is with spiritual wisdom, spiritual worship, and every one of the other terms listed above.

Thus the spirituality portrayed in the Bible is more than a warm feeling. One does not measure it in terms of pious talk or moral conduct. True spirituality, as portrayed in Scripture, is holy spirituality.

When the Spirit Comes

Nowhere does this concept stand out more clearly than in the expression "spiritual persons." A spiritual man or woman is a Spirit-filled, Spirit-moved individual, one who lets the Spirit live in and guide his or her thoughts and deeds.

This allows us to see some of the circumstances that are a part of Spirit-filled living:

1. When the Holy Spirit comes, He is in charge. We sometimes speak of having the Spirit or possessing the gifts of the Spirits. But it is more accurate to say that it is the Holy Spirit who has or possesses the believer. In fact, Scripture testifies that the Spirit at times directed people to do things contrary to their own wishes and ideas (see, for example, Acts 16:6).

The book of Acts tells about Simon the magician, who came to the disciples and offered them money for the Holy Spirit (Acts 8:16-20). Scripture does not condemn him, because he wanted to receive the Spirit and was willing to offer money to the apostles—they were not opposed to receiving donations. Rather, Peter criticized him because he thought that by paying money he could become the *owner* of the Holy Spirit and that the Spirit would then be under his control.

2. When the Holy Spirit is in charge, there is joy. At first this may seem contradictory, because spirituality is not a feeling. But Scripture tells us that Jesus, in spite of the crushing load He carried, was "full of joy through the Holy Spirit" (Luke 10:21, NIV). The apostles, after their expulsion from Antioch, "were filled with joy and with the Holy Spirit" (Acts 13:52, NIV). The Thessalonian believers "welcomed the message with the joy given by the Holy Spirit" (1 Thessalonians 1:6, NIV; see also Romans 14:17; Galatians 5:22).

3. Where the Holy Spirit is in charge, growth happens. Spirituality is not moral behavior, but a Spirit-filled life results in the development of true morality. And while spirituality is not moral transformation, the Holy Spirit does bring a reshaping of the inner being that leads to truly moral conduct.

"And we, who with unveiled faces all reflect the Lord's glory, are being transformed into his likeness with ever-increasing glory, which comes from the Lord, who is the Spirit" (2 Corinthians 3:18, NIV).

As the tree grows, the fruit will certainly appear. Love, joy, peace, patience, kindness, goodness, faithfulness, gentleness, self-control, tenderness, compassion, understanding, and quietness will increase.[8] Trust will take the place of anxiety (1 Peter 5:7), gentleness will overcome striving (Ephesians 4:3, 4) and purity will bridle passion (1 Timothy 4:12).

Outward Dimension

When this has happened, our spirituality, which is eminently inward and private, will be "evident to all" (Philippians 4:5, NIV).

If it is to be obvious to all, that means it cannot be stoppered up and kept on a shelf. It must be taken out of the cloister and onto the road, out of the pew and into the office and the shop.

In other words, true spirituality is bent-nail and smashed-finger spirituality. Steadfast in the face of drudgery, pain, and thankless toil, it is the spirituality of love for the unlovely and patience with the unreasonable. It rejoices with the Lord on the mountaintop, but then it hastens back to the valley, or to the inner city where people are bleeding and beaten down in life's struggle. True spirituality is one of tears and laughter, and maybe of sweat and exhaust fumes and dirty sidewalks.

In summary, people who have lives directed by the Holy Spirit will walk closely with God, live His life, and do His work in a sad and broken world.

How does this compare with the popular concept of spirituality that we hear so much about today?

We are not in a position to look into the hearts of the Lisa and Tom and others like them. Nor have we any reason to doubt their sincerity, but their concept falls far short of the ideal of true biblical spirituality. It fails to recognize not only the fullness of the transformation that must take place, but the direction from which it must come. Lacking a divine dimension, it is left spinning within the limitations of the human spirit, and as a result we must reject it as a pitiful counterfeit of God's ideal for His children.

Would you like to record a few words of gratitude and praise for this wonderful assurance?

_____

_____

---

[1] *Newsweek,* July 25, 1994, p. 60.

[2] *Modern Maturity,* November–December, 1994, p. 51.

[3] Michael Crosby, *Spirituality of the Beatitudes* (Maryknoll, N.Y.: Orbis Books, 1981), p. 82.

[4] Gordon James, *Evangelical Spirituality* (London: SPCK, 1991); Francis Schaeffer, *True Spirituality* (London: Hodder and Stoughton, 1972); Andrew Purves, *The Search for Compassion: Spirituality and Ministry* (Louisville, Ky. Westminster, 1988); Stephen C. Barton, *The Spirituality of the Gospels* (London: SPCK, 1992).

[5] Amanda Porterfield, *Feminine Spirituality in America* (Philadelphia: Temple University Press, 1980); Betsy Caprio, *The Woman Sealed in the Tower* (New York: Paulist Press, 1982); Christin Weber, *Womanchrist: A New Vision of Feminist Spirituality* (San Francisco: Harper and Row, 1987).

[6] Dody Donnelly, *Radical Love: An Approach to Sexual Spirituality* (Minneapolis: Winston Press, 1984).

[7] Charles Cummings, *Eco-spirituality: Toward a Reverent Life* (Mahwah, N.J.: Paulist Press, 1991).

[8] In addition to the fruits of the Spirit mentioned in Galatians 5:22, 23, the apostle mentions each of these characteristics in other texts, including Romans 1:4; 14:17; 15:13, 30; 2 Corinthians 6:6; Ephesians 4:3, 4; 2 Timothy 1:7; Philippians 2:1; see also, 1 Peter 3:4; James 3:17.

Chapter 5

Return to Reason

One of Jack London's famous stories is "To Build a Fire." It describes how a prospector in the Yukon freezes to death as he desperately tries to start a fire. I had an experience once that reminded me of this story.

The trail maps of the San Isabel National Forest in southern Colorado showed the path running beside a mountain lake. It was easy to imagine an idyllic campsite—moonlight reflecting off the water and the soft lapping of the waves on the shore while I drifted off to sleep on a fragrant bed of pine needles protected by the overarching arms of evergreens.

I left the trailhead about 3:30 p.m.—that was my first mistake. I was a teenager then, and strong, but at 8,000 feet and with a route pitched steeply upward, one does not make a lot of speed. Darkness found me still about five miles from my objective. The trail had reached 11,000 feet at that point, and was even steeper. Instead of the sheltering forest there were only a few gnarled bristlecone pines struggling to survive in the cold thin air. A short distance farther along even they had vanished.

I finally came to the lake just as a pale moon appeared from behind some scudding clouds. The temperature was close to freezing, and a gusting wind made walking a challenge. Instead of pine needles, there were boulders and angular rocks of all sizes, and underneath, a granite base swept clean of soil by the latest glacier.

Have you ever tried to strike a match or start a campfire under conditions like that? There may be a way to do it, but it was definitely not on my list of learned skills. Pitching a tent was also out of the question.

Jack London told of mistakes the prospector made that turned out to be fatal. It was clear to me by that time that the old man and I were pretty much in the same league. My dream of a warm sheltering experience was turning into an icy nightmare. Studying some of the issues related to origins reminded me of this experience not long ago.

The philosophers of ancient Greece talked about "physics" and "metaphysics." By "physics" they meant the physical universe—anything that you can see, touch, or somehow measure. *Metá,* in Greek, means "beyond." They believed there were things that were beyond physics, beyond the range of experimental knowledge, but that were nonetheless real. It was these things that they called *meta*physics.

Before long, they—especially Plato—came to believe that metaphysics is the actual reality. Since illusions abound and perception is fallible, anything we say about the physical is tentative and unreliable. You can't even be sure it exists, and if it does, it's only transitory, whereas metaphysical things—such as concepts, ideas, and values—are forever.

This viewpoint gradually became the popular wisdom, the politically correct opinion of the day, and for more than 1,000 years metaphysics ruled the world. Under the influence of this unbalanced view, fairies, leprechauns, spooks, and goblins abounded. Unseen forces governed every event on earth, and important decisions depended on the proper alignment of the stars.

More than anything else, such a philosophy put an end to discovery, to critical thinking, and to intellectual progress. Why observe? Why ask questions? Everything you see is only illusionary, and anyway, it doesn't matter. Whatever will happen, will happen, because strange and mysterious forces beyond our knowledge and control have fated it to be.

Then, starting about the twelfth century, the philosophical pendulum began to creep in the opposite direction. The movement was slow at first, but it began to pick up speed, until by the mid-nineteenth century Western civilization threw metaphysics off the throne, and rationalism ruled the world.

Rationalism exalts the importance of reason and the intellect. Above all an optimistic philosophy, its motto is "Yes, you can!" It taught people to hope, to believe in themselves, to reason and observe by encouraging them to use their brains to analyze and evaluate ideas. In countless ways rationalism has influenced our world for the better.

But the pendulum didn't stop there. Before that century ended, rationalism had gone a step further and had given birth to naturalism. Whereas the ancient philosophers believed that the true reality was metaphysics, naturalism considers that the only reality—absolutely the only thing that exists—is the physical world. If you can't see it, measure, or somehow detect it and explain it by natural law, it doesn't exist or ever happened.

It is an understatement to say that naturalism brought with it a radical change in worldview. Robert Ingersoll was one of its best-known proponents during the nineteenth century. Standing beside his brother's open grave, he said: "Life is a narrow vale between the cold and barren peaks of two eternities. We strive in vain to look beyond the heights. We cry aloud, and the only answer is the echo of our wailing cry."

A brilliant man, and completely logical, Ingersoll presented in stark terms the end result of a naturalistic worldview. Whatever hope it may have of a better future must rest on an unpredictable process of change through millions of years of evolution. And even that hope is fading today because the environment, the driving force behind evolution, far from bringing any encouragement, is plunging us toward disaster. "It is obvious to any thoughtful person that our world is in great trouble," wrote one observer recently, "that we are heading rapidly toward self-destruction due to overpopulation, destruction of nature, pollution of food, air, and water, climate change, etc."[1]

Under the rule of metaphysics, people were prisoners in a haunted house. Rationalism chased away the spooks, but naturalism tore down the house. It threw out faith and hope, and left us camping on a freezing bed of Precambrian granite.

Cold and Lonely

We find many signs of the existential loneliness—the absolute ophanhood—that naturalism brought with it. For example, humanity craves to know that other intelligent beings exist somewhere in the universe. As early as the nineteenth century, proposals emerged to send a message to people on the moon. One idea was to cut a huge swath in the forest to show them the Pythagorean theorem. Later, when telegraphy had become common, someone suggested a scheme for flashing Morse code signals to the moon with giant mirrors. In 1924 astronomers determined that the orbit of Mars was bringing the red planet closer to earth than usual, so they organized a project for scanning the radio frequencies, hoping that the inhabitants of Mars might be sending us a message.[2]

Today no serious scientist believes that people live on the moon or any planet of the solar system except our own, so the search has now extended far beyond. Since the 1960s, astronomers at the giant radio telescopic observatory in Arecibo, Puerto Rico, have spent thousands of hours listening to and analyzing radio signals, hoping against hope for any kind of communication from extraterrestrials. But they can report only continuing failure.

A number of other SETI (search for extraterrestrial intelligence) projects have joined the Arecibo investigators, all of them dedicated to providing an answer to the age-old question *"Are we alone?"*[3] Please, somebody out there, talk to us.[4]

Beyond Science

Science, the great benefactor of all of us, owes its origin and continuing viability to the principles of logic and reason taught by rationalism. Some believers in naturalism claim that rational reflection and the logical deductions of science have brought them to this position. They see naturalism as a logical conclusion based on observation and discovery in the world around us. We need to ask if such a claim is true or if, in fact, the opposite may be the case.

The most fundamental questions considered by any worldview are: Where did we come from? Why are we here? and Where are we going? The passage of time and the advance of scientific discovery have made it more, rather than less, difficult to answer from a purely naturalistic point of view.

Early proponents of naturalism had an easy answer to the question of the origin of life. They believed that life had sprung spontaneously from nonliving matter. Certain things have in them a "vital principle," they said. Thus manure or decaying meat can generate maggots, mud in the bottom of a pond can produce tadpoles, and mice appear spontaneously in garbage.

But by 1862 French chemist Louis Pasteur had conclusively proved such concepts to be false. So what was left? Well, really, nothing at all. "There is no rival hypothesis" [to the idea of life originating by itself] declared biologist H. H. Newman in 1924. None, that is, "except the outworn and completely refuted one of special creation, now retained only by the ignorant, dogmatic, and prejudiced."[5]

In 1954 Harvard University biochemist and Nobel Laureate George Wald wrote in *Scientific American*: "Most modern biologists, having reviewed with satisfaction the downfall of the spontaneous generation hypothesis, yet unwilling to accept the alternative belief in special creation, are left with nothing."[6] Wald, however, was not willing to let it go at that. The solution he proposed was a return to the theory of spontaneous generation.

Not that it was easy. During the 92 years between 1862 and 1954 advances in science had added an overwhelming load of difficulty to such an idea. With the invention in 1931 of the transmission electron microscope, it was possible to magnify objects up to 1 million times. Scientists were stunned as they began to realize for the first time the incredible complexity of the ordinary living cell.

Carl Sagan, an astronomer who became famous as an apostle of naturalism, wrote: "A living cell is a marvel of detailed and complex architecture. Seen through a microscope, there is an appearance of almost frantic activity. . . . It is known that molecules are being synthesized at an enormous rate. Almost any enzyme catalyzes the synthesis of more than 100 other molecules per second. . . . The information content of a simple cell [has] been estimated as . . . comparable to about 100 million pages of the *Encyclopaedia Britannica*."[7]

Of course, Wald, who was a biochemist, knew about this difficulty. In fact, he described it in considerable detail. The solution he proposed was time. Given enough time, he believed, anything is possible. And given even more time, it becomes inevitable.

British astronomer Sir Frederick Hoyle, intrigued by the idea, set out in the 1970s to calculate the mathematical probability[8] of the spontaneous origin of life in the way that Wald and others were proposing—an endless process of combining and recombining atoms in a primordial soup. To simplify his calculations, Hoyle decided to focus on one single aspect of the problem. He knew that the smallest conceivable life form needs at least 2,000 proteins to carry out basic life functions such as metabolism and reproduction, so he decided to calculate the probability of all the essential proteins forming spontaneously.

Hoyle concluded that it is one chance in 10 raised to the power of 40,000. That number is a one with 40,000 zeros behind it. We can also write it like this: $10^{40,000}$.

Let's think about what this means. Suppose you buy a ticket in a lottery that has sold 10 million tickets. Obviously your chances of winning are exceedingly slim—only one in 10 million. That is the same as one in 10 to the seventh power, because 10 million is a one with seven zeros after it (10,000,000) or 10^7.

Now what would be the chance that you could win a similar lottery every week for 80 years? When we calculate the possibility mathematically, you would have one chance in $10^{29,120}$. That is, of course, a 10 with 29,119 zeros after it. A tremendous number, but still *it is far less than $10^{40,000}$*. In other words, the spontaneous generation of just the protein in an amoeba is *much less likely* than winning the lottery every single week for 80 years.

In reporting his findings, Hoyle concluded with a famous comparison. He said that the likelihood of spontaneous generation of a bacteria is about the same as the probability that "a tornado sweeping through a junkyard could assemble a 747 from the contents therein." [9]

Hoyle's calculations, however, really don't reveal the full difficulty of the task. Remember, he was calculating only the probability of the spontaneous generation of the protein components of a cell. But that leaves out the problem of organizing of the cell with its cytoplasm, its mitochondria, endoplasmic reticuli, golgi apparatus, and the other parts inside the double membrane that holds it all together.

Harold Morowitz, a professor of molecular biophysics and biochemistry at Yale, studied the problem and concluded that the odds of a whole bacterium assembling by chance would be one in $10^{100,000,000,000}$. That is 100 billion zeros. It would be like your entire family winning the lottery every week for a million years. [10]

But wait! There's more: All of these esoteric calculations still leave unanswered the most fundamental question of all: Even if this ridiculously unlikely event were to occur, even if a cell could arise by chance with every component in perfect order, would it be alive? This question practically shouts for our attention. Why aren't the naturalists asking it? They know that a cell can die without being crushed or destroyed. It would still have all the essential proteins, all the enzymes, DNA, RNA, mitochondria, plasma, cellular walls, nutrients and every other component present, and in its proper place and order. All those things are there, but the cell is dead. There is no reason to believe that a cell assembled by such a totally unlikely chance would be alive. To hold otherwise is to assume that life is something that obviously it is not: simply the functioning of a machine.

Why Believe?

After describing at length the extreme difficulty of believing that life could come from spontaneous generation, George Wald concluded:

"One has to only contemplate the magnitude of this task to concede that the spontaneous generation of a living organism is impossible. Yet here we are—as a result, I believe, of spontaneous generation."[11]

Science does *not* support spontaneous generation. Neither does logic or common sense. But that apparently did not deter the eminent scientist. He chose to ignore science, defy logic, and fly in the face of reason. Why? Because of his philosophy. That is, of course, naturalism.

And it is precisely the message of *Darwin on Trial,* a powerful book by Phillip Johnson.[12] It has received widespread attention because its author is not an advocate for any creationist organization. He wrote from his perspective as a professor in the School of Law at the University of California at Berkeley.

Johnson used his training as a trial lawyer to analyze the validity of the evidences employed to support evolution. His conclusion was that evolution is not upheld by any type of evidence that would be considered valid under the rules of legally permissible evidence. Rather, it is based a priori on a philosophical bias. It is an arbitrary and unsustainable decision in favor of naturalism.

Optimistic rationalists of the nineteenth century expected to see the world improving constantly as the enlightenment continued to spread through programs of universal education. But it is strange and perplexing to see things going in the opposite direction as fundamentalism takes a stranglehold on the minds and lives of millions.

This greatly abused term (fundamentalism) has come to mean a fanatical and unreasoning adherence to one's beliefs while ignoring even the most basic principles of evidence, reason, and logic. The attitude usually accompanies intolerance, sometimes to the point of persecution, toward anyone who does not fully agree with the proponent's narrow view.

By this definition, naturalism has without question taken its place in the ranks of modern fundamentalisms.

Stopping the Trickle

Remember the story about the little Dutch boy who stuck his finger in the dike? He did so because he knew that if the dike continued to wash away, the trickle of water he was now stopping would quickly turn into a flood. Naturalists today are fighting against intelligent design theory because it is clear that behind the trickle there is a flood. You really can't admit that an "Intelligence" designed and put together the first cell, and then halt there. As soon as you accept the overwhelming evidence and admit the operation of such an Intelligence, it is clear that you are in the presence of some sort of splendor. What kind of awesome (and I do not use the word lightly) Intelligence could have done this? And if "It" could make a cell, what couldn't It do? Furthermore, what sense does it make to say that an Intelligence would make a cell and then assume that it would be uninterested or uninvolved in what happened after that? In this way science—true science—brings us face to face with God.

When Doubting Is the Thing to Do

When I found myself freezing in the glacier valley in Colorado, it didn't take too long to figure out that retreat was the better part of valor, and that any hope of finding safety and avoiding death from hypothermia lay in heading back as quickly as possible to look for shelter and safety at a lower elevation. It seemed nearly impossible, but that bitter night march did succeed in its purpose, and a few hours later I was able to get some rest and wake up to brighter prospects the next day.

Evidence suggests that more and more people in the scientific community today have begun to lose their blind faith in naturalism, and are considering a strategic retreat from its frozen heights.

As you think about this "Intelligence," this awesome Creator-God who made you and everything else, what are some of the adjectives that come to mind?

Why not put on paper a few words of your response:

_____

_____

[1] http://www.physics=philosophy=metaphysics.com/forum/wsm-in-logmans-terms-t530.html.

[2] A more detailed account of attempts to communicate with extraterrestrials may be found at http://www.wolframscience.com/nksonline/page-1189c-text.

[3] If you want to get involved in this search using your own PC, look up "Seti at home": http://setiathome.berkeley.edu.

[4] http://www.naic.edu/public/discovrs.htm. *National Geographic* reports that recent attention is focusing on five stars located between 27 and 50 light-years from earth that may have planets.

[5] Horatio Hackett Newman, *Outlines of General Zoology* (New York: Macmillan Co., 1924), p. 407.

[6] George Wald, "The Origins of Life," *Scientific American* 190 (August 1954): 46.

[7] Carl Sagan, "Life," *Encyclopaedia Britannica:* Macropaedia (1974)., pp. 893, 894.

[8] "Mathematical probability" is a calculation of how likely something is to occur. If you toss a coin into the air, the chance of getting heads is one out of two. If you toss a die (singular of "dice"), the chance of getting a particular number is one in six, because a die has six sides.

[9] Sir Frederick Hoyle, "Hoyle on Evolution," *Nature,* Nov. 12, 1981, p. 105.

[10] Anyone interested in a further discussion of this point can find it at http://www.direct.ca/trinity/origin.html.

[11] Wald.

[12] Downers Grove, Ill.: InterVarsity Press, 1993.

Chapter 6

Who Are You?

Thin and rugged as the surrounding crags, he guides his tractor over the steep-angled plot of ground by the fjord. Raising her apron, she fills it with a scoop of cracked corn. Then she steps briskly outside and scatters it while the chickens run wildly after it and the quacking ducks try to keep up.

He follows his water buffalo slogging along through the deep muck as he tills his paddy, getting it ready for the rice that he will plant there next week.

****

As she bends over the tomato vines in her dacha garden, she delights in their pungent fragrance as she checks the leaves for insects.

****

Her eyes nearly shut, she trips along the hallway, then leaps back just in time to avoid crashing into a friend. "Sorry!" she says with a laugh that rings out like a melody. "I've got Kylie Minogue on my iPod."

"I know," replies her friend. "Isn't she a ripper?"

****

These are some snapshots of the amazing and fascinating variety of people who share space on our shrinking planet. They roam its deserts and cities or journey across pampas, tundra, and permafrost. Their huts and houses cling to mountain slopes and hide in forest clearings. Many of them sleep eight or more in a single room and feel fortunate, knowing that outside thousands live on the streets and that others are three days' walk from the nearest market. Some spend their days breathlessly watching every surge and quiver of the stock market, while others are glad to find a bit of garbage off the street that they can pick up and eat. Everywhere, every day, they are on the move, seeking, fearing, struggling, and hoping.

Who are they? They are all of us—you and I—members of the great human family.

Right now, as you read this, thousands of us are riding the Metro in Mexico City, in Paris, in Moscow. What are we thinking? What are we hoping as we watch for our stop? See that little grandma in Dhaka? She holds a baby to her shoulder—it couldn't be more than a few weeks old. And she repeats softly, *"Allahu Akbar. Allahu Akbar* ["God is good"]." What is on *her* mind and heart? Is it something that you have never experienced?

This great commonality is the fundamental truth that springs from acknowledging the creatorship of God. It is the truth that all of us everywhere have the same Father. And we are all brothers and sisters.

The apostle Paul understood this. In Acts 17 we find him in Athens. It appears he may be going through some kind of culture shock. To the right, to the left, up ahead and everywhere, he can see altars, shrines, and temples with people hurrying in and out, burning incense, murmuring prayers.

It's a long way from Jerusalem, isn't it, Paul?

Then comes an invitation and an opportunity. Some Epicurean and Stoic philosophers gather every day on Mars Hill for no other purpose than to hear and discuss something new. Hearing about the strange foreigner, they wanted to know more about what "this idle babbler" had to say (Acts 17:18).

Paul begins his message to these people by observing, "I notice that you are very devout" —a tactful way of referring to all those images. He is acknowledging the cultural differences. But then he tells them: "God, who made the world and everything in it" "has made from one blood every nation of men to dwell on all the face of the earth" (verses 24, 26, NKJV).

The differences are obvious, he implies, but they are superficial. Why? Because we all share "one blood"! A common thread ties us all together.

****

It had not been easy to reach the village in the mountains of Chiapas, Mexico, but the welcome we got there made us forget the long hours on the trail. After the evening meeting and a meal of beans and handmade tortillas fresh off the grill, it was time for bed. Did I say "bed"? Well, if that's what you could call the uneven hand-hewn planks laid over a rough frame. No mattress or any sort of padding was in sight. It was not very wide and not nearly as long as I am, and I was sharing it with two other men. I'm not sure if we were better or worse off than the five or six others who slept on the rough plank floor in the same room.

But what impressed me and what I remember most about the experience was not the aching bones or penetrating chill that crept in before morning. Rather, it was the fun that we had because of Antonio. From the time we first arrived, the young man had attached himself to us as our guide and friend. It was soon clear that Tony was everyone's friend. And now that we were sharing his space, he was delighted to have an audience. Bubbling and enthusiastic, he kept us laughing far into the night.

And I thought, *I've met this guy before.* By a different name, yes, but we've met. He was in my graduating class in high school. She is a receptionist in my doctor's office. He is the spark plug of our youth group at church.

This particular Antonio's Spanish was heavily accented by his native Mixteco dialect, but there was no mistaking the extroverted sanguine personality. And I thought: *Despite the fascinating differences imposed by culture, people are people wherever you find them.*

Is that what Paul meant by "one blood"? Was he saying that what we have in common is very much more, and also much more important, than the cultural details that make us different?

As if we needed more evidence, the human genome project is proving it once again. There really is "one God and Father of all, who . . . works through all, and is present in all." That's why "everything you are and think and do is permeated with Oneness" (Ephesians 4:6, Message).

Privilege and Responsibility

Now take a look at the following Bible passage:
"God spoke:
'Let us make human beings in our image,
    make them reflecting our nature
so they can be responsible for
    the fish in the sea,

the birds in the air,
the cattle,
and, yes, Earth itself.' "
—Genesis 1:26, Message

What would you say are some of the things that make us human—characteristics that we have in common that distinguish us from other forms of life? Let's start with . . .

self-awareness (we are conscious of how we appear to others).

aesthetics (we recognize and appreciate beauty).

values (such as loyalty, honor, and decency).

moral conscience (a sense of right and wrong).

transcendent spirituality (we reach out to something beyond ourselves—to God).

Because of these things we strive for right and want to be better people. God "has put eternity into man's mind" (Ecclesiastes 3:11, RSV). "He has given men a sense of time past and future" (verse 11, NEB).

The unique traits that we hold in common identify us as human and show our kinship with people of other times and places. But there's more to it than that.

In Genesis 5:3 we read that "Adam . . . became the father of a son in his own likeness, according to his image." Do you notice an echo here of what God said about the creation of human beings? Adam's son was born "in his own likeness" and "according to his image." Seth resembled Adam in ways that none of the animals did. Because of this, Adam could relate to his son in a way not possible with any other creature. Adam could talk to Seth. He could nurture and train him. Beyond that, he could teach him values and life skills and show him how to be a man and live responsibly.

In a similar way, Adam, a "son of God" (Luke 3:38), was created in *his* Father's likeness and according to His image (Genesis 1:26, 27). The higher faculties he received made possible an interpersonal relationship with his heavenly Parent.

Furthermore, because Adam had these characteristics, because he was able to receive instructions directly from his Father, and because he was gifted with moral as well as with intellectual faculties, he was in a position to stand as God's representative—as ruler in God's stead—over creation. He could be responsible for "the fish of the sea," "the birds of the sky," the animals, and, yes, earth itself (verse 21).

The Unnecessary Tree

Sin not only brought about an estrangement between humans and God (Isaiah 59:1, 2)—it *was* an estrangement. That, in fact, was their sin. Before they ate the forbidden fruit, human beings had already turned their backs and walked away from God. They had rejected the parent-child relationship. That's what was happening when they took the fruit and ate it. The name, the overarching label of the relationship they were leaving, was "faith"—the simple, confiding trust that characterizes the connection between a parent and a young child.

They didn't really need that forbidden fruit in order to sin. Adam could have pulled a branch from a tree and used it to give Eve a whack. She could have been jealous of him because he was created first. So, in a sense, the tree was unnecessary. But God put it there and made a point of telling them about it, because He wanted to make sure they *knew* they had a choice, a decision. There can be no such thing as a moral person if moral choice is not real.

"Adam, I notice you are faithful and obedient to God. Why?"

"Ahhh, . . . well, I don't know. You mean I could have disobeyed?"

Because of the tree, such a conversation never could have happened. Adam *knew* he could disobey.

Eden is no more, but the tree of the knowledge of good and evil has remained behind. It is now planted in the heart of every one of us. Theologians call it our "fallen nature."

"Hello, friend. It is good to see you here in Paradise. How did you get here?"

"Well, you know . . . someone told me about the streets of gold, and I wasn't too busy, so I decided to come and check them out."

No one who has ever fought a battle against the dark evil of our souls could believe that such a conversation might be possible.

The Christian life is not a lake but a flowing stream. At some points the water goes rushing along, crashing over the rocks, while at others it is more peaceful. But it's always flowing. We can overcome, we can grow and move upstream only by effort—and sometimes by a hard or even titanic struggle against our evil nature that wants to hold us back and drag us down.

The psalmist recognized that truth. "I was brought forth in iniquity," he wrote, "and in sin did my mother conceive me" (Psalm 51:5, RSV). The apostle Paul used his own case as an illustration: "What I don't understand about myself is that I decide one way, but then I act another, doing things I absolutely despise. . . . I decide not to do bad, but then I do it anyway. My decisions, such as they are, don't result in actions. Something has gone wrong deep within me and it gets the better of me every time" (Romans 7:15-20, Message). With total frankness the great apostle confesses that he is a perfectly normal human being and that spiritual struggles are part of his life, just as they are for the rest of us.

But, of course, he doesn't leave it there. Paul has no intention of saying that the battle is hopeless. He immediately adds: "With the arrival of Jesus, the Messiah, that fateful dilemma is resolved. Those who enter into Christ's being-here-for-us now no longer have to live under a continuous, low-lying cloud. A new power is in operation. The Spirit of life in Christ, like a strong wind, has magnificently cleared the air, freeing you from a fated lifetime of brutal tyranny at the hands of sin and death" (Romans 8:1, 2, Message).

In Ephesians 4:24 he explains further: "Put on the new self, which in the likeness of God has been created in righteousness and holiness of the truth." Listen! Did you hear an echo of Genesis 1:26? Here is that phrase again: "the likeness of God." The apostle says that this "likeness," this "image of God," which has largely been lost, can be "put on" again. But how? In the same way we got it in the first place. It has to be "created"—this time *re*-created in each one of us. It is what makes it possible to hope again. God's new act of creation results in a relationship of "righteousness and holiness of the truth."

Giving Peace a Chance

In 1986 David Blumenfeld, an American rabbi, was on vacation in Jerusalem when a Palestinian teenager stepped out of a doorway and shot him in the head. It was a totally random incident—the boy was a member of a rebel faction of the PLO that had decided to kill as many Jews as possible to avenge the downing of a Libyan airliner by an American missile.

Blumenfeld survived his injury and returned to the United States, determined to forget what had happened and get on with his life. But his daughter Laura found herself haunted by a desire for revenge. She determined, however, that true revenge would be, not to hurt the shooter, but to make him sorry.

Through a series of unlikely events Laura was able to discover the young man's identity. His name was Omar Khatib, and he had been arrested by the Israeli government and sentenced to 25 years in prison.

Presenting her credentials as a journalist but without otherwise identifying herself, Laura began visiting Omar's family in Ramallah, on the West Bank. Through them she was able to communicate with him by letters that they smuggled in and out of the prison for her. She continued the contact for more than a year and was able to establish close ties of friendship with the family.

One day in 1999 the authorities scheduled a hearing to consider the possibility of an early release for Omar because of a serious health problem. Laura had returned to the United States by that time, but she flew to Israel to attend the meeting and asked to speak on his behalf. She told the judges that David Blumenfeld had forgiven Omar Khatib and believed that if he was ill he should be released from prison.

"Classic hearsay," snorted the chief justice. "You have no right to speak."

"I do have a right," she answered.

"No, you don't."

"Yes, I do."

"Why?"

"Because," she said, "I am his daughter. . . . I am Laura Blumenfeld."

The defense lawyer then told the judges about the close relationship that Laura had established with the family. They were astounded. Omar and his family were in shock, most of them crying.

"How did you present yourself to the family?" the chief justice said, trying to grasp what was happening.

"As a journalist."

"How long did you keep up this front?"

"A year."

"Why did you do this?"

At last Laura could explain. "I wanted them to know me as an individual and for me to know them. I didn't want them to think of me as a Jew, or as a victim. Just Laura. And I wanted to understand who they were, without them feeling defensive or accused. I wanted to see what we had in common."

It all still seemed more than the judges could fathom: "Why did you do such a dangerous thing?" they persisted.

"You have to take a chance for peace. You have to believe it's possible."

One of the judges commented, "I think it took a lot of guts to do what you did."

"I did it for one reason," she replied. "Because I love my father very much, and I wanted them to know—he is a good man, with a good family. I wanted them to understand that this conflict is between human beings, and not disembodied Arabs and Jews. And we are people. Not 'military targets.' We're people with families, and you can't just kill us."

Soon after Laura returned to America, David Blumenfeld received a letter from Omar Khatib. "God is good to me that He lets me know your Laura," he wrote. "She was the mirror that made me see your face as a human person deserved to be admired and respected. I apologize for not understanding her message early from the beginning. Laura chose a positive way of getting revenge from me, and she succeeded."*

That is the kind of "revenge" God has been trying to get on all of us for being so far from Him. He wants to save us from the foolish estrangement that has caused us so much suffering.

Maybe you're reading this but still don't know very much about God. Or maybe you have heard, but you have had a hard time understanding Him from the explanations that others have given you. Remember what Laura said: "You have to take a chance for peace." First of all, you have to stop turning your back and walking away when He wants to talk to you. You need to stop "feeling defensive or accused." This shouldn't be hard, because He doesn't come at you in this way—with an attack.

Giving you as much time as you need, He will patiently teach and answer your questions. He will reason with you. But what He desires is a lot more than that. The Lord did not give you a brain, with the ability to reason, just for you to have only information about Him. Nor does He want you just to understand Him in some abstract way, any more than parents want their children to have only an intellectual understanding about them. What

He desires is a relationship. It is through a relationship that we can truly learn to admire, respect, and love someone. Laura Blumenfeld understood this. And that is what the "image of God" in you is all about. Only it can make such a relationship possible.

When you accept and enter into this relationship, an amazing process of re-creation and restoration begins. Every day you will grow as you find yourself "with unveiled face, beholding as in a mirror the glory of the Lord, [while you] are being transformed into the same image from glory to glory" (2 Corinthians 3:18).

Before you put this down and get busy with something else, I encourage you—in fact, I would even urge you—to record in a few words your personal response to God's wonderful invitation:

_____

_____

_____

---

* Laura Blumenfeld, *Revenge: A Story of Hope* (New York: Simon and Schuster, 2002), pp. 347, 348.

Chapter 7

Can You Explain the Holocaust?

A few days ago you stopped in at the local school supervisor's office to see about work as a substitute teacher. They asked you some polite questions and had you fill out a form.

"OK," they said. "We'll let you know if anything turns up."

It didn't sound very hopeful. But last night your phone rang. And now, here you are, standing in front of 36 live-wire sixth graders. You look at your watch . . . again. It's 8:45. Three-thirty p.m. seems unimaginably far away.

You are clearing your throat—again—when you hear, "Teacher!"

"Um, yes?" It's the red-haired kid over by the window. Let's see. You just took the attendance record, so . . . what *was* his name?

"Could we just sort of talk about stuff?" he says. "I mean, Mrs. Packard, she, like, lets us have discussions, and sometimes we ask her questions."

Hey! That's a great idea!

"Sure, I guess we could. I notice on the schedule that you have social studies right now, so let's talk about the things you've been learning in that class."

"Well, I was wondering if maybe you could explain the Holocaust for us."

OK, that one's easy. "Sure, Jimmy."

"Jeremy."

"Oh, sorry! Well, the Holocaust happened in Germany. It was when Hitler killed 6 million Jews. He called it 'the final solution,' and he ..."

"We already know that part," the boy says, interrupting your flow of eloquence. "What I mean is: How could something like that happen?"

"Uh, well ... "

"Hitler didn't do it all by himself," he insists. "Mrs. Packard said that thousands of people were involved. How could so many people be so bad? And why did God let it happen?"

OK. Wake up! It's just a story. I mean, you're not really stuck with answering that question in front of a whole class of sixth graders. So relax!

But before we let it go . . . how *would* you answer? Of course, you could start out by saying that Hitler was an evil man. But that wouldn't get you very far. As Jeremy says, they already know that part. How many people do you think helped him? Well, obviously thousands if you count the camp employees, soldiers, cooks, civilian guards. Were they just "doing their job," or did they have some moral responsibility? What about the industrial barons who vied for lucrative contracts to supply the cyanide and other supplies involved, the engineers who designed and built the gas chambers? What about the IBM Corporation, which contributed to the meticulous record keeping with its primitive computers and punch cards? What about the scientists who researched methods to achieve efficiency in killing and disposing of the bodies? Then there were the researchers and doctors who used the Jews as human guinea pigs for gruesome experiments, such as injecting dye into people's eyes in an attempt to change their color, immersing people in vats of ice water to see how long it would take them to die that way. And the physicians who performed surgery, amputating limbs and other organs, fusing normal twins together to make them conjoined (Siamese).

Who were these sadists, these monsters? Here is the most chilling and frightening idea of all. A lot of evidence suggests they were just normal people, individuals like you and me. Think of the woman next door who waves at you every morning when she comes out to water her geraniums. Or consider the doctor who examines your kids and musses their hair in a friendly way.

Adolph Eichmann was in charge of rounding up and sending Jewish captives to death camps in Poland. He did his job so efficiently that in 1944 the German authorities dispatched him to do the same thing in Hungary. There, working day and night, he was able to send more than 400,000 people to their death before the Soviet invasion of that country forced him to flee. In 1945, with the Third Reich collapsing, Heinrich Himmler ordered a halt to the Jewish extermination program. When Eichmann heard this, he nearly went berserk. He was determined to kill as many as possible before it was too late.

By 1960 Israeli secret service agents had located Eichmann, who was living in Argentina as Ricardo Klement. They put him under surveillance and for months followed his every move. One of the things that impressed them was how normal "Klement" was. Holding an undistinguished job in the public water works, he was a conscientious family man. Every evening he would come home to kiss his wife and spend time playing with the children.

Can "normal" people do terrible things? Stanley Milgram, a researcher at Harvard University, carried out a series of experiments looking for an answer to this question. First he set up a simple test to examine the power of group pressure. He showed a group of five people a paper with two horizontal lines of unequal length.

"Which line is longer, A or B?" he asked them. The subjects gave their response orally one after another. But the first four people were actually cooperating with the psychologist who had coached them to give the wrong answer. The individual who was the actual subject of the test was always the last. The test subjects would listen in amazement as the others confidently stated that the short line was longer. Staring hard at the page as if doubting their own senses, they would frown, squirm, and fidget in their chairs—clearly they were under stress. Some of them would try to argue with the others, who would then turn on them and ridicule them. After the first four had given the wrong answer, it would be the subject's turn. Rather than go against the opinion of the group, 31 percent of the test subjects gave a response that was clearly and obviously wrong. One of them said later: "That line seemed actually to grow longer as I heard what the others were saying."

Next Milgram set up an experiment designed to test the effect of an authority figure on conformity. He recruited volunteers who were willing to participate in an experiment that he told them was designed to show the relationship between punishment and learning. Three individuals participated in each test: a stern, authoritative instructor and two subjects. The instructor explained to the two subjects that one of them would be the learner and the other would deliver the punishment. The instructor would first bind the learner to a chair with his or her hand on an electrode.

The instructor then ordered the punisher to deliver an electric shock to the learner by pressing a lever on a machine each time the learner made a mistake on a word-matching task. Each subsequent error led to an increase in the intensity of the shock in 15-volt increments, from 15 to 450 volts.

In reality the shock box was a well-crafted prop, and the learner was an actor who did not actually get shocked. The "learner" was strapped to the fake electrodes and could not get free. As the "shocks" increased, the "learner" would start to scream and protest against being tortured. "Stop! You can't do this. Let me loose. You've got to stop." If the "punisher" hesitated, the instructor would demand in a stern voice that he or she continue.

The result: 65 percent of the subjects continued to obey—believing they were delivering 450-volt shocks, inflicting severe pain, and even burning an unwilling subject—simply because the experimenter commanded them to do so.

Milgram's studies illustrated a truth that Nazi Germany had already made clear. Under the pressure of group opinion, many "normal" people will agree to something that is obviously wrong, and combining group pressure with an order from an authority figure greatly increases the conforming behavior. Under such circumstances, many ordinary people will do things that are morally reprehensible. Other researchers have replicated Milgram's studies many times, and always with similar results.

A more recent and disturbing example of this phenomenon was the mass suicide at Jonestown in Guyana in which Jim Jones commanded his followers to swallow an artificially flavored drink laced with cyanide. Victims of cyanide poisoning usually die from suffocation produced by spasms of the respiratory system. On a recording of the Jonestown event the first people to drink the poison can be heard screaming in agony while Jones, brandishing a pistol, continues to command the rest to come forward and drink. A few people ran off into the jungle and hid, trembling with terror, but hundreds obeyed and died.

French ethnologist Francois Bizot survived three months in a Khmer Rouge camp led by one of the regime's most notorious torturers. Meditating on the horrors that he witnessed, Bizot later wrote: "There are forces that can make a man cowardly, destructive, heartless. When the rule of law disappears, these forces that exist even in normal times suddenly can make us killers, make us aspire to positions that turn us into monsters, into people we never thought we'd become."[1]

The Christian Filter
As is so often the case, the Bible looks at this aspect of human behavior

and peels back a few layers, allowing us to see deeper and to understand more.

The apostle Paul talks about the mindless acceptance of group think, and warns us against it: "Do not be conformed to this world," he says (Romans 12:2). *Don't let the "world"* —that is, popular culture—*squeeze you into its mold.*

But Paul is not setting up Christianity as a counterculture. There is no virtue in touting difference just for its own sake. Not everything in our culture is bad, and if something is popular, that doesn't necessarily make it evil. Instead of being "conformed to this world," the Christian needs to be "transformed by the renewing of your mind, that you may prove what the will of God is, that which is good and acceptable and perfect" (verse 2). There's the secret: a mind that is transformed and renewed through a relationship with God will be able to "prove," that is, to "test," to "check out," what the "world" offers. It will know what is "good and acceptable and perfect"—what is in harmony with "the will of God" and what is not.

In 1969 long-simmering tension between El Salvador and Honduras exploded into the "100-Hour War." Passions on both sides of the border ran high, especially in Honduras, where rampaging mobs massacred hundreds of Salvadorans. Traveling between the two countries shortly after that, I heard Christians on both sides of the border vehemently echoing the line of hatred pouring from the respective news media. But not everyone. Some people rejected hatred—and many acts of quiet heroism occurred as Hondurans risked their lives to save Salvadorans from the mobs.

As we study the Word of God, the Holy Spirit impresses its sacred principles on our hearts until they become part of our lives. Then we are able to "prove [that is, test] all things; hold fast that which is good" (1 Thessalonians 5:21, KJV). A Christian who lives this way could never fail Milgram's test. He or she will understand that popular opinion is not a safe guide and that no human authority can command our conscience.

An Inside Track for the Enemy

Two fundamental things are in play in the matter of conformity to evil. The first is a reason that exists deep within us, and the other lies outside and beyond us. We can label them by using two terms that seem to be in vogue today. They are the existential and transcendental reasons.

For more than 20 years William Bennett was a commanding general in the fight for morality. As Ronald Reagan's chairman of the National Endowment for the Humanities, he railed against academic permissiveness. Later as secretary of education, and as "drug czar" under the first president Bush, he traveled and lectured promoting morality and family values. After leaving public office, Bennett wrote *The Book of Virtues,* which sold millions of copies. A popular lecturer, he commanded $50,000 for speeches on the lecture circuit that were practically sermons.

Then the Washington *Times* reported that Bennett had won a $200,000 jackpot at the Mirage Resorts Bellagio casino in Las Vegas. Bennett's office quickly issued a denial, leading reporters to investigate further. They soon discovered that the report was, indeed, erroneous. Bennett had won $25,000 rather than $200,000 . . . and had lost $625,000 on that same weekend.

Further digging revealed that the "king" of values had a long-standing addiction to high-stakes gambling, and that he commonly lost $150,000 or more in a single session. In one two-week period he wired $1.4 million dollars to the casinos to cover his losses.

It is not that hard to *think* values, and neither is it difficult to *preach* them. But living them—bringing them into the press and grind of daily life—is not nearly as easy.

Psychologists Peck and Havighurst draw a grim picture. In their book *Psychology of Character Development* they say that to attain truly moral behavior "requires a great deal more self-restraint and a great deal more effortful, thoughtful foresight than most of us have learned or really find welcome. What most of us have to cope with in ourselves is a welter of childishly intense desire, often curbed only by sheer force, mixed with some milder, more satiable urges. We are a turmoil of unorganized, undirected, highly irrational thoughts, out of which we wrest an acceptably logical idea only now and then. We are a mass of preconceptions, only reluctantly willing or able to entertain a real new, different outlook. We have loving impulses, but we also have a great many aggressively selfish desires; and we experience more intense resentments and hatreds than polite society is ever supposed to admit. This is not a pretty picture, and the terms are somewhat vague, but it seems to be generally accepted as true by most students of human nature. (Indeed, it is not a little achievement to be able to view this picture without turning away either in disgust or despair.)"[2]

The Bible uses different terminology to paint this same picture. It says: "For the sinful nature desires what is contrary to the Spirit, and the Spirit what is contrary to the sinful nature. They are in conflict with each other, so that you do not do what you want" (Galatians 5:17, NIV).

Ever since the beginning of sin, these two forces—the will of the "sinful nature" and the will of the higher spiritual nature—have been locked in mortal combat. We all have noble, altruistic impulses, creating a longing to be better people and to stand up for right. But time and again the good impulses get overwhelmed by our deep-rooted bent to selfishness. What Paul is saying is that it is an unequal contest, and that the evil nature, if left to itself, will always win.

Cosmic Conflict

The second important idea the Bible teaches about the struggle between good and evil is that it is not only personal and existential; it is also cosmic and transcendent. "We wrestle not against flesh and blood, but against principalities, against powers, against the rulers of the darkness of this world, against spiritual wickedness in high places" (Ephesians 6:12, KJV). "Therefore, take up the full armor of God, so that you may be able to resist in the evil day, and having done everything, to stand firm" (verse 13).

The Message, a contemporary-language Bible, puts it this way: "This is no afternoon athletic contest that we'll walk away from and forget about in a couple of hours. This is for keeps, a life-or-death fight to the finish against the Devil and all his angels. Be prepared. You're up against far more than you can handle on your own."

Revelation 12 places the cosmic struggle in the context of historical time. First we see the symbol of a beautiful woman. Clothed with the sun and her hair spangled with the stars of heaven, she is a symbol of the church—God's people. Next a red dragon comes roaring in (verses 1, 3). It is "the serpent of old who is called the devil and Satan" (verse 9).

Finally, we see a war, not between the dragon and the woman, but between the dragon and his angels on one side, and God and the angels of light on the other. The struggle starts in heaven, but then moves to the earth, where it goes on for centuries . . . but not forever. It moves toward a definite conclusion. And when the war is over, the peace will never end (Isaiah 9:7; Daniel 2:44).

The prophecy also reveals that when the drama draws close to its climactic finale, the struggle will be especially intense. A voice from heaven cries out: "Woe to the earth and the sea, because the devil has come down to you, having great wrath, knowing that he has only a short time" (Revelation 12:12). "So the dragon was enraged with the woman, and went off to make war with the rest of her children" (verse 17).

Jesus also spoke of this cosmic conflict. He made it clear that the most important part would be the struggle for hearts and minds. As the story nears its grand conclusion, He said, millions of people will find themselves overwhelmed by a powerful and sophisticated deception. Highly convincing religious leaders will "show great signs and wonders, so as to mislead, if possible, even the elect" (Matthew 24:24; see also 2 John 7 and Revelation 13:3).

Notice especially the phrase *"if it were possible."* Praise God for that wonderful "if." And Christ added: "But those who stand firm until the end will be saved" (Matthew 24:13, Clear Word).

Revelation 12 also speaks of these steadfast people. It calls them a "remnant" (verse 17, KJV). Neither fooled or afraid, they are unimpressed by groupthink. Even angry threats or the loud commands of the "dragon" and his friends cannot frighten them into conformity.

You Have to Love It

The apostle Paul reveals the secret of their success. First he echoes the words of Jesus, saying that the end-time deception will be supported by powerful "signs and false wonders . . . for those who perish, because they did not receive the love of the truth so as to be saved" (2 Thessalonians 2:9, 10).

Did you notice why so many people will succumb to deception? *It is because they do not love the truth.*

What does it mean to love the truth? What do people who love it do?

1. If we love the truth, we will search for it. It will seem important to us to discover it. We will take the time and make the effort necessary (John 5:39). Bible study and prayer for understanding will be a normal part of our lives (Acts 17:11). Like the psalmist, we will pray earnestly, "Lead me in thy truth, and teach me" (Psalm 25:5, KJV).

2. If we love the truth, we will value it. Jesus told a story about a man who was plowing in a field when suddenly his plowshare struck something hard.

It was an ancient box filled with treasure. Without hesitation the man sold all that he had and bought the field. Jesus added that the man did so with "joy" (Matthew 13:44). Why the joy? The answer is obvious, isn't it? He was happy because he recognized the value of what he had found. The man knew that the treasure in the box was worth far more than anything that he already owned.

The "field" in Jesus' story represents the Bible, the Word of God. The treasure is the truth that it contains. If we really love truth, we will experience this same joy as we study Scripture and discover the beauty of its teachings (1 Corinthians 13:6). It will be more precious to us than silver or gold (Job 28:15; Proverbs 16:16)—even more than life itself.

3. If we love the truth, it will change us. The Bible makes it plain that something is not really truth to us unless it makes a difference in how we live and how we behave (Galatians 5:7; Romans 2:8).

4. If we love the truth, we will be eager to share it. Once we have seen the beauty of truth and experience its power (1 Peter 1:22), we will be excited about it, and it will seem natural for us to give it to others.

When the Israeli government placed Adolph Eichmann on trial for his crimes, he advanced the same argument used by the defendants in the war crimes trials at Nuremberg: He said he was not responsible for what he had done because he only followed orders. What do you think about his reasoning? The Israeli court, like the judges at Nuremberg, was unimpressed, and it condemned Eichmann to be hanged.

I leave you with this question: What do you think the court of heaven will say to people who argue: "But that's what everybody believed." "All my friends and neighbors thought it was true." "That's what my parents taught me." "My boss told me I had to do it." "My husband ordered me." "It was the law—didn't I have to obey the law?"

Describe the individuals who will win in the cosmic conflict. What do you think are their most important characteristics?

_____

_____

_____

[1] http://detailsaresketchy.wordpress.com/2007/08/27/the-man-and-the-monster.
[2] Robert Peck, R. J. Havighurst, Ruth Cooper, Jesse Lillenthal, and Douglas Moore, *The Psychology of Character Development* (New York: John Wiley and Sons, Inc., 1960), pp. 101, 102.

Chapter 8

Whatever It Takes

She came out of the forest.

That's the only thing we know for sure about the strange woman who became the focus of media attention in January 2007. Some loggers in northeastern Cambodia complained that somebody had been stealing their lunches. Then one day they caught her—an emaciated creature with long hair and a strange crouching walk who could communicate only by signs, grunts, and shrieks.

Soon the news got around, and a crowd of curious people gathered, among them Sal Lou, the village constable. After watching the cowering captive for a few minutes, a memory stirred deep inside Lou, and he went to call his wife. Eighteen years earlier their daughter, Rochom, then 9 years old, had disappeared while herding buffalo. "Do you suppose . . . ?"

"Remember, Rochom had a deep scar on the inside of her wrist close to her hand," his wife said as they hurried toward the place. Gently they took the strange woman's arm and looked. They saw the scar.

The questions were many and the answers few. What was the story behind all of this? Could this girl, or anyone, have survived 18 years in the jungle? What had she eaten? And how did she avoid being eaten?

But for the moment none of that really seemed important. The joyful thing was that they had their daughter back. With songs and celebration they took her home, hearts overflowing and eager to give her the pent-up love of all those lost years.

What a change for Rochom! No more nights in the jungle, no more grubbing or snatching for food, no more cowering, running, and hiding. Now she could have security and a comfortable bed at night, clean clothing, proper nourishment, and above all, people who cared for her, who could love and talk to her.

But Rochom's family was in for a terrible surprise. First of all, they discovered that she didn't really like their food all that well. Most of the time she preferred to take a stick and grub for roots and worms. Nor did she enjoy wearing clothes, and she definitely didn't appreciate it when they tried to give her a bath. Before long they had to set up a watch around the clock to keep her from bolting back into the forest.

All of which leads to a question that is even more fundamental than the first ones: Is it really possible to have access to something better, and prefer something worse? Rochom's frustrated parents will assure you that it is. After having lost their daughter 18 years ago, they now thought they had gotten her back, but they discovered that they really hadn't.

And they are not alone in their suffering. Here is a message posted on the Web site of a parental support group: "My oldest son is addicted to crack, painkillers, and pot, and I think he has done just about every drug there is. . . . Most of the time I feel like if I'm the only mother in the world that is going through this. I love my son more than life itself. I would die for him if he would just get well."[1]

What can be harder or more painful than seeing someone you love make devastating choices?

And for Rochom's parents, things soon got even more complicated. Before long they found themselves under the gun of human rights activists. "This woman is an adult," the people protested. "Is it ethical to hold her against her will, to force her to follow your lifestyle? If she prefers to live like an animal and grub for roots and larvae, who are you to tell her that is a wrong choice?"

Here is the anguish and dilemma that God has been dealing with for a long time. Sometimes people who don't really understand the issues will say: *If God is good and if He is powerful, why doesn't He stop evil in its tracks? Why doesn't He make all the bad people good, and fix everything that's wrong with the world?*

It sounds logical, doesn't it? A lot of evil lurks out there. Think of what God could do with a few well-placed bolts of lightning! The first to go would be those monsters responsible for mass murder and genocide in places like Kosovo. Next He would zap the truck bombers and pedophiles. But hey, that would be just warming up. Before long He would get around to the people who tell lies and who don't go to church regularly. That would take care of a lot of things, wouldn't it? Think how devout everyone would be! All of us would run for the nearest church and pray really hard. And the offerings would be spectacular.

But that's not the way He does things, because that's not the way He is. God is love, and love and freedom are inseparable. Furthermore, as we noticed earlier, there can be no such thing as a moral person without moral choice, and moral choice includes the freedom to be immoral.

To choose the path of evil means to opt for the way of self-destruction. In fact, the two terms are synonymous. This is why God warned Adam and Eve that to choose evil was to select death (Genesis 2:17). But He also told them: "If you want to make that choice, if you want to root and grub in the dirt, to live on cockroaches and worms, then, as painful as it is for Me, I will let you."

Tough Choices

He will let us, yes, but He is not indifferent. Neither is He neutral or dispassionate about what happens. Because He loves us, He cares intensely. And He has devised a rescue strategy, a way for setting the captives free. What Christians usually call "the plan of salvation," it is difficult and slow precisely because He does not do it with thunderbolts. Instead, He does it without violating the twin principles of love and freedom.

It seems strange, doesn't it, that God has to urge and beg us to accept something that is for our own good? After all, it shouldn't be that hard to see the difference between a lifestyle that brings health, dignity, peace of mind, and self-respect and one that sets our feet on the road to personal disaster. What's wrong with people, anyway? Why can't everyone understand this?

On February 4, 1974, an urban guerrilla group called the Symbionese Liberation Army (SLA) kidnapped 19-year-old Patricia Hearst. In a message to her parents, the group said that it had made an "arrest" and that Patty was in "protective custody." They were fighting, they claimed, for poor people. Responding to the demands of her captors, Patricia's wealthy parents bought and distributed food worth millions of dollars to the poor of the San Francisco Bay Area.

The SLA, however, did not release Patricia. Instead they sent another communiqué saying that the food distribution had not been nearly enough and that it was of poor quality.

Then, on April 15 four women and a man armed with submachine guns held up the Sunset District branch of the Hibernia Bank in San Francisco. Police reviewing the surveillance video were amazed to see that one of the women holding a gun appeared to be Patricia Hearst. Could it be possible, the newspapers asked, that she had actually been brainwashed to the point of doing such a thing?

Forty-eight hours after the robbery the SLA released a tape in Patricia's own voice. In a defiant tone, she stated that she was, in fact, one of the bank robbers. "My gun was loaded, and at no time did any of my comrades intentionally point their guns at me." The crime was necessary, she claimed, to finance "the revolution." She called her parents "pigs," dismissed her fiancé, and said, "As for being brainwashed, the idea is ridiculous beyond belief."[2]

After she took part in several other violent crimes, Patty Hearst was arrested and eventually sentenced to 35 years in prison. The sentence was later reduced to seven years, and she served only two of those. In 1979 President Jimmy Carter commuted her sentence. "It should be clear to anyone," he said, "that this woman was brainwashed."

Hearst's captors had, in fact, subjected her to strenuous psychological pressure, and they achieved spectacular success. Without doubt she became totally convinced that their ideas were right and that their violence was fully justified.

As Rochom's parents and the Hearsts—and thousands of others have discovered—it really is possible to get your brain turned inside out. If you wallow in the dirt and eat grubs long enough, they will eventually seem good to you. Here is the key to understanding how some people fervently insist that evil is good and good is evil, and they scream that no one has a right to take it away from them.

Alexander Pope talked about this phenomenon back in the eighteenth century:

"Vice is a monster of so frightful mien,
As to be hated needs but to be seen;
Yet seen too oft, familiar with her face,
We first endure, then pity, then embrace."[3]

The plan of salvation, working from the foundation principle of love, rests on the twin principles of illumination and persuasion. Illumination means sharing information. It involves education to awaken the conscience and make the options clear.

Several years ago *Reader's Digest* published an article about smoking. After referring to advertisements that show a brawny macho cowboy smoking a cigarette, the article asked, "Do you want to see what *real* smokers' country looks like?" And it took the readers, not to a cattle ranch, but to a cancer ward. Then it described people drooling uncontrollably after the removal of their jaws because of bone cancer. It showed people suffering from radiation burns, people with faces horribly disfigured, unable to speak or eat normal food for the same reason. Others endured violent paroxysms of coughing or struggled desperately for air because emphysema and lung cancer were destroying their lungs. The article ended with a memorable line: "Somebody told these people a lie, and they believed it."

Think about that phrase. It is a perfect description of what has happened to millions of people today. They have been misled, deceived, and fooled, and not just with regard to smoking. Sin is destructive in all its shapes and forms. And "somebody" has been working hard to make it look like a cool, macho thing to do.

After 40 years as leader Moses stood before his people for the last time to deliver a farewell message. With an abundance of practical examples he described the benefits of following God's way. He contrasted the blessings of obedience with the despair and ruin of a self-destructive lifestyle. Then he said: "I call heaven and earth to witness against you today, that I have set before you life and death, the blessing and the curse. So choose life in order that you may live, you and your descendants" (Deuteronomy 30:19).

The apostle Paul gives us a solemn warning: "Don't be misled," he says. "No one makes a fool of God. What a person plants, he will harvest. The person who plants selfishness, ignoring the needs of others—ignoring God!—will harvest a crop of weeds. All he'll have to show for his life is weeds! But the one who plants in response to God, letting God's spirit do the growth work in him, harvests a crop of real life, eternal life" (Galatians 6:7, 8, Message).

This struggle for people's brains takes place not only in cases that make the headlines. Destructive and self-damaging behavior—"sin"—stalks the pathway of every one of us. Millions of people do stupid things that ruin their lives and hurt people they love—things that damage their usefulness and keep them from enjoying a sense of fulfillment and inner peace.

Jesus, too, talked about these drastic alternatives. He said that His mission was to give people their lives back. And not just the same as before: "I have come that they may have life, and have it to the full" (John 10:10, NIV). "I came so they can have real and eternal life, more and better life than they ever dreamed of" (verse 10, Message).

When Moses led the children of Israel out of Egypt, they had been living there as an ethnic minority for more than 200 years. Under the hypnotic drumbeat of popular culture, they had little concept of holiness or awe in the presence of God, no sense of the "exceeding sinfulness of sin," no horror at the terrible damage and estrangement it brings. In other words, their situation was a lot like the one that we face today.

Moses soon discovered that he could get the people out of Egypt, but that it was a lot harder to get Egypt out the people's hearts. This is the problem we are dealing with here, the most difficult one of all.

Because of this, God told Moses to set up a "sanctuary." It was a worship center rich in symbolism that included a detailed system of rituals and observances, all of them designed to teach important lessons for life.

For the forgiveness of their sins, God instructed the people to bring what He called a "sin offering." It was an animal. Repentant sinners had to come personally to the sanctuary with the creature and place their hands on its head. In this way they would symbolically transfer their sins—their guilt—to the animal.

Then they had to cut its throat.

There is no way to soften this picture or make it nice. A sheep or a goat—the animals most commonly used for sacrifice—does not die quietly. It struggles desperately and cries like a child as its blood pours out. But that was part of God's plan of instruction. He was trying to break through and bring reality home to their dull senses.

Such cruel and bloody animal sacrifices represented a reality that was even more impressive. Isaiah talks about the coming Messiah, and shows how He relates to what went on in the sanctuary:

"It was our sins that . . .

ripped and tore and crushed him—*our sins!*
He took the punishment, that made us whole.
Through his bruises we get healed.
We're all like sheep who've wandered off and gotten lost.
We've all done our own thing, gone our own way.
And God has piled all our sins, everything we've done wrong,
on him, on him."
—Isaiah 53:5, 6, Message.

Millions of people have been spiritually brainwashed. Their moral sense is almost gone. Believing that evil is fun and good is passé, they don't hesitate to indulge in a polluting, careless, overspending, self-destructive lifestyle while millions are starving and dying in slavery and oppression. And they dare to ask, "What's wrong with it?"

What can God do for such people? How can He get through to someone whose spiritual life is comatose? The answer is the cross.

Did you see Mel Gibson's movie *The Passion of the Christ?* It attempted to show the terrible brutality, the cruelty, of the Crucifixion. But the blood and gore are only part of the truth. On the cross Jesus experienced the darkness, the awful ophanhood of a soul without God. He went through what sinners will feel at the end of time when they know at last the full meaning of the decisions they have made.

By this horrifying spectacle Jesus sought to overcome our brainwashing and somehow get through to us. He tried to show us what sin is in reality, and God's incredible willingness to absorb the blows that would otherwise fall on us.

We live in a world in which hyperbole and exaggeration are common, but there is none at all in the cross. Exaggeration is impossible here. Nothing can adequately describe or portray the magnitude of Jesus' sacrifice, and no one will ever be able to fully comprehend it.

The theory of the "big bang" postulates that all matter, all the energy of the universe, and even space and time, sprang from one infinitesimally small point. Calvary was the moral equivalent of that point. The cross of Jesus Christ is the epicenter of the ages, the place in which all the evil and all the darkness concentrated. There, the horror of sin and all the suffering it has caused, all the loneliness and despair, all the cruelty and injustice from the beginning and until the end of its existence, came together in one spot. And from this same point grace and love, hope and eternity, sprang out.

As we begin to grow in understanding, we become spiritually alive. Then the anesthesia of our brainwashing starts to fade, and something happens that can be extraordinarily painful. Jesus talked about the work of the Holy Spirit and said: "He will convict the world of sin" (John 16:8, NKJV). When that happens, the horror of the cross increases, but at the same time, so does the hope and peace it offers, and we begin to see the truth of Isaiah's words: "The punishment He took . . . made us whole" (Isaiah 53:5, Message).

Here is how the apostle Paul puts it: "We're speaking for Christ himself now: Become friends with God; He's already a friend with you. How? you say. In Christ. God put the wrong on him who never did anything wrong, so we could be put right with God" (2 Corinthians 5:20, 21, Message). That, my friend, is the meaning of the cross: God put the "wrong" on Jesus.

The cross is part of God's whatever-it-takes decision to bring us to our senses, to break the stranglehold of our brainwashing, to push through the barricades that we have set up to keep out His love. At the cross we find our hearts broken and our pride overwhelmed by the reality of an unexplainable, incomprehensible love. "And I, if I am lifted up from the earth, will draw all men to Myself" (John 12:32), Jesus declared. In eternity we will never cease to study the meaning of the cross, and will never fully plumb its depths nor scale its heights.

Reflecting on this, the apostle Paul falls to his knees, exclaiming: "O the depth of the riches both of the wisdom and knowledge of God! How unsearchable are his judgments and unfathomable His ways!" (Romans 11:33).

"God was in Christ reconciling the world to Himself" (2 Corinthians 5:19). When His great work of reconciliation has accomplished its purpose, when we open our hearts at last to His love, then a wonderful process begins. Energy from above illuminates every corner of our darkened minds, clearing out the cobwebs and the clutter. Every day our sense of awe, our joy in the reality and purity of God, will grow. Then, when there is "nothing between us and God, our faces [will be] shining with the brightness of his face. And so we are transfigured much like the Messiah, our lives gradually becoming brighter and more beautiful as God enters our lives and we become like him" (2 Corinthians 3:18, Message).

This growth, this transformation brings with it a reordering of values and priorities, a realignment of loyalties. Reflecting on it, Paul made a list of the things that had been most important in his life before he knew Jesus: He had taken great pride in his nationality, his racial and ethnic purity, and his family name. Paul had been proud of his excellent education and, above all, his personal accomplishments. The apostle had looked down on people who did not share his religious zeal, and he had despised anyone who disagreed with his viewpoints. "I once thought that all these external things would save me," he wrote, "but now I know they're worthless. My hope is not in myself and what I have done, but in Jesus Christ. Everything I did before and all the honors I received are worthless compared to the priceless treasure of having Jesus Christ as my Savior and Lord" (Philippians 3:7, 8, Clear Word). And as if he is afraid we may still not get the point, Paul adds emphatically: "Whatever I had and did was nothing but *rubbish* in comparison to knowing Jesus Christ" (verse 8, Clear Word).

In the pure religion of Jesus we find openness, peace, and an incredible sense of freedom. The gospel enables us to love other people sincerely and purely with no hidden agenda, to accept them with their faults and weaknesses. As we linger in God's presence, His Spirit gives us growth and maturity and a balanced view of life and love and reality. Then the trials and even the tragedies of life turn into blessings, stepping-stones to higher ground.

Such an opportunity, such an invitation, calls for a response. Maybe sometime in the past you've felt a good impulse, a longing in your heart, to be more spiritual and to live a truly consecrated life. Maybe you've felt that, and thought: *Sure, that'd be nice,* but that's as far as it has gone.

I would encourage you—urge you—right now to do more than that. God has committed Himself to a whatever-it-takes plan to rescue you and bring you to Himself. Isn't it time for you to respond in the same way?

Jesus said: "The one who comes to Me I will certainly not cast out" (John 6:37). That takes us all in. Maybe you are coming with hesitation, half doubting, half believing, hardly understanding, and still wondering if hope is possible at all. None of that matters. The key word is "Come!" Whoever comes will be "accepted in the beloved" (Ephesians 1:6, KJV).

You can respond in your heart, and God will see and accept you fully into His loving embrace. At the same time, it will confirm your decision and make it even more concrete and permanent if you take a minute to record a few words expressing your personal decision and commitment as you respond to His invitation.

_____

_____

_____

[1] From a note posted on http://www.mothersofaddicts.com/Other_Mothers_Tears.htm.
[2] Based on an article by Katherine Ramsland at http://www.crimelibrary.com/terror-ists_spies/terrorists/hearst/3.html and information from other sources.
[3] Alexander Pope, "Essay on Man," Epistle I, lines 217-220.

Chapter 9

Beyond the Beginning

Sprouts tend to look alike. Take tomatoes and eucalyptus, for example. When that first little sprig of green pushes up, you really don't notice a lot of difference. It's what happens afterward that makes it easy to tell.

If you sense an analogy here, you're right. There is one, and it has to do with the subject of this chapter, which is about what happens after the beginning.

A lot of the people who read this will already be beyond the beginning in their spiritual life, but not everyone. Some are just starting to sprout spiritually, or even just considering their first thoughts about it. Before going on, I want to address a few words specifically to those individuals.

Maybe you have noticed something happening in your life, something of a spiritual nature. Perhaps hard to explain or even describe, it could be sort of a "softening." Thoughts and inclinations that you never were aware of before or that you had almost forgotten now creep into your mind. Have you responded to them in some way? Have you made a commitment to link up with God? If so, I fervently praise Him for that. Even if you haven't yet, and you are only beginning to feel less resistant to the idea, here is a little prayer for you:

"Dear God, thank You for watering my soil. It's been pretty dry. Something is definitely going on. Just the fact that I've been willing to listen must be Your doing, because it's new to me. Is something growing? Yes, it must be. I'm almost afraid to say it, but I will: 'Thank You!' And, yes, I want more."

If this prayer speaks to you in how you feel or where you are right now, then take courage, and read this chapter with care. It's about growing, because sprouting isn't enough.

Oh, and by the way—I'm not implying that this is only for beginners. A tomato grows to a certain size and stops, but a eucalyptus as long as it lives will keep on trying to reach higher. So whether you are recently sprouted or have been growing in God's garden for quite a while, the ideas discussed here will be helpful. This chapter is not one to skip or skim over lightly. It contains fundamental principles of Christian growth.

The KC Method

Early on April 9, 1892, 25 heavily armed men surrounded a four-room cabin on the KC Ranch in Johnson County, Wyoming. Their object was to hold a "necktie party"—that is, they planned to lynch Nate Champion, a cowboy whom they suspected of cattle rustling.

The attackers planned to finish the job quickly and get on with other business, but they had not counted on the valor of their intended victim. By rushing from window to window, Champion was able to return their fire so effectively that no one made any move to charge the house. From daybreak, when the first shot rang out, until about 5:00 p.m. Champion continued to hold off his attackers single-handed, coolly recording in a pocket memorandum book (whenever there was a lull in the gunfire) the circumstances and progress of the attack.

His story illustrates one idea of how it is possible to grow, to change, and to overcome in the Christian life. According to this model, we run desperately from window to window, blazing away at temptation, holding the devil and his friends at bay by will power and fierce determination. We could also call it the gritted-teeth and white-knuckles method. At times it involves holding our breath and counting to 10 (and maybe far beyond).

For Nate Champion, unfortunately, the method was ultimately unsuccessful. Around 5:00 in the afternoon his attackers set fire to a wagon loaded with hay and sent it rolling down a slope and crashing into the rear of the cabin. In a few minutes the little wooden structure burned furiously. Soon someone shouted, "There he goes!" The Winchesters blazed, and for Champion the fight was over.[1]

The Beanstalk Method

Like Jack in the famous children's story, some people believe that Chris-

Simply Put

tian growth is a matter of climbing the beanstalk or ladder of Christian achievement, until one day you finally arrive at the higher regions of spiritual achievement. This approach is more positive than the KC method, because it involves adding strength to strength, virtue to virtue, as we get rid of bad habits and acquire good ones.

Changing the analogy a bit, we find that it consists of incorporating into our list of character traits virtues such as generosity, humility, honesty, efficiency, order, temperance, respect, love, purity, patience, caring, discipline, order, modesty, kindness, forgiveness, unselfishness, trust, hopefulness, spirituality . . . I pause here, but the list really never does stop. It is infinite, because the perfection we are to achieve is measured by the perfection of God Himself (Matthew 5:48).

The Endorphin Method

Science is still learning about endorphins, those "happy hormones" produced in the brain. They reduce inflammation and pain and promote digestion, alertness, and a sense of well-being. Exercise increases them, and stress inhibits them.

If spiritual growth is a matter of happy feelings, then we achieve it by doing whatever promotes endorphins. We could define a "good" sermon or song as one that leaves us with a happy glow. Likewise, we would evaluate our personal devotions, meditation, faith-sharing, and all other things spiritual in terms of their endorphin value.

One could also call the endorphin approach the feel-good or cloud-nine method. When I was a boy, we used to sing a chorus about being "in-right, outright, upright, downright happy all the time." Maybe that's what some people equate with spiritual growth

The Right Answer

Now as you consider these alternatives, you are probably thinking that the correct answer is "none of the above." Well, maybe it is, but not necessarily. The various approaches are not always and not entirely wrong.

Fighting against temptation. The apostle Paul, using a figure of speech, said that he "beat" his body and made it his slave, so that after he had preached to others he himself would not end up being disqualified for the prize

72

(1 Corinthians 9:27). Near the end of his life he said that he had "fought the good fight" (2 Timothy 4:7). The book of Hebrews rebuked its readers because "in your struggle against sin, you have not yet resisted to the point of shedding your blood" (Hebrews 12:4, NIV). So maybe the KC method does have something to say for it. The Christian life really is a battle and a march.

Adding Christian virtues. And we mustn't entirely discount the beanstalk or climbing idea, either. In fact, it too has a basis in the Bible. The following passage has become known as "Peter's ladder":

"Now for this very reason also, applying all diligence,

in your faith supply moral excellence,

and in your moral excellence, knowledge,

and in your knowledge, self-control,

and in your self-control, perseverance,

and in your perseverance, godliness,

and in your godliness, brotherly kindness,

and in your brotherly kindness, love.

"For if these qualities are yours and are increasing, they render you neither useless nor unfruitful in the true knowledge of our Lord Jesus Christ" (2 Peter 1:5-8).

So the idea of progressively exchanging evil habits for good ones, of adding virtue to virtue, is not wrong.

Spiritual growth is more than behavior modification, but we cannot separate spirituality—a Spirit-filled life—from morality. As we continue in His presence, the Holy Spirit brings a transformation of the inner being that leads to a truly moral conduct. "And we, who with unveiled faces all reflect the Lord's glory, are being transformed into his likeness with ever-increasing glory, which comes from the Lord, who is the Spirit" (2 Corinthians 3:18, NIV).

As the tree grows, the fruit will certainly appear. The Bible mentions specifically love, joy, peace, patience, kindness, goodness, faithfulness, gentleness, self-control, tenderness, compassion, understanding, and quietness.[2] Trust will take the place of anxiety (1 Peter 5:7), love that of quarrelling (Ephesians 4:3, 4) and purity that of passion (1 Timothy 4:12).

One of the gifts that we receive from the Holy Spirit is joy (Romans 14:17). Jesus, our example, was "full of joy through the Holy Spirit" (Luke 10:21, NIV; see also Acts 13:52; 1 Thessalonians 1:6; Romans 14:17; Galatians 5:22). Therefore, it is not wrong to expect spiritual growth to reveal itself by happy feeling, and maybe that means that it might involve something like endorphins.

The Enoch Method

The problem comes when we take any of these methods without the central unifying principle that we could call the Enoch method.

The Bible tells us that Enoch "walked with God" (Genesis 5:22, 24). Evidently his method of achieving spiritual growth was successful, for we read that "he was commended as one who pleased God" and that he "was taken from this life, so that he did not experience death; he could not be found, because God had taken him away" (Hebrews 11:5, NIV).

The Bible is full of metaphors. They are figures of speech that help to illustrate truth. But unless we take time to think about their meaning, they can actually obscure the truth rather than clarify it. "Walking with God" is a metaphor. The translators of *The New English Bible* sensed this barrier and tried to break through it. In Genesis 17:1, in which God says to Abraham, "Walk before Me," they wrote: "Live always in my presence."

Living in God's presence means to educate the heart and mind to be aware of His presence. It involves the spiritual discipline of meditation: keeping our thoughts directed toward Him. And prayer: talking with Him, not just to fulfill our duty at certain specific hours, but breathing thoughts and words toward our Friend at every hour of the day. "Pray without ceasing," the apostle Paul urges us (1 Thessalonians 5:17). It means flashing a word toward heaven wherever we are: "Lord, walk with me today." "O God, help me to be patient with this person and remember my own mistakes." "Wow! What a beautiful rose! Thank You, Lord." "Please comfort Jeff today, Lord—he needs You a lot." When we can't sleep, when we are tempted, when we are happy, when we are peaceful or troubled: there is no time or place in which it is not appropriate to pray.

Practical Results

When we are walking with God, living always in His presence, the KC method is no longer a self-centered, muscle-tensing effort to fight off temptation. We will not be passive, of course, but we will direct our efforts toward staying in the sheltering presence of Jesus. We will spend more time and energy thinking about God and His love than thinking about the sin we are trying to resist. That was how the psalmist did it: "I have set the Lord always before me. Because he is at my right hand, I will not be shaken" (Psalm 16:8, NIV).

And what about the ladder or beanstalk way of achieving spiritual growth by climbing and gaining higher ground? Notice that the Enoch method does not involve sitting with Christ, but "walking" with Him, and walking implies movement. The people that God is leading "follow the Lamb wherever he goes" (Revelation 14:4). They may not have a sense of climbing, because they are simply always with Jesus. But the way He leads is ever upward.

Apart from Jesus, the endorphin method is also highly self-centered. The believer is always chasing after emotional highs. "How am I feeling?" becomes the central issue of the day, and ecstasy, the measure of religious experience. But in Jesus—that is, in His presence—we find "the peace of God, which transcends all understanding" (Philippians 4:7). Here is the great paradox: that we can have peace even while hurting, peace even while beset with troubles on all sides. Jesus said: "In me you may have peace. In this world you will have trouble. But take heart! I have overcome the world" (John 16:33, NIV). And David sang of the believer: "Surely you have . . . made him glad with the joy of your presence" (Psalm 21:6).

As we walk with God in the present life, the journey will reveal more and still more of His glory. The more we know of God, the more intense will be our happiness. Even in this life we can be filled with His love, satisfied with His presence. No one can have any greater hope or aspiration than this. And it is the one and only essential preparation for the eternity that God is preparing for His children.

This, then, is the Enoch method, God's perfect plan for spiritual growth. It means walking with Jesus, cultivating a sense of His presence, until every breath is a prayer and thoughts of God become intertwined with every act and circumstance of life. It is the divine remedy for self-centered living and the false values that the popular culture tries to force on us.

And it is not just a nice idea—it is our only hope of being prepared for eternal life.

You may be able to think of some specific ways in which spiritual growth has come to your life: changes in your way of thinking, maybe your attitudes or behavior. It would be good if you want to take a moment to thank God for them and also to focus on some changes that you would like to see in the near future.

_____

_____

_____

---

[1] Everett Dick, *Tales of the Frontier* (Lincoln: University of Nebraska Press, 1963), pp. 373–375.

[2] In addition to the fruits of the Spirit mentioned in Galatians 5:22, 23, the apostle cites these characteristics in other texts, including Romans 1:4; 14:17; 15:13, 30; 2 Corinthians 6:6; Ephesians 4:3, 4; 2 Timothy 1:7; Philippians 2:1. See also 1 Peter 3:4; James 3:17.

Chapter 10

Crossing the Line

The Danube River was neither blue nor beautiful[1] that evening in October of 1981 as Victor Bardan stood looking at its dark expanse. He was terrified, and for a good reason: a weak swimmer, he had always been afraid of water, but now he was planning to cross to the other side. The river was more than a mile wide at this point, its swirling current made even more dangerous by a recent storm.

But the alternative was grim. Behind him the secret police of Romanian dictator Nicolae Ceau escu were closing in. Capture would mean imprisonment, torture, and, almost certainly, death. On the other side was freedom, and with it, hope for a new beginning.

As the fading day gave way to darkness, Victor used a rope to lower an air mattress down the steep embankment, followed by a plastic bag into which he had sealed a change of clothing. Then, after scrambling down, he lay facedown on his flimsy craft and began to paddle.[2]

So what does this story have to do with "church," the topic of the present chapter? you might be asking yourself. *This guy is running away from something, not sitting there listening to a sermon.*

You may be surprised to know that "church" in the Bible is, in fact, about getting away from something. The root meaning of the word is "called out." The church is a group of people who have taken a stand and separated themselves from the crowd.[3]

The Bible writers, of course, remembered that God summoned Abraham, the founding father of their nation, to leave a great pagan city, to worship Him in the silence of the desert. "By faith," says the record, "Abraham, when he was called, . . . went out, not knowing where he was going" (Hebrews 11:8). He was leaving a prosperous city and the lifestyle that went with it (see Joshua 24:2). Eventually he came to Canaan, and there God and Abraham entered into a solemn "covenant"—a pledge of mutual commitment. It was these two apparently opposite things—separating (leaving Ur and the life it represented) and joining (pledging himself to God and a life of faith)—that made Abraham and his descendants God's chosen people, His "church" in ancient times.

The apostle Paul says that the Christian church is built on this same plan: "Remember," he wrote to the early believers, "that you were . . . excluded from the commonwealth of Israel, and strangers to the covenants of promise. . . . But now, in Christ Jesus you who formerly were far off have been brought near by the blood of Christ. . . . So then you are no longer strangers and aliens, but you are fellow citizens with the saints, and are of God's household" (Ephesians 2:12-19).

In another place the apostle uses a metaphor to give the same idea. He says that the church is not a new plant in God's garden, but a branch grafted into the root stock of Israel. So to understand the church—God's people today—we can take our cue from Abraham and the covenant that God made with him, because being one of God's children today, belonging to His church, involves the same two things it always did: leaving and joining, coming out and coming in. "Leaving" is a conscious decision to stand separate from the false values and destructive lifestyle of the "world." "Joining" means to take the covenant pledge, to unite ourselves to Jesus Christ and to identify publicly with Him and His cause. The visible expression of such joining is baptism.

Half of the Equation

Victor Bardan's "baptism" in the Danube River was a critical point in his journey to freedom, but the conditions and convictions that brought him to the edge of the water began a long time before. They started with an awareness that things were not right in the world in which he lived, and a refusal to close his eyes and pretend otherwise. And soon—much sooner than he expected—it became clear that he could no longer remain a part of this world, that to linger was to die.

A lot of Victor's friends were unhappy about his decision. They could see the same things he did, but the idea of actually making a change seemed overwhelming to them. *My family lives here and always has. This is where my friends and my job are. It's the only life I've ever known. My uncle works for the government, and my cousin is a party member. What would my parents say?*

And so they chose to stay. Are you are sensing an analogy here?

It is clear that a rapid change is taking place in the society we live in. The past 30 years have seen a steady deterioration in values. We see the shifting standards reflected in the media, the arts, and the Internet. A lot of people are upset and disturbed by what they witness. Surveys reveal that at least 70 percent of people are unhappy with the changes. Such people are not fanatics. In fact, most of them are not even religious. But they find their sense of morality and justice offended. But too many of them, however, have chosen to make an accommodation in order to survive.

The Bible employs the ancient city of Sodom as an example of scandalous public immorality. It is interesting to note that a righteous man was living right there in the middle of all the corruption—Abraham's nephew Lot. The Bible says that Lot "felt his righteous soul tormented day after day with their lawless deeds" (2 Peter 2:8). He was "tormented," yes, but he stayed. For one thing, his wife was not eager to leave behind her comfortable home in the city to go back to dwelling in a tent. Furthermore, their daughters were involved in the social life of the city. So it was easy for Lot to rationalize and stay.

Victor Bardan's friends would have agreed.

And maybe Jesus wouldn't have been too hard on him, either. In fact, He talked about this issue one time. He said: "I have other sheep, which are not of this fold" (John 10:16). Such "other sheep" are people like Lot. They live out their lives as honest citizens. Not cold and uncaring, they are ready to serve and help someone when they see a need. As a result, they belong to the 70 percent who have not caved in, who disagree with what is going on in society today.

Jesus is not casting doubt on their sincerity. In fact, He says that they have a special place in His heart.[4] He says they belong to Him. They are His sheep, yes . . . but they are not "of the fold."

Is that a problem? Most people today seem to think it is not. Living, as they do, in a society that is almost totally secular, they see absolutely no relation between being a good person and belonging to a church.

But Jesus' analogy of the sheepfold tells us a different story. In the mountains near where I live in northern Mexico, one finds many sheep with their shepherds, usually young boys, taking care of them. I have often seen them coming down at nightfall with their bells tinkling to take shelter in the sheepfold. For sheep being left on the mountain in the dark would be a terrifying thing. In a land in which the coyote is king, the possibility of a lone sheep surviving the night would be almost nonexistent.

That's what Jesus means when He talks about His "other sheep" not being in the fold. He is not just casually discussing the situation as OK. In fact, He uses an urgent imperative, saying that He "must call" those other sheep. As night falls and dangers abound, getting into the "fold" (which, of course, is the church) is the most important thing that a sheep can do.[5]

As a sincere and conscientious person, you may be one of God's chosen ones, His very own sheep. You may have right now the assurance of His love and care for you. But if you are not in the "fold," you are definitely not where you ought to be.

The Church as a Shelter

Invisible cords within any group of people bind heart to heart and mind to mind. Researchers have explored these powerful influences, especially since 1947, when Kurt Lewin pioneered the study of group dynamics. Today a wide variety of recovery and support groups harness the ability of the group to influence people.

During the past few years such study has taken a new turn. Scientists are dedicating intense research to what they call "swarm" behavior. In a way not fully understood, large groups of animals seem to develop a collective intelligence, as seen, for example, in insects, and also in flocks of birds or schools of fish. With no visible leader, the entire group makes instant decisions to change direction or take action against a predator. In 2003 Karsten Heuer, a wildlife biologist, followed a vast herd of caribou for five months, traveling more than 1,000 miles with the animals on their migration from winter range in the Yukon to calving grounds in Alaska. He described this collective intelligence: "It was as though every animal knew what its neighbor was going to do, and the neighbor beside that and beside that. There was no anticipation or reaction. No cause and effect. It just was."[6]

Something similar appears to function in human society as well. The group is a powerful influence, and people drawn together by a common purpose can truly have a life-changing effect on one another. Human beings "are wired to connect," says social scientist Daniel Goleman. There is a kind of "neural WiFi."[7]

The Dynamo Behind Church Dynamics

It is hardly surprising that the power of group dynamics is at work in the church. The church is a group consisting of people who interact, and obviously they will influence one another.

But more—much more—than that is involved.

When Jesus decided to talk to His disciples about church for the first time, He didn't begin by mentioning an organization and inviting them to join. He said: "Who do you say that I am?"

"You are the Christ," Simon replied, "the Son of the living God" (Matthew 16:16).[8]

It was at this point that Jesus mentioned the church for the first time, because at last He had somebody who was ready to be part of it. Jesus' next statement made it clear why Simon was now ready: "You are Peter, a rock," He said. "This is the rock on which I will put together my church, a church so expansive with energy that not even the gates of hell will be able to keep it out" (verse 18, Message).

We noticed in chapter 1 how Peter himself later clarified the meaning of those words when he wrote: "And coming to [Jesus], as to a living stone, . . . you also, as living stones, are being built up as a spiritual house" (1 Peter 2:4, 5).

Jesus Christ is the great "living stone." He is the cornerstone of the church. But the cornerstone is not the whole building. Whoever comes to Jesus and connects with Him, as Peter did, will also, by the grace of God, become solid material, a "living stone" just like Peter (verse 4; Matthew 16:18). It is by focusing on our relationship with Jesus, by keeping it strong and constant, that we ourselves become living stones, material that God can use to build up His church. This is so important that I am going to repeat it: It is by focusing on our relationship with Jesus, by making sure that it remains strong and constant, that we ourselves become living stones that God can use to construct His church.

If we focus our relationship to the church in any other way, we will find ourselves wobbling and wavering with every passing breeze, and we will contribute to the weakness and instability of the structure rather than helping it grow and adding to its strength. If our relationship to Jesus is not active and strong, then the only dynamic remaining in this equation is the influence of the group, and the only resource available to us is the strengths or weaknesses of the individual members. But if we concentrate on our connection to Jesus Christ, then we will draw strength from His strength, purity and holiness from His perfection. When this happens, the group dynamics that are at work in the church will have a powerful sanctifying influence on each member, and the church will truly be a force for good in the community and the world. Not even "the gates of hell" can "prevail" against a church that takes as its basis a relationship with Jesus Christ.

It was exactly the same message in Abraham's time. "Coming out"—leaving behind Ur and all that went with it—was not enough. Abraham also had to "come in." He had to enter into a covenant relationship with God. "Live always in my presence," God said to him, ". . . so that I may set my covenant between myself and you" (Genesis 17:2, NEB).

Living as honest citizens while we quietly disagree with the evil that surrounds us is good, of course. It's a lot better than joining the forces of evil, but it's not enough.

Stop right now and listen. Hear that quiet voice? It's the Shepherd, and He's calling *you*. He wants you in His fold. "Today, please listen; don't turn a deaf ear" (see Hebrews 3:7, 15). *Now* is the time to stand up and be counted. Night is definitely falling. Please, don't waste another minute. Get inside the fold while you still can.

How to Stay Inside Once You Get There

"Naw, I don't go anymore," Jerry told me the other day when I talked to him about church. "I finally woke up and realized I wasn't getting anything out of it, so I quit."

Like a lot of other people in his generation, Jerry is infected with a click-click mentality. At home he never sits down to watch TV without the remote control, the "clicker," in his hand.

What does he want to get out of the TV? Something quite specific, actually: a happy feeling, maybe a laugh, something that will stir his emotions.

OK, let's see, here's channel 27: Yikes! Some skinny woman is talking about how she gets her calcium by drinking milk. "Click." Channel 28: The local school district is floating a bond issue. "Click" goes Jerry again. Another rerun of *Seinfeld!* "Click, click, click."

The last time Jerry dragged himself to church, he sat there for a while longing for a clicker. Before the sermon was over, he got up and left. Maybe he'll be back again, but it's not for sure.

Going to church with a click-click mentality means sitting there passively, waiting for something to happen, something that will tickle your emotions and give you a happy feeling. It's treating church as if it were some kind of show—as if it were the preacher's job to give you a feel-good experience.

As we noted earlier, the Lord gathered His people at Mount Sinai to talk to them about church—not under that name, of course, but that's what He was doing when He spelled out the terms of the covenant. Here's what he said to them:

"If you will listen obediently to what I say and keep my covenant, out of all peoples, you'll be my special treasure. The whole Earth is mine to choose from, but you're special: a kingdom of priests, a holy nation" (Exodus 19:5, 6, Message).

This passage offers us a foolproof way to get rid of the click-click mentality, to vitalize our religious experience and overcome boredom and apathy in the church. God is not calling His sheep into the fold just to mill around and baa at each other. He has given us a responsibility, a work to do.

We need to care about the people who don't have the beautiful experience that God has given us. We have to care enough to pray for them. Interceding with God on their behalf is part of the priestly ministry described in the covenant. It also involves interceding with the people on behalf of God, urging them to be reconciled to Him, telling them about the night-and-day difference He made for us.

Furthermore, He wants us to be a holy people. Thus we must focus constantly on our relationship with Jesus Christ, keeping it strong, growing, and active. When we do this, then the songs, the prayers, the sermons, and everything else that happens in church will come alive for us. They will be deeply meaningful.

As we live this way, we will no longer sit slumped in the pew waiting for church to do something for us. We will realize that *we* are the church, and that it is up to us to vitalize the experience and make it meaningful.

Crossing the Line

The line we cross by joining the church causes a shift in the social fabric of our lives. It involves new goals and values, a new sense of purpose and of mission and more than likely a change in lifestyle as well. Baptism, the public ceremony by which we become part of the church, signals our acceptance of the covenant. It is a visible statement, a public acknowledgment that something has been going on in our life.

But it does *not* mean that this "something" is finished and complete. And you don't have to wait until it is before you can join the church. Just as a wedding is neither the beginning of love nor its full maturing, so it is with baptism, the public act that declares our entry into the church. But it is a critical and essential point.

For Victor Bardan, crossing the Danube was a frightening thing to do, and not only because of the difficulty involved in the physical act. It almost seemed as if he were turning his back on people he loved, and the way of life that he knew best.

When he finally emerged dripping on the other shore, he was hardly home free. But God placed in his path wonderful people who helped him on his way and offered him the encouragement he needed. Even with their assistance, some dark hours still awaited him. Many of his former acquaintances ridiculed and denounced him. It took time to form new connections and feel completely at home in the new world that he had chosen. But even in his darkest hours Victor never doubted that he had done the right thing, and each passing year confirmed the value of his decision.

I encourage you to record here a brief prayer in which you ask for God's guidance and express your decision with regard to His church:

---

¹ An allusion to "On the Beautiful Blue Danube," a waltz by Johann Strauss.

² The name is fictional, but the incident is real. See http://as.uwb.edu/voices/EN.html.

³ By the time the New Testament was written in the first century, the word *ekklesia* (church) had become a common term that meant "assembly" or "meeting."

⁴ Corinth was famous for a degree of immorality that was scandalous even by the loose standards of the time. The apostle Paul went through something like culture shock when he arrived there. But that night the Lord spoke to him in a dream and said, "I have many people in this city" (Acts 18:10; 1 Corinthians 6:9-11).

"The blood shall be a sign for you on the houses where you live; and when I see the blood I will pass over you, and no plague will befall you to destroy you when I strike the land of Egypt" (Exodus 12:13).

⁵ The apostle Paul says something that also reflects this same idea. He comments that anyone who rebels against the principles of the faith has to be excluded from the church. He refers to it as handing over the person to Satan (1 Corinthians 5:5-9). It is equivalent to putting someone out of the sheepfold and leaving them exposed, away from the protecting cover of the church.

⁶ Reported in Peter Miller, "Swarm Theory," *National Geographic,* July 2007, pp. 141, 146.

⁷ *Social Intelligence* (New York: Bantam Books, 2006) See also *Newsweek*, Oct. 23, 2006. This effect also appears in "mob psychology." People who are normal and otherwise good neighbors—individuals such as you and me—will commit acts of savagery under the influence of the group.

⁸ A quiet conviction held in some secret place deep within your heart is good. In fact, it is essential. But it is not enough. We also need to make a visible, public commitment. And that was what Peter was doing.

Chapter 11

Finding the Remnant

My grandpa Talbott used to tell about a hired man who worked hard every day in the fields. Plowing, planting, weeding, harvesting—you name it. He never slacked off.

Everything was fine until one day in the spring when it started to rain. Everyone on the farm was trying to get the crops in, but nobody could work the ground in that soggy weather. So the farmer's wife got together the eggs and butter that she'd been saving to sell in town. Then they hitched their horse to the wagon and started off.

They left the hired man down in the cellar with instructions to select the seed potatoes for planting. If any were shriveled or showed signs of blight, he was to throw them onto a pile to be used as feed. The good ones he would cut into two or three pieces, selecting the best for planting.

Well, they'd gotten almost to town when the farmer's wife remembered a shawl that she'd been fixing up for an old widow, and she insisted they had to turn around and go back for it. When they arrived back home, the cellar door was open, and as they went by they said "Howdy" to the hired man, but he didn't answer. So they went down to check, and they found him lying on the floor.

"You all right?" they asked him.

"Not hardly," he said, opening his eyes partway. "I don't think I was ever so tuckered out."

"How could you be tuckered out, jest from settin' there and sortin' potatoes?" the farmer asked.

"I know, I know," he answered. "It don't seem like nothin', but it's them decisions. It's the decisions that gets me down."

I think Grandpa liked this story because it tells a fundamental truth about life—and maybe about Grandpa himself. He was a good man, always fair and honest. You could count on him to keep his word, and he'd go out of his way to help someone in need, but he had no use at all for religion of any kind.

I asked him about it one day, and he didn't say "It's the decisions that gets me down." What he said was "There are a lot of churches, Loron. And you know something? All of them are right—and they can prove it, too!" Grandpa's solution to all the conflicting claims was to give up and not even try to sort it out.

You've got to admit, of course, that he had a point: when it comes to religion there really are a lot of choices. Even the little town where I live in northern Mexico has Catholics, Baptists, Methodists, Adventists, Presbyterians, Jehovah's Witnesses, Mormons, and several kinds of Pentecostals. If you go a little farther afield you can find Wesleyans, Moravians, Lutherans, Presbyterians, Swedenborgians, Unitarians and Trinitarians, Shakers and Quakers, and a very long list of others. No wonder a lot of people adopt Grandpa's approach.

In fact, some take it even further. The other day one of them said to me: "There's no right or wrong in religion. The only thing that matters is love. And if you claim your religion is right, that's wrong, because it's not loving. And besides," he said, eyeing me suspiciously, "it's elitist." When he said that, of course, I backed off in a hurry, because who wants to be an elitist?

It would appear, however, that Jesus' disciples were not quite so timid. One day Peter began talking about which was the right religion in his time, and he didn't say: "There are a lot of choices, but it doesn't matter. The important thing is to be loving." What he declared was: "There is salvation in no one else [but Jesus]; for there is no other name under heaven that has been given among men by which we must be saved" (Acts 4:12). You wouldn't expect somebody like Peter would be an elitist, would you? But it seems clear that he thought his religion was right, and if so, that meant he assumed the others were wrong.

Of course, the idea of a right religion didn't start with the apostle. We've been talking about something called the covenant. Now, there's an "elitist" document for sure. It singled out the children of Israel (the Jews) as God's chosen people. And if they were "chosen," that meant the others weren't—it was just that simple.

Was That Fair?

But we need to ask if such an idea would have been fair or even reasonable. I mean, don't you think there were good and sincere people among the Moabites, the Egyptians, and others who lived in those days?

Of course there were. In fact, the Bible gives specific examples of such individuals.[1] Furthermore, it says that God loves everyone—even the people who don't love Him (Matthew 5:45; Romans 5:8). It also declares that He "is not one to show partiality, but in every nation the man who fears Him and does what is right, is welcome to Him" (Acts 10:34, 35).

So how could we believe that He would select one specific people group for salvation, leaving all the others out in the cold? The answer is that He wouldn't. The question comes from a mistaken idea about what it means to be chosen.

Paul said the disobedient Jew would be lost, and the faithful Gentile saved. He realized this idea would shock some of his Jewish readers, so he deliberately raised the question he knew they would ask: "Then what advantage has the Jew?" (Romans 3:1). If being one of the chosen people—having the right religion—doesn't give you a ticket to eternal life, what does it offer you?

Paul answered his own question by emphasizing that the advantage of the Jew was "great in every respect" (verse 2).

Well, then, what was it?

"First of all," the apostle explained, "that they were entrusted with the oracles of God" (verse 2).

The oracles were communications, messages that God sent through the prophets (Hebrews 1:1). Eventually they were collected and became known as Holy Scripture, or the Bible.

This gives us a fundamentally different idea of what the "chosen people" or the right religion is all about. By designating the descendants of Abraham as His people, God was not giving them a monopoly on His love or an automatic guarantee of eternal life. Rather, He selected them to be His messengers, His channels of truth for the world.

"Darkness shall cover the earth, and gross darkness the people" (Isaiah 60:2, KJV). God's solution was to find a people through whom He would shed light.

He told them:

"The Lord will rise upon you [like the sunrise],

and His glory will appear upon you.

Nations will come to your light,

And kings to the brightness of your rising."

—Isaiah 60:2, 3

God planned that through Israel all the nations of earth would come to the light. Then "the earth will be full of the knowledge of the Lord as the waters cover the sea" (Isaiah 11:9).

" 'They shall not teach again,

each man his neighbor and each man his brother,

saying, "Know the Lord,"

for they shall all know Me,

from the least of them to the greatest of them,'

declares the Lord."

—Jeremiah 31:34

So God's "elitist" plan of calling a chosen people was actually the most nonelitist one in history. It was His way of reaching the Moabites, the Egyptians, the Africans, and all the rest with the message of His love.

How to Tell the Difference

Does this bring us any closer to answering Grandpa's question? A little, because it tells us that God really did have a "chosen people" in ancient times. But Grandpa didn't live in ancient times (contrary to what I once believed). His problem was that he couldn't figure out how to tell the difference between the true and the false today. "They all look alike," he said, so he gave up.

He's gone now. I wish that he were still here and that I could tell him that there really was an answer, and that he could have found it.

We have noticed before that when God called His people out of Egypt He spelled out the terms of the covenant that would establish them as His chosen people. He said that they would be (1) a kingdom of priests and (2) a holy nation (Exodus 19:6).

A royal priesthood. First of all, they—the whole nation—would be His priests. By definition, a priest is a go-between, a mediator between God and human beings. This term is directly related to what we just observed—that God had selected them to represent Himself among the nations of earth. They were to intercede with the people on behalf of God, urging them to accept His love and sharing with them the oracles, the truth that He had been sending through the prophets. Furthermore, they were also to intercede with God on behalf of the people through their prayers.

A holy nation. The second important characteristic of God's people was they were to be a holy nation. "Holy" means wholly dedicated and consecrated to God. The terms of their holiness were specific. "The Lord spoke to you from the midst of the fire. ... He declared to you His covenant which He commanded you to perform, that is, the Ten Commandments; and He wrote them on two tablets of stone" (Deuteronomy 4:12, 13).

What Happened When Jesus Came?

Now let's fast-forward to the time Jesus arrived and the Christian church started to make its way in the world. Who was the "chosen people" at this point?

Here is what the apostle Peter wrote to the Christian believers: "But you are a chosen race, a royal priesthood, a holy nation, a people for God's own possession, that you may proclaim the excellencies of Him who has called you out of darkness into His marvelous light" (1 Peter 2:9).

Do you notice that he is citing the terms of the covenant from the passage that we just looked at in the book of Exodus? But now he applies them to the church. The church—he is saying—has become the new chosen people, and true believers are those who show the same two characteristics: they are a "royal priesthood, a holy nation."

Royal priesthood. The priestly service of God's ancient people devolved upon the first Christians. They went everywhere, saying: "We are ambassadors for Christ, as though God were entreating through us; we beg you on behalf of Christ, be reconciled to God" (1 Corinthians 5:20). The church was the channel that God had chosen to receive and transmit the "oracles," or prophetic messages to the world. We know of at least seven prophets in New Testament times, although probably more existed.

A holy nation. Some people, knowing that Paul says that we are no longer "under the law," have concluded that God doesn't take into account our behavior and that a life of holiness is optional. But Peter declares that Christians, like their ancient counterparts, are to be "a holy nation."

The "Chosen People" Today

We have identified two important characteristics of the chosen people, and we have seen that they are applicable not only in Moses' time but in the Christian Era as well. This brings us closer to finding an answer to Grandpa's question about identifying the "right religion," the true church today.

In Revelation 12 we find a prophecy that outlines the history of the church from the time of the apostles down to the end of time. It begins with Christ and His victory over Satan. Next it describes the long centuries of persecution and apostasy that would come, and in the last verse it offers a vision of God's people in our own day: "The dragon [Satan] was enraged with the woman [the church] and went off to make war with the rest of her offspring, who

[1] keep the commandments of God and

[2] hold to the testimony of Jesus" (verse 17).

The word "rest" means "remainder," "remnant," something that is left over. But we need to ask: a remnant of what? Obviously, this term ties them directly to the past. They are the continuation of God's people, His church in ages past.[2] As a result, they are the same "holy people" described in the Exodus covenant and are committed to a life of faithfulness and obedience.

We live in a society in which any idea of submission to the will of God and obedience to His commandments is definitely not part of the landscape. In fact, the Ten Commandments are under attack today even among people who read the Bible and claim to believe it: As John MacArthur notes: "The gospel in vogue today holds forth a false hope to sinners. It promises them that they can have eternal life yet continue to live in rebellion against God. Indeed, it encourages people to claim Jesus as Savior yet defer until later the commitment to obey Him as Lord. It promises salvation from hell but not necessarily freedom from iniquity. It offers false security to people who revel in the sins of the flesh and spurn the way of holiness. By separating faith from faithfulness, it teaches that intellectual assent is as valid as wholehearted obedience to the truth."[3]

So even among Christians we find that some do not always believe or appreciate the importance of the Ten Commandments. But Jesus stated that obedience was one of the marks of a true follower. "Not everyone who says to Me, 'Lord, Lord,' will enter the kingdom of heaven; but he who does the will of My Father who is in heaven" (Matthew 7:21).

They hold to the testimony of Jesus. And what about the second characteristic of God's last-day chosen people, the one that declares that they hold to the testimony of Jesus Christ? We get more specific information about the "testimony of Jesus" from two parallel passages that appear later in the book of Revelation. The angel messenger who brought the revelation to John told him:

"I am a fellow servant of yours and *your brethren who hold the testimony of Jesus.*" —Revelation 19:10	"I am a fellow servant of yours and of *your brethren the prophets.*" —Revelation 22:9

In other words, the "brethren" who have the "testimony of Jesus" are "the prophets," a conclusion confirmed in the first passage (Revelation 19:10), which declares categorically: "The testimony of Jesus is the spirit of prophecy."

As with God's people in ancient times, the remnant of the last days shares the "oracles"—the messages received through the prophetic gift. Once again God has chosen a people to speak for Him, to testify about His love, to transmit to the world His message because they possess and give to the world "the testimony of Jesus."

This characteristic of the true church in the last days corresponds to "royal priesthood," the special ministry that belongs to God's true church in every age,

The "Chosen People" Today

It should be clear that the same two characteristics have identified God's people in every period. The true church is one that defends and honors the law of God and that carries out a royal priesthood, sharing with the world the testimony of Jesus received through the gift of prophecy.[4]

You shouldn't have given up, Grandpa. There really is a right religion today just as there always has been, and God has given us clear signs by which to identify the chosen people, God's remnant church today. As has always been true, the "chosen people" do not claim to have a monopoly on God's love. They are, rather, a people with a mission—messengers specially designated by Him to communicate truths specific for the time. They summon men and women everywhere to know God and to turn to Him in obedience and love.

Why do you think it is part of God's plan to have a designated people rather than just recognizing every sincere person in the world as His messenger?

_____

_____

_____

_____

---

[1] We remember, for example, Ruth the Moabite and Naaman the Syrian officer.

[2] The "remnant" is a persistent theme in the Bible. See Gerhard Hasel, "The Remnant," *International Standard Bible Encyclopedia,* rev. ed. (Grand Rapids: William B. Eerdmans, 1988).

[3] *The Gospel According to Jesus* (Grand Rapids: Zondervan, 1994), pp. 201, 202.

[4] Chapter 16 will provide further light on the testimony of Jesus manifested through the gift of prophecy in our time.

Chapter 12

Getting Along

If you and everyone else in your family are less than five feet tall, if your native language is a series of clicks and guttural sounds, and if you wear leather garments and get your food by chasing it down in the bush, then the chances are pretty good that you are a Bushman and you live in the Kalahari Desert of Botswana.

One bright morning William Moyo, a Seventh-day Adventist pastor in Tsessebe, Botswana, heard a polite cough outside the open doorway of his home. When he went to see who was there, he was startled and more than a little afraid. Standing before him was Bushman carrying a hunting knife and a bag that hung partially open, revealing a number of poison-tipped arrows. Tsessebe is more than 180 miles from the tribal homeland of the Bushmen, and it was practically unheard-of for any of them to wander so far from their familiar haunts.

"*Dumelong*" ("Good day"), the Bushman said politely. At that the pastor was even more astonished, because it meant that his visitor could speak Tswana, the common language of the Bantu people.

But Moyo's typical African courtesy prevailed: "Will my brother please come in?" he said, and soon the little man was seated before him.

"My name is Sekuba," the visitor explained, "and I am looking for the people who obey all of God's commands."

The Bushman explained that some days before, he had been awakened during the night by a blinding light. In the midst of the flames was one who told him that he must go in search of a people who have a black Book with the words of the great Creator God, a people who keep all of God's commands.

"How will you speak to the Bantu?" Sekuba's family asked him in alarm when he told them that he was going on a journey.

"The Book talks," he replied calmly. "The shining one taught me words from the book. I understood them, and I will be able to speak them."

It was a difficult journey, one that took many days. Several times Sekuba suffered mistreatment and insults from the Bantu. At one point he was arrested, marched 40 miles, and made to appear before a magistrate, who listened to his amazing story and then released him. But through it all, the little man quietly persevered. He told Pastor Moyo that he had been following a small, mistlike cloud that appeared each morning on the horizon. As he approached Tsessebe the cloud disappeared, letting Sekuba know that it was the place he had been seeking.

Pastor Moyo went for his Bible. When Sekuba saw it, he bowed low. "Yes!" he said. "That is the Book."

For two weeks Sekuba remained with Pastor Moyo. They spent hours each day studying the words from the Book. The pastor soon discovered that the Bushman was quick to learn and grasp the message. Before leaving, the little man extracted a promise from Pastor Moyo to visit him and his family. "There are many more who will listen if you come to teach us about God's words," he explained.

A short time later Moyo traveled on his bicycle to fulfill this promise. On the first visit he stayed a week, teaching and explaining while the Bushman translated. A few months later Sekuba received the fellowship of Jesus and His church through baptism, the first from his tribe to do so. Later his wife, brother, and sister were also ready for baptism. Before long the number of Bushmen believers had grown to 40. Sekuba was ordained an elder and appointed to lead the Bushman church.

Now I want to leave Sekuba for a minute and tell you about someone else.

I don't recall anyone among the doctoral students at the theological seminary at Andrews University who was not somewhat in awe of Professor Carsten Johnsen. Profoundly intellectual, he was also articulate and original. He was as creative in his way of presenting his ideas as he was in his reflection. More than anyone I ever knew, his discourse was free from clichés and trivia. I never heard him tell a story or crack a joke. He never waved his arms or abandoned his quiet conversational tone, but he absolutely held your attention. His classes were deeply rooted in Scripture and warm with his own personal spirituality and piety.

Now let's fast-forward a few years and imagine a scene that might happen one day. Jesus has returned, and His people are still amazed as they try to take in the incredible beauty of their new home. They are reveling in the glorious music and in the love that flows as freely as the water of life.

Suddenly someone announces, "Look! Over there! That's Dr. Johnsen!" At that moment we spot Carsten heading to where Jesus is sitting and talking with a little man from Africa.

"Carsten!" we hear Jesus say as he comes up, "it's good to see you! Here, I want you to meet a friend of Mine. Carsten, this is Sekuba."

Now, I want to ask you a question: Do you think those two will find anything to talk about?

"Tell me about yourself, Sekuba," Carsten Johnsen says.

"Well, I was a sinner," Sekuba replies. "My mind was filled continually with wicked thoughts, fear, hatred, and confusion. Then one glorious day Jesus found me."

But that's as far as he gets, because Carsten Johnsen breaks in. "Amazing! That's just what happened to me! And how was your life after that?"

"When Jesus came in, the darkness disappeared, and everything was different. My entire existence changed. After that, life had meaning, a deep purpose . . ." Their conversation goes on, and before long we see the two of them walking along the golden street in close conversation like old friends.

It's a beautiful picture, isn't it? I enjoy thinking about this because I find it hard to imagine two individuals who apparently would have less in common. And yet they did share the thing that matters most.

When Jesus is the centerpiece, when our thoughts are dominated by gratitude for what He has done and our soul is at peace in Him, then nothing else is as important. Here is the great commonality of the gospel. Nothing but the gospel can be so effective in bridging every gap and overcoming every human barrier.

It's Not Easy

When Richard Nixon was running for president of the United States, at one of his campaign stops a teenage girl held up a sign that said: "Bring us together." Nixon decided to adopt the phrase as a campaign slogan. "That will be the great objective of this administration, at the outset—to bring the American people together." It was a beautiful ideal, of course, but the bitter end of the Nixon presidency illustrates how difficult it is to achieve.

We live in a world torn by sectionalism, tribalism, and many kinds of social prejudices and hatreds passed along mindlessly from one generation to the next. In many places people still seek to avenge offenses suffered by their ancestors hundreds or even thousands of years ago.

Maybe that shouldn't surprise us too much, because we live in a sinful world. But the saddest things is that even the church, the institution established by Jesus Christ to bring people to Himself, has not escaped such strife.

Jesus could see it coming, and it weighed heavily on His heart. In His last prayer with His disciples He tells His Father: "I'm praying not only for them [His disciples], but also for those who will believe in me because of them and their witness about me [that's you and me]. The goal is for all of them to become one heart and mind—just as you, Father, are in me and I in you, so they might be one heart and mind with us. Then the world will believe that you, in fact, sent me. The same glory you gave me, I gave them, so they'll be as unified and together as we are—I in them, and you in me. Then they'll be mature in this oneness and give the godless world evidence that you've sent me and loved them in the same way you've loved me" (John 17:20-23, Message).

Jesus here prays that His followers will draw together in unity and love. And furthermore, He is explaining to us how we can do it: "I in them," He declares, "and they in me."

When we come to Jesus, we approach closer to each other. We cannot be united with Christ without being united with each other. And we cannot be separated from one another without also drifting apart from Jesus.

That is what the apostle John tells us: "If someone says, 'I love God,' and hates his brother, he is a liar; for the one who does not love his brother whom he has seen, cannot love God whom he has not seen" (1 John 4:20).

Maybe you remember a line from chapter 10: "It is by focusing on our relationship with Jesus, by keeping it strong and constant, that we ourselves become living stones, material that God can use to construct His church. . . . If we focus our relationship to the church in any other way, we will find ourselves wobbling and wavering with every passing breeze, and we will contribute to the weakness and instability of the structure rather than helping it grow and adding to its strength." It is equally true that it is only by keeping our relationship with Jesus strong and constant that we can be united with one another.

For longer than most of us could remember, Laura had been a pillar in the church. She seemed like everyone's mother. Every time the doors opened, she was there. As the others arrived, she never failed to have a smile, a hug, or a word of encouragement for each one.

Then one sad day Roxana, a young woman hardly out of her teens, stood up and announced, "I saw it with my own eyes: The last time the church received a shipment of clothing for the poor, Laura took several bags, stuffed them full of clothes, and gave them to her family and close relatives."

Some glanced nervously at Laura and noticed that she was staring at the floor. After the meeting, several looked for her to offer a word of support and encouragement, but she had vanished. For the first time that anyone could remember, she didn't stay around to speak to the young mothers or help the deacons to put things away before they locked up the building.

One of Laura's friends stopped by her house the next day. Tears came as they talked about what had happened. "Aren't my poor relations as worthy of help as anyone else?" Laura asked. "Just because they are related to me, does that mean I can't help them? Why didn't Roxana tell me, if that's how she felt? Why did she get up and accuse me in front of the whole church?"

"You're absolutely right," her friend said, with a sense of indignant sympathy. "It's just terrible what she did."

Within a week it seemed that everyone in the church had lined up on one side or the other. The older women, in general, sided with Laura while most of the younger members said they admired Roxana for her courage. A few even commented that Laura acted as if she owned the church, and that it was good that somebody had put her in her place.

After that, if Laura came at all, she arrived late and left early. And for a lot of us, the church seemed like a different place.

A number of weeks went by this way. Then one day the head elder announced that the next week we would be celebrating Holy Communion, the rites of the Lord's Supper.

Laura came to the meeting that day. You could see her sitting in one corner toward the back.

The Communion table was resplendent and colorful. The bread and the wine, representing Jesus' broken body and blood, were laid out on silver trays. The sweet fragrance of the grape filled the little church. The pastor began reading the familiar texts from the Gospels. "This is my body, which is broken for you." "This is my blood …, which is shed for many for the remission of sins" (1 Corinthians 11:24, KJV; Matthew 26:28, KJV).

Roxana said later that as she heard these words, her eyes seemed to focus on the bleeding Savior, and the Holy Spirit touched her soul. She saw herself a forgiven sinner, covered by the mercy and grace of God, and then she thought of Laura. *She's a sinner too, struggling against the power of a fallen nature, just as I am. How could I set myself up to pass a harsh judgment on her for what she did?* As Roxana opened her heart to the work of the Spirit, she was horrified to realize the deadly effect that the controversy was having on the congregation.

Laura was thinking too. In fact, she had spent nearly every waking moment since that terrible day dwelling on how Roxana had hurt her, how unfair it had been, and how some of the other members had turned their backs on her after her years of faithful service.

But now, in the presence of Jesus' loving sacrifice, her eyes too began to focus in a different direction, and before long her feelings of anger and self-pity began to melt away. *Roxana's a young woman, just starting in life,* she thought to herself. *I've made enough mistakes myself. After what Jesus went through for me, how could I continue to cherish feelings of resentment for what she has done?*

Just then she noticed Roxana coming toward her, tears in her eyes. "Laura, I'm so sorry," Roxana exclaimed, and they embraced while both of them wept openly.

As the rest of us witnessed the scene that day, it seemed as if a ray of sunshine had flashed down from the sky, and the power of the Spirit had filled every heart.

Jesus Christ, His life and sacrificial death, His ministry of reconciliation, His loving fellowship with the believers—these are the great themes of the gospel. They are the center point, not only of salvation, but also of reconciliation.

"For all of you who were baptized into Christ

have clothed yourselves with Christ.
There is neither Jew nor Greek,
There is neither slave nor free man,
There is neither male nor female
[Bantu nor Bushman, Black nor White,
Old nor young, rich nor poor];
 for you are all one in Christ Jesus."
—Galatians 3:28

"This," Jesus proclaimed, "is how everyone will recognize that you are my disciples—when they see the love you have for each other" (John 13:35, Message).

It wouldn't be surprising if you know someone who tends to get on your nerves, who seems to require an extra amount of patience on your part. Would you like to record here in a few words your decision regarding this situation?

_____

_____

_____

_____

Chapter 13

Peace Child

When Don and Carol Richardson went with their 7-month-old son to live among the Sawi people of Irian Jaya, they knew it would be tough going. For a while it seemed more than that—it seemed impossible.

The picture that emerged as they got acquainted with the people and their culture was not pretty. Malaria, dysentery, and hepatitis took a heavy toll, but that was not the worst part. They found that Sawi culture glorified violence and treachery. A popular idea was to spend a great deal of time and effort cultivating the friendship of someone you planned to kill and eat. People who could do it skillfully were regarded as great heroes.

As their ability to communicate improved, Don and Carol began to share the story of Jesus and attempted to explain the difference that He can make in our lives. One day, while Don was telling how Judas betrayed Jesus with a kiss, he noticed a strange excitement among his listeners. *Maybe at last the message is getting across,* he thought. Then, to his amazement, the people begin laughing and cheering—but for Judas! "Oh, Don," they said, "that man Judas is what we call *otary duhan,* 'a master of treachery.' He betrayed Jesus with a kiss! We call that *tui asnaman,* 'fattening him for slaughter.'" In their view, Judas was a hero and Jesus was a dupe to be laughed at.

"While they were laughing," Don wrote later, "I was sitting there in utter discouragement, praying: 'Lord, how can I find a key to break through to these people and get them to understand Your love?'"

Soon after that, things got worse. Warfare broke out between Haenam and Kamur, the two Sawi villages closest to the Richardsons. For months no one worked. Women and children hid in terror, and day after day one could see groups of men racing back and forth bent on slaughter.

Don tried to use his influence with the leaders of both clans, pleading with them to make peace, but to no avail. "Maybe it is easy for you *tuans* [their name for outsiders]," they told him. "You can just shake hands and everything will be fine, but it's not that way with us."

How can anyone make peace in a society that idealizes treachery? Any peace initiative would obviously be seen as a setup for greater slaughter.

"So what can you do?" Don asked them. "Isn't there any way peace can come back?"

Finally the villagers admitted that there *was* a way—but only if someone could be found willing to make a sacrifice so profound that everyone knew an insincere person could never summon the courage to do it. It involved giving up one of your own children to the enemy—what they called a *tarop tim,* a "peace child."

Late that night the Richardsons heard a shout outside their back door. Don went out and found a group of leading men from both warring factions. "Tuan, tomorrow we are going to sprinkle cool water on each other!" they told him. "Cool water" is a Sawi idiom for "peace."

Hardly anyone slept that night. Shouting and excitement filled the village. The next morning at dawn people from both villages emerged from their houses and stood facing each other at a safe distance.

Here is Richardson's account of what took place:

"Strange, opposing forces of attraction and repulsion were building up an incredible tension between Haenam and Kamur. From my vantage point between the two villages, I could feel those forces crackling around me with an almost physical violence. Then, out of the corner of my eye, I half noticed a husky Kamur man named Kaiyo turn away from the crowd and climb up quickly into his longhouse. Kaiyo had only one child, 6-month-old Biakadon. Naturally, if anyone would bring himself to the point of handing over a child, it would be someone who had many children and therefore would not miss one of them too badly. But a moment later Kaiyo emerged from the doorway of the longhouse, holding Biakadon close to his chest and began to walk toward Haeneman, his limbs trembling and his face contorted by grief.

"Kaiyo's chest was heaving with emotion as he reached the edge of the village. The leading men were massed in front of him. Kaiyo scanned the row of enemy faces. Then he saw the man he had chosen and called his name. 'Mahor!' he cried.

"Mahor came and stood before him.

"'Mahor!' Kaiyo challenged. 'Will you plead the words of Kamur among your people?'

"'Yes!' Major responded, 'I will plead the words of Kamur among my people!'

"'Then I give you my son and with him my name!' Kaiyo held forth little Biakadon, and Mahor received him gently into his arms.

"Both villages thundered with cheers and shouted until the earth seemed to quiver with emotion.

"Suddenly Mahaen, a Haenam elder, stepped forward holding aloft one of his baby sons, and cried, 'Kaiyo! Will you plead the words of Haenam among your people?'

"'Yes!' cried Kaiyo, 'I will.'

"'Then I give you my son and with him my name!'

"Next Mahor turned and shouted an invitation to the entire population of Haenam: 'Those who accept this child as a basis for peace come and lay hands on him!'

"Young and old alike, male and female, filed eagerly past Mahor and laid their hands in turn upon tiny Biakadon, sealing their acceptance of peace with Kamur. The same ceremony took place in Kamur as soon as Kaiyo returned with Mahaen's baby in his hands. Kaiyo now began to go by the name of Mahaen.

"I was electrified by the sudden vaporization of the atmosphere of war, hardly daring to believe the new beginning tingling in the air. After six months of horror, shock, and tension, I had virtually forgotten how to feel light and cheery. But 300 Sawi had laid hands on a peace child. Now they were singing and laughing and dancing for joy."[1]

Emotion overwhelmed Don Richardson as he watched the scene. *That's it!* he thought. *Here is the key we have been praying for that will open the door for the Sawis to understand the gospel.*

And it proved to be true. Don explained to them that "God, the creator of heaven and earth has sent His one and only Son; He has given Him to us forever. Jesus is our *Ton Tabatin.*"

As the idea became clear to them it amazed and deeply moved the people. They were also filled with horror. "But these people killed the Peace Child!" they exclaimed.

"When Kaiyo handed the Peace Child to his enemy," Don told them, "he was confirming and guaranteeing a peace that everyone wanted, but God gave His Son to a world that was still fighting against Him. He did this knowing full well the terrible consequences that would come. He did it because it was the only way."

Jesus "presented Himself for this sacrificial death when we were far too weak and rebellious to do anything to get ourselves ready. And even if we hadn't been so weak, we wouldn't have known what to do anyway. . . . But God put his love on the line for us by offering his Son in sacrificial death while we were of no use whatever to him" (Romans 5:6-8, Message).

Like the Sawi peace child, Jesus didn't come simply as an observer or a weekend visitor. He came to join our clan—He became our blood relative, our kinsman, forever. What greater proof, what stronger guarantee, could we ask for regarding the inalterable character of God's peace?

"If God didn't hesitate to put everything on the line for us, embracing our condition and exposing himself to the worst by sending his own Son, is there anything else he wouldn't gladly and freely do for us? . . . I'm absolutely convinced that nothing—nothing living or dead, angelic or demonic, today or tomorrow, high or low, thinkable or unthinkable—absolutely *nothing* can get between us and God's love because of the way that Jesus our Master has embraced us" (Romans 8:32-39, Message).

Making It Our Own

As the Sawi people passed one by one and laid their hands on the peace child, they personalized their acceptance of the gift. They committed themselves individually to the peace agreement that the child had brought.

A key word in the Bible shows how *we* are to lay our hands on God's Peace Child, how we commit ourselves to the covenant that He offers. It is the word "into" (Greek, *eis*). [2] The apostle Paul says that we are "baptized into [*eis*] Christ." Through baptism we signify our personal relationship with the Peace Child and ratify His covenant to ourselves.

What do you think it means to be baptized "into" Christ?

_____

_____

_____

As you analyze this question, consider the following from the apostle Paul:

"We each used to independently call our own shots, but then we entered into a large and integrated life in which *he* has the final say in everything. (This is what we proclaimed in word and actions when we were baptized)" (1 Corinthians 12:13, 14, Message).

I encourage you to read and reread this passage, thinking about what it says. You will find it throws a flood of light on the meaning of baptism.

Here's another one: "All of you who were baptized into [*eis*] Christ have clothed yourselves with Christ" (Galatians 3:27).

As Christ's life is imparted to us, as we learn to follow His example and live by His values (Philippians 2:5), people will begin to see in us a family resemblance. We become "saturated" with Christ—that is, with His character—and then we begin to imitate His life.

It is only as spiritual rebirth takes place that water baptism has any real meaning. Jesus said: "Unless one is born of water *and the Spirit,* he cannot enter into the kingdom of God" (John 3:5). Water baptism is a visible, physical act. It is a public ceremony that others can witness, photograph, and certify. Spiritual birth is invisible and inward, the work of the Holy Spirit in our hearts. A realignment of values and attitudes, it results in a change of behavior.

Baptized Into His Name

We are also baptized into *(eis)* His name (Matthew 28:19; Acts 8:16; 19:5). It means that from now on we will go by the family name. Identifying ourselves openly as Christians,[3] we will belong to and actively participate in His church, because that's what it means to live as members of His family.

As part of a natural sequence of events, we first make a decision to join ourselves to Christ, and this prepares us to be part of His visible body, which is the church.

It is natural for all of us as human beings to jealously guard our own turf, to take quick offense and defend our ideas and opinions. I say that it is "natural" because that's the way we are born. But Jesus prayed for His followers "that they may all be one; even as You, Father, are in Me and I in You, that they also may be in Us" (John 17:21). There's the secret: when we have been born of the Spirit, when we are in Him and are one with Him, then we can have peace and unity with one another.

Each of us who has been baptized into Jesus' name "is now a part of his resurrection body, refreshed and sustained at one fountain—his Spirit—where we all come to drink. The old labels we once used to identify ourselves—labels like Jew or Greek, slave or free—are no longer useful" (1 Corinthians 12:13, Message). Such "old labels" formerly kept us apart because they classified us according to culture, gender, nationality, skin color, social and economic condition, and many other things. Under the false value system that ruled our lives, the "old labels" were extremely important, but we now consider them worthless. Our new family name, our new identity as members of God's family, is the only honor or distinction that we care about.

Paul said this had happened to him. He formerly took enormous pride in his pedigree, his good connections and personal success. But one day all of that changed. "Why? Because of Christ. Yes, all the things I once thought were so important are gone from my life. Compared to the high privilege of knowing Christ Jesus as my Master, firsthand, everything I once thought I had going for me is insignificant. . . . I've dumped it all in the trash so that I could embrace Christ and be embraced by him" (Philippians 3:7, 8, Message).

Going Down and Coming Up

The minister who, as Christ's representative, lowers us into the waters of baptism is putting us into the grave. "Don't you know that all of us who were baptized into *(eis)* Christ Jesus were baptized into [*eis*] his death?" Paul asks. "We were therefore buried with him through baptism" (Romans 6:3, 4, NIV).

What do you think it means to be "baptized into his death"?

_____

_____

_____

The transition from our old tribal village to members of Jesus' family involves a change of identity. It means leaving behind the culture of pride, the self-centered lifestyle into which we were born, the way we used to live and think. The persons we once were are now gone. Baptism is the burial of those dead sinners.

It is what we talked about in chapter 12 in which we noticed that before we can join we have to unjoin; that before we can come in we have to go out; that we have to leave behind and let go of what we used to be.

But Jesus didn't stay in the grave, and of course, neither do we. Going down into the water represents burial. The coming up is a resurrection, the beginning of a new life. "We were therefore buried with him through baptism into death in order that, just as Christ was raised from the dead through the glory of the Father, we too may live a new life" (Romans 6:4, NIV).

Our emerging from the water symbolizes this resurrection. It is the "joining" part of the covenant transaction.

The Beginning of Life Eternal

One of the clearest promises of the Bible is the resurrection of the body that will take place when Jesus returns. On that glorious day, "those who have fallen asleep in Jesus," "the dead in Christ," "will rise" (1 Thessalonians 4:14, 16).

While it is a beautiful promise for the future, we need to understand that for those born of water and the Spirit the resurrection life has already begun. The life that Christ imparts *is* eternal life. "Whoever eats my flesh and drinks my blood *has* eternal life, and I will raise him up at the last day" (John 6:54, NIV). Baptism is not only a statement of our faith in the resurrection—it *is* a resurrection.

"Christ became one flesh with us, in order that we might become one spirit with Him. It is by virtue of this union that we are to come forth from the grave—not merely as a manifestation of the power of Christ, but because, through faith, His life has become ours. Those who see Christ in His true character, and receive Him into the heart, have everlasting life. It is through the Spirit that Christ dwells in us; and the Spirit of God, received into the heart by faith, is the beginning of the life eternal."[4]

How Shall We Escape?

The non-Christian Kaiyo made a personal sacrifice that I find impossible to understand. I shudder even to think about doing what he did. But it is still nothing—absolutely nothing—compared to the sacrifice that God made for us.

The question for me to answer is: How will I stand if, after all of that, I refuse to step forward and place my hand on the Peace Child, if I fail to be baptized and thus ratify to myself the covenant that He has validated for me at such a cost?

"How will we escape if we neglect so great a salvation?" (Hebrews 2:3).

Here is a simple prayer of response. I encourage you to make it your own:

"Lord, I'm astonished and deeply moved by Your incredible sacrifice for me. And I do want to respond. You know my heart, Lord. By faith I'm stepping forward right now to place my hand on Your Peace Child. And as soon as possible I want to seal this decision by being baptized.

Name_____ Signature_____ Date_____

---

[1] From Don Richardson, *Peace Child* (Ventura, Calif.: Regal Books, 1974), pp. 192-206.

[2] From the Greek *eis.* For an extensive discussion of this word, see E. Stauffer, in *Theological Dictionary of the New Testament* (Grand Rapids: William B. Eerdmans Pub. Co., 1964), Vol. II, pp. 434-442.

[3] I recognize that under certain circumstances and in some parts of the world it would be unwise or even dangerous to make an issue of our Christian identity. Jesus said: "I send you out as sheep in the midst of wolves; therefore be as shrewd as serpents, and innocent as doves" (Matthew 10:16).

[4] Ellen G. White, *The Desire of Ages* (Mountain View, Calif.: Pacific Press Pub. Assn., 1898), p. 388.

Chapter 14

In My Father's Arms

The strange drama began early one Saturday morning on the campus of Centro Educacional Adventista, the secondary-level boarding school in Honduras of which I was the principal. Ruth Ann and I had just left our house and were walking toward the church when we saw a red pickup turn in the gate and pull up in front of the administration building.

The feelings I had when I recognized the well-dressed woman stepping out of the vehicle were not pleasant. She was an official from the Ministry of Education, general supervisor for the entire north part of the country. My encounters with Doña Olga in her office 35 miles (45 kilometers) away in San Pedro Sula had not been pleasant. Often I could hear her scolding voice as I walked down the hall, and that tone seldom changed as we spoke. "Why are you people trying to operate a school out there in the bush? Why are you taking students away from the government schools?" and on and on. Nothing that I could say or do seemed to satisfy her.

Now, it appeared, she had chosen today to pay us a surprise visit. Many schools in Honduras operate six days a week. Evidently she thought we did too, and would be expecting to visit some classes.

Trying to appear calm, I went over to greet her. As I did so, a burly man also climbed out of the pickup, followed by two teenagers.

"Welcome to our campus," I told her. "This is certainly a surprise" (quite an understatement).

Doña Olga smiled and, in a tone of voice that I'd never heard her use, she said, "I suppose it is. But don't worry. We haven't come on official business. It's just that . . ." She seemed to hesitate a bit. "Well, everybody needs to take some time for some spiritual reflection, and we've come here to find it with you."

Was I hearing right? Or was this some sort of setup? It was then that I noticed . . . was it actually possible? Madam supervisor carried a black book in her hand that looked a lot like a Bible.

By this time the burly man stood with his arm around her, and she said, "This is my husband, Rolando." The teenagers, she explained, were their children.

If you had taken a photo about that time, it would probably have shown my jaw dropped and my eyes staring widely. My brain tried to process what I was hearing.

The events that followed during the rest of the day were no less astounding and inexplicable. We invited them to our home for lunch. Never in all our experience had we seen anything like the love and devotion of that family for their wife and mother. It was clear that they practically worshipped her. While Ruth Ann and I were getting things ready, she sat in the center of the sofa in our little living room. Her teenagers occupied a place on either side of her. One of them had his arm around her while the other held her hand. "Would you care for a drink of water, Mom?" one asked. And the other jumped up to get it. Her husband sat across from them on our piano bench and looked lovingly at his wife the whole time.

After they left, Ruth Ann and I turned to each other. "Did you ever see anything like that?" I asked her.

"Never!" she agreed. "I've never seen such a devoted and loving family."

None of it seemed to make any sense. Was this really the fearsome ogre that I had known?

A few weeks later I again had occasion to visit the supervisor's office on school business. Naturally, I was looking forward to a different reception this time.

"She's not in," the man I found sitting at her desk informed me.

"Oh, sorry," I told him. "I'll come back later."

"Ah, well, I don't think she'll be back."

To my questioning look, he responded: "She's in the hospital with cancer in an advanced stage."

Many thoughts whirled through my mind as I left the office that day. Everything that had seemed so strange and incomprehensible was suddenly clear. Now I understood why Doña Olga was suddenly looking for spiritual comfort, why her husband was so devoted, and why those teenagers outdid themselves at being thoughtful and considerate of their mother. They hadn't told us, but they already knew: she was a woman living under a sentence of death.

And I thought: *Why does this kind of family devotion seem so strange and unusual? Why do we nearly always fail to value something while we have it in our hands?* Not until we are faced with losing it do we wake up and realize how precious it really is.

In His Father's Arms

Jesus told the story of a boy who was like that: he had it all, and he couldn't care less. The son of a wealthy landowner, he was hateful and ungrateful, and finally, he ran away.

A long time went by, until the day that, after tremendous suffering, the youth came to his senses and turned his steps toward home. Here is where we find one of the most beautiful verses in the entire Bible. It says:

"But while he was still a long way off,
  his father saw him
    and was filled with compassion for him;
  he ran to his son,
    threw his arms around him
    and kissed him."
—Luke 15:20, NIV

How many times do you think the father had hugged that boy when he was little? How many embraces had the young man rejected during those years of teenage rebellion? I don't know. Probably it was a lot. But there is one thing I can tell you with absolute certainty: for him, there was never another embrace like that one.

His clothes were ragged and torn. He was still sweaty from the road, and an aura of the pigpen lingered about him. "I'm so unworthy, Dad," he started to say. "I know I don't deserve it, but . . ."

Do you know what that son really desired—what he wanted with a longing that was more intense than anything he had ever felt in his entire life? It was forgiveness. And I am not talking about some sort of legal pardon that would get him out of trouble. The kind of forgiveness he craved meant a restoration of the broken relationship, a return to the loving communication and sharing that he had once enjoyed with his father. That's what forgiveness meant to him. At this point the word "communion" comes to mind. He longed to be restored to communion with his father.

But even before the son heard his father's words, he knew the answer. That wonderful embrace, being held once more in his father's arms, gave him the answer. It told him that he could hope again. And for the first time ever, he realized what his father's embrace really meant.

Yes, You *Can* Come Home Again

Wouldn't it be wonderful if we never went away? If we never had to say, "I'm sorry"?

I wish that I had always remembered to treasure my Father's love and rejoice in His presence.

Maybe it's a dim comfort, but the Gospels tell us that even Jesus' disciples had such an experience. They were sincere . . . of course they were! Loving Jesus, they had dedicated their lives to His service and had spent three and a half years with Him.

But when the time came for them to sit down with Him for the last supper—the very first "Communion" service—they were busy looking out for number one. The questions uppermost in their thoughts were not: "How can I walk more closely with Jesus? How can I be more like Him? How can I show more gratitude for what He has done for me?" No, their minds were focused on: "Which one of us is the greatest?" (see Luke 9:46; 22:24). Who gets the biggest office, the fanciest desk when Jesus sets up His kingdom?

While this was going on—the silent pushing and shoving—they were gathering around the table for the Last Supper. It was Passover, and the time had come for the ceremony to begin, but there was one problem: nobody had been designated to wash the road dust off their feet. That was an invariable custom in those days. You had to do that before you could eat. The trouble was that it was a servant's job . . . and in that crowd there sure wasn't anyone who wanted to be thought of as a servant.

So, OK, let's see, who's going to do it? Peter glances at Nathanael, raises his eyebrows, and gives him a little nod. Nathanael looks away and frowns . . . and *he* nudges Thaddaeus. No one says anything, and everyone avoids eye contact.

The seconds tick away ... but not very many, because Jesus gets up from the table. As the disciples watch unbelievingly, He ties a towel around His waist, pours water into a basin, and begins to wash their feet.

Try to visualize this scene as it happens. Slowly Jesus moves around the table. Stopping by each one, He bends low and takes those dirty feet in His hands, washes, and then dries them with the towel. If it were your feet that Jesus was washing, what thoughts would be racing through your head?

Do you know what I feel as I look at this picture? Ashamed. How many times has selfishness gotten in the way of *my* service for the Master? How many times have I known the right answer but failed to have the right spirit? How often have I taken for granted the richness and abundance of the Father's table, and then run off to that far country? *Dear God, I'm so unworthy! How can you give me a place at Your table?*

Now Jesus has finished, and He returns to His place. Then, through my tears, I see Him holding out a piece of bread, and He says to me quietly: "Take, eat. This is my body; it was broken for you." And a moment later, a portion of the wine, adding: "This is my blood, which is shed for the remission of your sins."

Do you recognize what this is? If you do, then you know the true meaning of Communion. It is the Father's embrace. It's His voice saying, "Dear child, My love for you has never changed. You do still have a place at My table."

The Happy Ending Is Only the Beginning

If someone had written the gospel story in Hollywood, we wouldn't need Communion. In fairy tales Prince Charming marries Cinderella and they all live happily ever after. But in real life Cinderella discovers that the prince snores quite loudly, and before long he realizes that the wedding bells didn't magically turn her into a good cook. The wedding doesn't really make a marriage. The true union of hearts is a process, and it takes a huge amount of patience, a willingness to adapt and learn, to laugh and overlook—and quite a lot of time.

It is also true that baptism doesn't automatically transform one into a mature Christian. I wish it did, don't you? I wish that I'd always been a perfect Christian after my baptism. I wish that I'd understood the Christian life better and had been more faithful in doing the things that I did grasp. There's no excuse for the stupid things I've done that have hurt Jesus and others.

Yet He has never turned His back on me, never left me alone. Sometimes by whispering in my ear, and at others by giving me a pretty good whack, the Lord has been speaking to me. And I've been listening, and learning as we walk together.

But while this has been going on, I never cease to be amazed and very glad that He keeps inviting me back to His table. There, His blood reminds me once again that He is the source of my forgiveness, my only hope. His broken body reassures me that He is eager to provide for all my needs and that He can give me strength for every one of the changes that I need to make.

So please don't hesitate. Don't say, "Maybe later." Don't wait for some terrible crisis to make you appreciate the richness of the Father's grace. You can know what the prodigal took so long to learn without all his suffering. Our Father really does provide for all our needs. Accept His invitation, and you too will receive the incredible gift of the body and blood of Christ at the Communion service.

As I think of this wonderful invitation, my response is

Chapter 15

You, Too, Are Gifted

When you hear the word "gifted," does anyone in particular come to mind?

Such as, maybe . . . Mozart? You may have heard what happened during Holy Week of 1770 when he was 14 years old. His father took him to hear Gregorio Allegri's *Miserere* performed in the papal chapel. Now, it happens that this particular work is—shall we say?—rather complex. It features intertwining melodies from two antiphonal choirs placed on opposite sides of the chapel, one with four-part and the other with five-part harmony. The church so prized the *Miserere* that the pope had forbidden anyone to copy the score or remove it from the Vatican under penalty of excommunication. As soon as he got back to his room, Wolfgang sat down and wrote out the whole thing note by note. Later he attended a second performance to make sure that he'd gotten it right. And he had.

Day and night, music sounded in Mozart's head. He often composed entire musical works in his mind while partying with friends. Writing them down was sort of an afterthought, and sometimes he didn't bother unless his wife, Constanze, got after him. Unlike her husband, she worried about paying the bills, and seemed to believe that if you don't write it down you can't sell it.

Or perhaps you have heard of Daniel Tammet. Danny knows the value of pi to 22,514 decimal places. He calculates square roots in his head almost before you finish saying the words and can do quite a few similar feats. On language, well, maybe he's a bit slower—it takes him about a week to become fluent in a new one. So far, he has learned only 11, so I guess that he hasn't really tried all that hard, but he's busy inventing another one from scratch.

And then there's Amanda García. Never heard of her? Well, I met Amanda a few hours after the terrible earthquake that devastated Managua. At the staging center where a number of us gathered that night to plan relief efforts for ADRA (the Adventist Development and Relief Agency) there was initially a good deal of confusion. Part of our team had come in from Costa Rica, and others were arriving from El Salvador, Honduras, and Miami. People milled around. Our Nicaraguan friends, in a state of post-traumatic shock, were telling their story to anyone who would listen. They seemed eager for someone to understand what they'd been through.

That's when I noticed Amanda. Quiet and unassuming, she wasn't taking charge or trying to run anything. She was just moving quietly from one nucleus of people to another. "Let me take those wet jackets," I heard her say to one group. "I'll hang them in a safe place so they can dry out a little." To another: "You need some paper to take notes, don't you? I think I can find some." And a few minutes later: "Here, I've brought some sandwiches."

Maybe you're thinking: *I thought we were talking about "gifted" people. Have we changed the subject or something?*

This question is not just a matter of curiosity. It brings into focus the most important question of all: Who is gifted, and what does the term really mean, anyway?

In 1904 the French government commissioned psychologist Alfred Binet to develop a test for identifying children who needed help to achieve success in school.

Binet developed an instrument that involved asking children to do such things as follow simple commands, copy patterns, name objects, and put things in order. He gave the test to Paris schoolchildren and created a standard based on the data he collected. For example, if 70 percent of 8-year-olds could pass a particular test, then success on that test represented the 8-year-old level of intelligence. As a result of Binet's work, the phrase "intelligence quotient," or "IQ," entered the vocabulary. The IQ is the ratio of "mental age" to chronological age. So an 8-year-old who passes the test for 10-year-olds would have an IQ of 10/8 x 100, or 125.

The evaluation of mental ability through IQ testing soon became immensely popular. It worried Binet, who insisted that we cannot describe something as complex as intelligence with a number. "Intellectual qualities," he wrote, "cannot be measured as linear surfaces are measured." However, educators and psychologists in the following decades paid little attention to Binet's concerns, and they at times treated IQ scores like a pronouncement from the throne regarding the possibility of achievement and success in life. A running debate developed as to what score confirmed that someone is "gifted" or, beyond that, a "genius."

Now, a century later, studies of intelligence have come full circle, and educators recognize the truth of Binet's words. Just as intelligence is not always the same size, neither is it always the same shape. Harvard professor Howard Gardner has proposed what he calls a "theory of multiple intelligences." Here is Gardner's list of types of intelligence.[1]

1. **Verbal-Linguistic.** Facility with words and language.
2. **Logical-Mathematical.** Ability to reason and perform complex calculations.
3. **Visual-Spatial.** Ability to visualize and mentally manipulate objects.
4. **Bodily-Kinesthetic.** Aptitude for activities that involve physical movement.
5. **Musical.** Sensitivity to sounds, rhythms, tones, and music.
6. **Interpersonal.** A natural sense of how to deal with others through communication and empathy.
7. **Intrapersonal.** Introspective and self-reflective capacities.

I never asked about Amanda García's musical ability, and I'm not sure how much she knows about the value of pi. But she has an outstanding gift of interpersonal intelligence. I became better acquainted with her over time, but I never once had any reason to doubt that my first impression about her was right.

I'm pretty sure that Daniel Tammet would recognize her gift as well. By his own account, Danny is seriously limited when it comes to people skills. He knows the meaning of the word "empathy," but says that he has almost none and that he is likely to be hit by a panic attack if too many people are around.

The apostle Paul would probably have recognized Amanda's gift too. He included "helpfulness" in a list of "spiritual gifts" found in 1 Corinthians 12. In this chapter the great missionary apostle reflected on giftedness. He compared the church to Christ's body and said that the people in it are like "members" or parts of the body, such as the hands, the feet, the eyes, etc. We differ in skills and functions, and that is good, because that way our abilities can complement one another. He goes on to offer some examples of the different attributes that members may have:

1. **Prophecy.** By this he evidently means proclaiming the word, what we might call "preaching."[2]
2. **Service.** Helpfulness, supplying the needs of others, contributing to their success.
3. **Teaching.** Instructing, clarifying the truth, enabling people to learn and grow.
4. **Exhortation.** Offering encouragement, guidance, and counsel.
5. **Generosity.** Contributing our skills, time, and money to benefit others.
6. **Leadership.** Facilitating and coordinating the work of the group, helping it identify its goals and achieve them.
7. **Mercy.** Working with the disadvantaged, those who need compassion and support.

Personally, I find a lot of encouragement in this list and the idea behind it. Maybe I'm not a prophet, but I can offer a word of encouragement and counsel, or at least a listening ear. I have trouble remembering the value of pi even to two decimal places, and I don't rate nearly as high as I would like in social skills, but I do have verbal-linguistic ability, and I can use that to teach and write.

For more than 20 years I have lived near the Universidad de Montemorelos, a Christian university in northern Mexico. During that time I have attended thousands of meetings at the university church. Music and song are an important part of nearly all of those services, but (can you believe it?) in all that time nobody has ever asked me to sing a solo. Not even once!

Now, if you are thinking to write the university president or the church pastor and complain on my behalf, never mind. Because singing—well, that's not my line, not where my talents lie at all.

I'm glad that we don't all have to shine in the same thing, aren't you? That way I can sincerely applaud my friends who are good at things I can't do. And I don't need to be Mozart or Tammet to recognize that God, in His mercy, has given me some nice gifts too.

Remember the words of the old spiritual?

"If you cannot preach like Peter,

If you cannot pray like Paul,

You can tell the love of Jesus,

You can say, 'He died for all.'"

Yes, I can do that. I can tell them, and—praise God!—there isn't anybody who can't.

One day Jesus healed an insane man near the town of Gadara. Even after he was well and in his right mind again, the fellow probably still couldn't preach like Peter. And I doubt if he was up there with Paul in his ability to explain justification and all that it implies. He might not have known even a single Bible text. But no matter: he had received a precious gift, and that placed him under a solemn responsibility. Jesus said to him: "Go to your family and loved ones and tell them what great things God has done for you, and how He has had mercy on you" (Mark 5:19). He was held responsible, not for what he didn't have, but for what God had given him. That he was to share.

And that's where we need to begin as well. Don't wait until you are full of knowledge and running over with eloquence. And don't wait till you have enough loaves and fishes to feed the whole 5,000. First, stop and make an inventory of what it is that you do have. Then take those few loaves and those tiny fishes, and put them in Jesus' hands. That's the most important thing you can do. Then, after He blesses them, do what the disciples did: start giving them away. When you do that, they will multiply.

"What I do, you cannot do;

but what you do, I cannot do.

The needs are great,

and none of us, including me,

ever does great things.

But we can all do small things with great love,

and together we can do something wonderful"

—Mother Teresa of Calcutta

You are gifted. Yes, of that I am absolutely certain. That is an awesome and humbling thought. By the infinite grace of God, take those precious gifts and put them to work for the Master.

I believe my gifts include:

_____

_____

Things that I can do to develop these gifts and improve them:

_____

_____

Ways that I can put these gifts to work for God and others:

_____

_____

---

[1] Gardner later added an eighth category he called "naturalist" intelligence: the ability to sense patterns and make connections to elements in nature. Other educators have suggested additional categories, such as "spiritual intelligence."

[2] An interpretation based on a study of Paul's use of the term in 1 Corinthians 14.

Chapter 16

A Hand Reaching Out

The most terrible poverty is loneliness and the feeling of being unloved."—Mother Teresa.

What do you think? Was Mother Teresa right?

The fact that you're reading this tells me that you're probably not one of the people she dealt with most often. And you probably don't live in the slums of Calcutta, or any place where thousands of the people sleep, eat, and do everything else on the sidewalk.

More likely you belong to the connected generation. You take for granted your cell phone, your e-mail, and the communication satellites orbiting overhead.

It seem strange, doesn't it, and tremendously ironic, that many experts regard the most connected generation in the history of the planet as the loneliest? In fact, sociologists today are talking about an "epidemic of loneliness."[1] They say that "more and more [people] are starving for significant relationships."[2] "Loneliness is a bigger problem for more people today than at any previous time in history."[3]

So if Mother Teresa was right, then this kind of poverty is immense, and it is growing.

Somehow, the story of Danny, the Romanian orphan, seems like a parable of modern life. Dumped at birth into a squalid orphanage, he received minimal food and clothing, harsh discipline—and nothing more.

Then one day in 1996, when Danny was 7, with no explanation or forewarning, a stranger picked him up, took him to the reception area at the local airport, and handed him over to a middle-aged couple, John and Carol Solomon, who had come from the United States to adopt him.

It sounds like a Cinderella story. I mean, here is a boy who has had a nightmare existence. He has never been hugged in his life, never owned a pair of shoes, and never been outside the orphanage. Now suddenly he finds himself overwhelmed by love and by more material things than he even knew existed. You would expect him to be ecstatic with gratitude, wouldn't you?

But he wasn't. Danny had left the orphanage behind, but he took the nightmare with him. And for the good people who had adopted him a new one was beginning.

Danny is 18 now and able to explain. "I was convinced," he says, "that it was these people [his adoptive parents] who had abandoned me in that terrible place, and left me there so many years." He reacted with rage and violence.

Not that the Solomons didn't try. Again and again they told him the truth about his situation, but nothing they could say or do seemed to make a difference. Something more than the language barrier was standing in the way. Repeatedly schools expelled him. Three times he was placed in a psychiatric hospital. Several times his parents had to call the police because of his violence at home. Psychologists and counselors pronounced him incurable and encouraged the Solomons to have him locked away.

Think of it! What did these people owe Danny? Absolutely nothing. Not needing to put up with his abuse, they could have annulled his adoption and abandoned him to the absurd course of self-destruction that he seemed so determined to follow.

But they didn't. At an enormous cost to themselves in effort, money, and personal trauma, they persevered, trying, trying, always hoping that somehow they could get their message across. Why? Because they never stopped believing that there must be some way to make him understand.

Mother Teresa was wrong—there really is something worse than the poverty of being lonely and unloved. It's self-imposed loneliness, making ourselves impervious to love when it's all around us.

That's why I said that Danny's story is like a parable of the human dilemma, because the Bible offers a picture of a God who really is there, and He is not silent.[4] He is reaching out, calling, seeking to get through to us. The Lord longs to hold us close and let us feel the security of His love. But too often we squirm and twist away. Or even rage and fight against Him. So why does He persist? Why doesn't He give up on us and leave us to the consequences of our incredible folly?

Because He knows that most of the people who reject His love are confused. Popular culture fills our ears with a deafening noise. Today's pressure-cooker lifestyle leaves little time for our families and even less for spiritual reflection. Our very connectedness adds to the din and thus wars against true spirituality. The constant yammering makes us hard of hearing and keeps us from stopping to reflect on eternal values.

The prophet Elijah achieved tremendous results in getting the whole nation to return to God. His methods were dramatic and effective. But then, at his moment of greatest success, he fell into a terrible funk, a bottomless pit of despair. That's when God came to him and said: OK, now I want you to go outside and stand on the mountain.

When he got there, "a great and strong wind was rending the mountains and breaking in pieces the rocks . . .

but the Lord was not in the wind.

And after the wind an earthquake,

but the Lord was not in the earthquake.

And after the earthquake a fire,

but the Lord was not in the fire;

And after the fire, a sound of a gentle blowing."

—1 Kings 19:11, 12.

"A sound of a gentle blowing"—a whisper. What do you think God was trying to tell him?

It shouldn't be too hard to figure out: In his tremendous campaign to get the whole nation back on track, Elijah had fallen into a danger that stalks every one of us. Caught up in a whirlwind of activity and busily trying to shake the earth, he had stopped listening to God's gentle whisper. He had lost the only contact that really matters. That's why, when the terrible darkness and spiritual fatigue overwhelmed him, he could see no light, no way out. Here is the greatest aloneness and poverty of them all.

God's voice to Elijah was a "gentle blowing." Interesting, because another Hebrew word for blowing is *ruach,* a word that also means "spirit." Notice the word "gentle." The Holy Spirit doesn't usually shout, but He is persistent.

Please look closely at the following verse, which tells us more about how God works to get through to us, even when we're not that much into listening.

"God . . . spoke to our fathers through the prophets,
many times
   and in a variety of ways."
—Hebrews 1:1, Clear Word

He Still Whispers

At the beginning of the book of Exodus, Moses received a commission from God to free His people from slavery. What worried him most about his task was how to get his message across to the king who was enjoying their free labor.

So God told him: "Your brother Aaron shall be your prophet. You shall speak all that I command you, and your brother Aaron shall speak to Pharaoh that he let the sons of Israel go out of his land" (Exodus 7:1, 2).

Did you notice that Aaron would be Moses' "prophet"? The passage throws light on the meaning of the word. Aaron would be Moses' designated spokesperson. And that's what a "prophet" really is—someone officially authorized to speak on behalf of another person. God chooses His prophets to communicate messages from Him to the people.

In the popular mind a prophet is someone who knows the future. You would want to have one around, for example, if you were planning to play the stock market. It is true that prophecy does sometimes deal with future events. But a prophet's work is much broader than this. And even when it deals with the future, prophecy is never about satisfying our curiosity or doing parlor tricks on demand. Rather, it is part of God's "whatever it takes" effort to get through to us.

Not an Easy Job

The biblical prophets were people with a passion and a mission. They were evangelists, and usually reformers as well. Often they had to stand for God against an overwhelming flood of evil. Some of them had spectacular success, but more often than not, they suffered rejection and abuse. A number of them ended up as martyrs. At the close of the second book of Chronicles the author observed: "The Lord, the God of their fathers, sent word to them [His people] through his messengers again and again, because he had pity on his people. . . . But they mocked God's messengers, despised his words and scoffed at his prophets" (2 Chronicles 36:15, 16, NIV). It's not a job you would want to volunteer for.[5]

When you look at the Bible record, the first thing that strikes you is how often God used the prophets in times of crisis and rebellion. Consider, for example, the following examples:

1. Responding to the first widespread rebellion, God sent Enoch.
2. As the wickedness of the earth continued to increase, He enlisted Noah.
3. After the Flood came Abraham, father of the "chosen people."
4. Moses was a prophet and lawgiver who led the people out of slavery and into the Promised Land.
5. The Lord summoned Deborah as a prophet and leader of the nation at another time of great national crisis.
6. When Ahab and Jezebel were leading Israel into violence and wickedness, God dispatched first Elijah and then Elisha.
7. In the difficult years that followed, God employed Isaiah, Jeremiah, Ezekiel, and others, many of them unnamed.
8. God had Anna and Simeon announce the birth of Jesus.
9. A few years later He sent John the Baptist to "prepare the way" for Jesus' public ministry.
10. Prophets in the early Christian church included Agabus and the four daughters of Philip the evangelist.
11. The apostle Paul also had the gift of prophecy.
12. As did John, who wrote the book of Revelation.

Prophecy in the End-time

Bible prophecy warns that the end-time will be the greatest crisis of them all, leading to an "overwhelming spread of evil" (Matthew 24:12, Message) and a "time of trouble, such as never was" (Daniel 12:1, KJV). The apostle Paul declares that in the last days "terrible times" will come (2 Timothy 3:1, NIV). Sinners will become bold and unashamed. Multitudes will "abandon the faith and follow deceiving spirits and things taught by demons" (1 Timothy 4:1, NIV). No wonder Jesus said that when He returns, true faith will be rare (Luke 18:8).

In the past, in times of crisis and rebellion, God has responded by sending His messengers, the prophets. It is hardly surprising to find several Bible prophecies that tell us that as the end-time approaches, the prophetic voice would once again make itself heard. "Behold, I am going to send you Elijah the prophet before the coming of the great and terrible day of the Lord" (Malachi 4:5). It does not mean that Elijah himself would return to life, but that someone would come "in the spirit and power of Elijah" (Luke 1:17) to do the work that he did, a mission of healing and reconciliation (Malachi 4:6), and to call people to return to God in the time of "overwhelming evil" (see also Joel 2:18, 31).

Such texts tell us that as part of the end-time scenario we should expect to see two powerful currents pulling in opposite directions: (1) an increase in wickedness and evil and (2) a renewal of the prophetic gift.

The prophecy about the remnant that we studied in chapter 13 also talks about the end-time restoration of the prophetic gift, calling it "the testimony of Jesus" (Revelation 12:17; 19:10). The gift of prophecy is Jesus' testimony. It is His seal of approval, one of the signs that He has given to identify the people that He has chosen as His special channels of light.[6]

Testing! Testing!

In still another important prophecy about prophecy, Jesus predicted that before the end many "false Christs and false prophets" would come. These phonies would not be strange-looking freaks—they would appear legitimate and highly convincing. Jesus said that they would "show great signs and wonders," so much so that if it were possible they would convince even God's chosen people (Matthew 24:24). His warning puts us on alert. It means that the false will seem true to the point at which it will be hard to tell the difference.

The apostle Paul says that we are not to "despise prophetic utterances" (1 Thessalonians 5:20). We should not reject a message out of hand just because someone tells us that it came from a prophet. That would amount to blind prejudice. What we should do, he says, is to "examine everything carefully; hold fast to that which is good" (verse 21).

So if people tell you that they have discovered a prophet in our time, it's not wrong to be skeptical. Don't accept anything until you examine the evidence. That applies to what I am going to tell you here, as well as to any other claim you might hear about prophets in our day.

If the false will seem true, how can we tell the difference? As in everything else, we need to take the Bible as our guide. If we try to figure it out for ourselves, we will surely get confused.

The Bible offers an image of a true prophet than can serve as a basis for comparing and testing anyone who claims to have the gift:

1. A true prophet will uphold the Bible (Isaiah 8:20; Deuteronomy 13:1-4).
   a. will have a message that rings true to anyone who knows and studies the Bible.
   b. will understand, support, and promote biblical values, attitudes, and ideals.
   c. will lead people to Scripture and will encourage them to study it, love it, and follow its teachings.
2. A true prophet will point people to Jesus (John 15:26; 1 John 4:1-3; Revelation 19:10).
   a. will help them understand His work and mission.
   b. will lead them to bow at His feet in praise and worship (Revelation 19:10).
3. A true prophet will have a wholesome message (Mathew 7:15-20).
   a. a message that motivates us to be better people.
   b. a message that promotes views and attitudes characteristic of common sense and of sound mental and spiritual health.
   c. a message that is sensible and balanced, not fanatical or extreme.
3. A true prophet will speak the truth (Deuteronomy 18:22).
   a. New truth given through the prophet will be largely falsifiable—that is, it can be tested. For example, predictions will come true or statements or revelations about situations or people can generally be verified.

With a sense of gratitude and something akin to awe, I want to introduce you to someone whose work and ministry did reflect these characteristics in a remarkable way, and whose practical counsels and devotional writings have blessed my own life and that of millions of other people. I'm talking about Ellen G. White. My approach will necessarily be personal, because for me it's like introducing you to a friend.

Please Meet My Friend

I had the privilege of growing up in a home with loving Christian parents. Morning worship was part of our daily routine. But our parents wondered what more they could do to offer spiritual nurture. So when I was about 8 years old and my brother 10, they decided to do something about the situation. That was when they put into practice a new plan. Instead of reading a brief verse or inspirational thought before breakfast, they decided to dedicate the entire breakfast time to reading books of lasting value. Thereafter, every morning, after giving thanks, one of our parents would read aloud while the rest of us ate.

The first book they took through this plan was called *Early Writings,* by Ellen White. After that, they read *The Desire of Ages,* her great masterpiece on the life of Christ, followed by the rest of the series, in which she covers the entire Bible: *Patriarchs and Prophets, Prophets and Kings, The Acts of the Apostles,* and *The Great Controversy.* Since they were substantial books, several of them more than 600 pages, the plan I am describing continued for years.

Much later I heard of people raising questions about those books. I could only wonder if they had actually read them or were speaking out of ignorance of their true significance. For me, the most important evidence of their inspiration does not lie in any of the stories about how they came to be written. It is in the powerful impact they had on my life. They made Scripture come alive. Bible characters were as real and as familiar as our next-door neighbors. The books upheld Bible values and applied them to modern living. Morning after morning we would go off to school thinking about Elijah facing up to the prophets of Baal on Mount Carmel, about David caring for his father's sheep, the boy Jesus talking with the elders in the Temple, and similar themes.

When I was 14 years old, Mother left a copy of another Ellen White book, *Messages to Young People,* near a spot where I often sat. She knew my habit of picking up and reading anything at hand. After glancing through the first chapter, I began to get interested, and soon had read it all and then reread some parts many times.

This came at a time that I felt a sense of despair as a Christian. It seemed to me that the standard of being like Jesus was so high, and my weaknesses so many, that I could never make it. I still remember vividly the powerful emotion I felt when I read: "Yes, tell it in words full of cheer, that no one who perseveringly climbs the ladder will fail of gaining an entrance into the heavenly city" (p. 95). And I thought: *I can do that. I am weak and often fail, but I can persevere.* And hope came back to my heart.

That's the Ellen White I came to know. Hers was a ministry of encouragement. No one can read her writings very long without feeling inspired to be a better person.

Seventh-day Adventists believe that her insights were not the result simply of her own intuition or personal reflections on Scripture. She wrote literally thousands of letters of counsel, warning, and encouragement. Many of them went to individuals that she had never met. She said that God had opened their cases to her, and we have many stories of how her words were precisely to the point. People who read them were convinced that only God could have shown her the truth about situations that no human being knew anything about.

In 1905 my grandfather, Pitt Wade, was a young physician starting his medical practice in southern Colorado. He dreamed of establishing a sanitarium similar to the world-famous institution founded by John Harvey Kellogg in Battle Creek, Michigan.

Eager to get Ellen White's support for his plan, he contacted her, describing the project in the most glowing terms possible. As time went by and he received no reply, he grew increasingly frustrated by her silence.

Finally, a letter did arrive. But her message was not at all the one he wanted to hear. She began by stating that she had not replied earlier because she was careful not to write when she had no "light from the Lord" regarding matters that people asked her about.

"But I am now prepared to speak positively," she added. "Last Thursday night [Sept. 28, 1905] the matter was presented to me."

She told the young doctor that the project he dreamed about was good in itself. But the Lord had shown her a serious difficulty that made it advisable for him to cease and desist. The problem, she wrote, was his tendency to give way to "passion"—he was hot tempered. He would cherish feelings of hatred and bitterness and lash out against anyone who did not agree with him and support his plans.

"My brother," she wrote, "you need a new spiritual life. ... For the reasons that I am presenting to you, I beg of you to keep free from the burdens that would come to you in connection with a sanitarium."[7] The letter went on for a number of pages. Tenderly she urged him to recognize that the Lord was warning him with a longing desire to have him avoid bitter heartache and sorrows. She pictured a dark and difficult path ahead if he failed to make the changes in his life that he so urgently needed.

When I read that letter more than 50 years later, I was astounded. How could she have described his personality and character with such vivid insight? How could she have known and outlined the problems that he did, in fact, face later in life?

The word "prophet" has been badly misused and is likely to be misunderstood. Therefore, Ellen White hesitated to apply the term to herself. However, a careful examination of her work and writings has convinced me and millions of other people who have considered the available evidence that her ministry did correspond to the Bible description of a prophet's role and that she was, in fact, a messenger from God for our day.

The gift of prophecy in modern times stands as a testimony to God's amazing love. It shows His persistence and unwavering effort to get His message across and break through our self-imposed isolation and ignorance. And it tells us how eager He is to convince people everywhere to return to a relationship of love and trust in Him. The same Holy Spirit who spoke through godly men and women of old has spoken again in our time. Once again, He has used a human instrument to bring us a message of encouragement and change.

I encourage you to come to your own conclusions about this. As an aid, I have made arrangements for you to receive, at no cost or obligation, a copy of Ellen White's brief devotional book called Happiness Digest. *If you live in the United States or Canada, ask for your free copy by calling 1-800-253-3002. From any country in the world, log on to www.ellengwhitetruth.com/ and click on "free resources."*

[1] Miller McPherson, Lynn Smith-Lovin, Matthew Brashears, "Social Isolation in America," *American Sociological Review* 71 (June 2006): 353-375; http://www.asanet.org/galleries/default-file/June06ASR-Feature.pdf.

[2] An unsigned editorial in *Christianity Today,* November 2006

[3] See http://ctrldotlife.blogspot.com/2007/07/how-to-deal-with-lonelyness.html. See, for example: "Britain Singled Out as Lonely Nation," http://news.bbc.co.uk/2/hi /uk_news/692150.stm.

[4] See Francis A. Schaeffer, *The God Who Is There* (Downers Grove, Ill.: InterVarsity Press, 1968).

[5] Stephen, the first Christian martyr, said to the religious leaders about to take his life: "Which of the prophets did your fathers not persecute?" (Acts 7:52; see also Luke 11:47-51).

[6] Prophecy is also a testimony about Jesus. Every gift of the Holy Spirit, including this one, is designed to draw attention to Jesus, to call men and women everywhere to worship Him (John 15:26).

[7] Ellen G. White manuscript 285, 1905.

Chapter 17

Knowing the Right Answer Isn't Enough

The other day Dr. Sawbones came into our ad agency. He wondered if we could do something to help him get more patients.

Yes, of course we could. Hadn't we just completed a successful campaign for a used clothing store?

So we cranked up our trusty laptop and located the display ad that we had prepared for the retailer. It looked pretty good, so we made a few adjustments here and there, and voilà! The new piece for the doctor was ready to go.

Here it is. See what you think.

Bargain Prices on Surgery With Dr. Sawbones!
Don't Miss This Chance!

- Attention! Attention! One day only! You'll never get a better deal on appendectomies! Thirty percent discount! But only on Thursday of this week! So come in and have yours out while the price is right!

- The doctor will also remove your heart and lungs at the same discount! Just cut out this ad and show it to the receptionist when you arrive!

- Huge discount on amputations if done on more than one member of the same family, so bring in your wife and children!

- Have one leg put in a cast any day this week, and we'll do the other one for only $1!

So are you already on your way to see Dr. Sawbones? Why not? Well, that's not hard to answer, is it? People don't have their appendix out just because it's cheap on Thursday. They will have it removed only when it hurts.

That's What the Law Is For

The apostle Paul said that at one point in his life he was fine—nothing was hurting him. "I was once alive apart from the Law," he wrote. The Greek word for "I" is *ego*. Paul's ego was alive and well—he was comfortable and self-confident.

"But when the commandment came,

sin became alive

and I died" (Romans 7:9).

Think of how your face becomes "alive" when the Novocaine starts to wear off. As soon as the law caught Paul's attention, his spiritual nerves started to jangle. All of a sudden they were raw, and he was sensitive to sin in a way that he never had been before. It was his ego that died, his "nothing is wrong with me" attitude.

I can tell you something about how that works. I was "comfortable and self-confident" one windy day when I stopped in at a local convenience store. While there I noticed some people looking at me and smiling, but that's easy to understand, because I happen to be a pretty good-looking fellow. Well, everything was fine until I went into the washroom and saw myself in the mirror. Wow! My hair stuck out in about six different directions! Discovering the truth made me uncomfortable and embarrassed.

Like a good friend, the law tells us what we need to hear. It is our family physician reading a report from the pathologist. "I'm afraid the news isn't good," Dr. Law says. "You are definitely a sinner."

Is This Really Possible?

But wait a minute! Something's wrong here. How could Paul say that he had been formerly "apart from the law"? After all, he was a Jew. More than that, he was Pharisee, a sect famous for strict obedience to the law. Jesus said that its members would pay tithe even on the mint and dill and cummin—tiny sprigs of green that grew in their herb gardens (Matthew 23:23). That's how strict they were. So if Paul was a Jew, a rabbi, and a Pharisee, how could he possibly say that he was formerly separated from the law?

Incredible as it may seem, he wasn't kidding, because in the matter of lawkeeping, more is less. Here's how it works:

First, we need to ask, Why were Paul and his friends so fanatically strict about keeping the law? Because for them, salvation was a matter of obeying it perfectly.

Now, suppose I go to the market here in Montemorelos and say to the man at the vegetable stand: "How much for that cabbage?" And he answers: "Ten pesos."

Do you think that I am going to reply, "What? Ten pesos! I'll give you 12, and not a penny less"? Of course I'm not going to say anything like that! If I'm paying for something, I want to get it as cheaply as possible.

In the same way, if I'm purchasing my ticket to heaven by doing "good works"—that is, by obeying the law—I want to get a bargain on that, too. Why pay more than I have to? So I have to figure out how much I absolutely have to do in order to be saved. Like a skillful lawyer, I will examine and press the wording of the law. I'll study the semantics and develop hairsplitting legal definitions of what the law really means. Legalism (salvation by obedience to the law) makes it inevitable.

During Jesus' time a whole group of people made it their job to interpret the law and tell people exactly what they could or could not do under every circumstance.[1]

Q: Suppose I am harvesting my barley on Friday afternoon, and I'm not quite through when the sun goes down. (The Sabbath begins at sundown on Friday, remember?) May I go ahead and finish?

A: No, reaping is one of the 39 kinds of manual labor defined by the rabbis,[2] and all of them are forbidden on the Sabbath.

Q: But what if I see a dark cloud approaching? It might rain, and I could lose the whole year's crop and my family would starve.

A: In that case you can pick up the barley sheaf that you already cut and carry it into the granary, but you can't continue to cut any more.

Q: What about the sickle I was using to cut the barley? Can I carry it in too, so it won't get rusty from the rain?

A: No, but you can put the sickle in the sheaf of barley. Then it will go into the shelter when you carry in the barley, and that's OK.

The specific words they used were different from what I am giving here, but the "doctors of the law" discussed and resolved these very kinds of issues.

We have no reason to doubt their sincerity. They really wanted to do God's will, but somehow they failed to see that they were making the wrong connection. Going at it this way weakens the law, because it gets us to nit-picking and bargaining over details.

Consider the following insights from a beautiful devotional book by Ellen White called *Steps to Christ:*[3] "There are those who" "seek to perform the duties of the Christian life as that which God requires of them in order to gain heaven" (p. 44). Here is a good definition of "legalism". But Ellen White notes: "Such religion is worth nothing" (p. 44).

Then she goes on to say "When Christ dwells in the heart . . ." Here we have a definition of authentic Christianity. It's neither a set of ethical rules nor a matter of getting all the doctrines fine-tuned and perfectly lined up. It is "Christ in you, the hope of glory" (Colossians 1:27). A friendship with Jesus, it involves a love relationship with our Creator.

Legalism is unavoidably self-centered. The focus is always on me. "How am I doing?" becomes the question of the day. And, inevitably, it gets us into comparing ourselves with others. Even more insidious, legalism also contaminates motivation—what Ellen White calls "the spring of action." Under legalism, love for God has nothing to do with salvation. Instead, we obey because of what we hope to get out of it—we want to be saved. When the center of our lives is a love relationship with Jesus Christ, however, "self will be forgotten." Only then can "love to Christ" be "the spring of action."

Bible religion is Christ-centered while legalism is self-centered, the extreme opposite.

Christ-centered religion leads to a completely different result. "Those who feel the constraining love of God do not ask how little may be given to meet the requirements of God; they do not ask for the lowest standard, but aim at perfect conformity to the will of their Redeemer" (p. 45).

True religion—righteousness by faith—results not in a lower standard of obedience, but in just the opposite. An amazing paradox, but it is true, because we no longer ask "How much do I really have to do in order to be saved? The question changes from "How good do I have to be?" to "How good do I get to be?" We do not ask for the lowest standard, but aim at perfect conformity to the will of our Redeemer.

Comparison and Contrast

In the Sermon on the Mount Jesus draws a sharp contrast between the results of legalism and true religion. "You have heard that it was said, 'You shall not commit adultery'" (Matthew 5:27). As soon as legalists hear this, they immediately demand, "Exactly what does this mean? How far can I go and still be saved? How much can I get away with?" Naturally they will interpret the word "adultery" in the narrowest possible sense. OK. I haven't actually gone to bed with this person, so I haven't broken any law. But "those who feel the constraining love of God" understand that spiritual obedience, motivated by an intense love for God, is far greater and broader. That's what Jesus meant when He said: "But I say to you that everyone who looks at a woman with lust for her has already committed adultery with her in his heart" (verse 28).

The legalist interprets obedience as a mechanical response to a dictionary definition of the words in the law. Paul calls this going by the "letter of the law" (see 2 Corinthians 3:2-6). But spiritual obedience that springs from an attitude of love will be far broader and deeper. It will also be less rigid and unforgiving, less judgmental and condemnatory. In the salvation-by-works mode we are always climbing a ladder toward heaven. It quickly gets us into comparing ourselves with others, looking down on anyone who has not yet reached our level of achievement or has not understood their duty exactly as we have.

As we noted earlier, Paul was
"a Hebrew of Hebrews;
as to the Law, a Pharisee; . . .
as to the righteousness which is in the Law,
found blameless" (Philippians 3:5, 6).

He was all that, and yet he could say that he was formerly "apart from the Law." Before he met Jesus, Paul knew all about the law in a legalistic way. He could tell you the definition of every word. But he understood nothing at all about the true law in its boundless spirituality. Paul later said that his approach had turned the law into a dead "letter"—that it was frozen in stone (2 Corinthians 3:2-6).

As a "transcript" of the divine character, the law attempts to describe in human language what God is like. Its purpose and great objective is not to bring us up to a certain standard of behavior that can be expressed in finite terms through studying the definition of each word. Rather, its goal is to lead us always upward, higher and higher into the holy atmosphere of heaven.

As Paul's vision cleared, he began to understand the infinite perfection to which the law pointed him. When he compared that perfection with his own selfish existence as a religious person, he found the revelation overwhelming. That is why he says that when the law came, "I died" (Romans 7:9).

But this function of the law is not an end in itself, any more than the doctor's job is finished when they have made their diagnosis. The idea is not to humiliate us and leave us in despair. In his letter to the Galatians Paul notes that the law first condemned us. It put us in jail as it "shut up everyone under sin. . . . We were kept in custody under the law" (Galatians 3:22, 23). In this way "the Law" became "our tutor to lead us to Christ, so that we may be justified by faith" (verse 24).

And that is the point. The law tells us the truth, and once we realize that we are sick, once we start hurting, we will be willing to go to Dr. Jesus to be healed. That is the great search-and-rescue mission of the law. And that is how the law is our true friend.

Why not take a moment to record a few words of your response to His offer of friendship:

_____

_____

---

[1] That's what the New Testament refers to when it talks about lawyers.
[2] Mishneh Torah "Shabbos" 8:3-5; 21:6-10. Chayei Adam "Shabbos" 12.
[3] This book has been widely circulated as *Happiness Digest*.

Chapter 18

Finding Peace and Lasting Happiness

I have no idea how many times I've traveled by passenger launch to the port of Livingston on the northeastern coast of Guatemala, but it's been a lot. Nevertheless, one such trip was like no other.

It was only about 5:00 p.m. when we pulled away from the dock in Puerto Barrios, but the sky was dark, and an insistent rain was falling. As soon as we left the shelter of the seawall the storm struck us with its full fury.

Violent gusts of wind lashed the rain against the windows of the cabin. With one hand I clung to the forward bulkhead to keep from falling and with the other held my head, longing for a way to calm the nausea that only grew worse with each heave and pitch. Conversation was impossible, but I could hear moans and, at times, prayers or curses from the other passengers.

The voyage usually took about 90 minutes, but this time it seemed eternal. In fact, I was beginning to think that the captain must have lost his way and that we were heading out to open sea, when suddenly the most incredible calm overtook us. Instead of tossing and pitching, the little ship began gliding steadily across the water, and, up ahead, we could see through the rain the cheerful lights of our destination.

What made the difference? The storm was not over, but we had entered the shelter of the harbor. Out in the open ocean the waves still raged as wildly as ever, but they could no longer terrify us, because we had come into the refuge and were safe.

The Bible says that in the beginning a storm incomparably worse than the one we experienced that night swept across the earth. Wrapped in impenetrable darkness, water, air, rocks, and earth churned about in a chaotic maelstrom (Genesis 1:1, 2).[1]

Then God spoke, and the darkness gave way to light. He spoke again on the second day of Creation week, and the atmosphere sprang into existence, continents appeared, mountains rose up, and the sea was contained in its bed. What such details tell us is that the process of creation was a movement from disorder to order, from turbulence to calm.

The next day at His command the earth put on a green dress. Grasses and broadleafs, mosses and ferns appeared. Majestic trees raised their arms toward heaven. Pines and flowers added color to the landscape and perfumed the air. Vegetation, with its marvelous process of photosynthesis, produced food and oxygen for animal life.

On the fifth day and early on the sixth, God ordered the sea and earth and skies to teem with creatures that swam, flew, walked, or crawled.

"Then God said,
'Let Us make man in Our image,
according to Our likeness;
and let them rule
over the fish of the sea and
over the birds of the sky and
over the cattle and
over all the earth, and
over every creeping thing
that creeps on the earth."
—Genesis 1: 26

The creation of intelligent beings to govern the earth was the last step in bringing order out of chaos. Then, with infinite joy, the Creator contemplated His finished work, and He said that "it was *very good*" (verse 31).

Contrary to Nature

Physicists have synthesized a number of laws of thermodynamics. The second law states that all systems in nature show an invariable trend toward disintegration, disorder, and loss of energy. Scientists call it the principle of entropy.

Creation involved precisely the opposite. Through biochemical and physical transformations of immense complexity, God turned a chaotic planet into a world of order. When He said that it was "very good," it was because the storm was over, disorder had been conquered, chaos was gone, and the whole earth was a peaceful symbiosis in all of its different parts and relationships. God had designed each element and every detail of creation to serve others. With one voice everything testified to the love and infinite wisdom of the One who had brought it all into existence.

God's final pronouncement at the end of the Creation account tells us that:

(a) God saw that it was very good, and then

(b) He rested.

It is clear that the Creator's rest has nothing to do with fatigue. It is rest that comes when order takes the place of chaos—the peace and the calm that follow the storm. God saw that the earth was at rest—and then He Himself rested.

The Work Is Finished

Here is the passage in which God's declaration appears. Notice especially the terms I have numbered:

"God saw all that He had *made* (1), and behold, it was very good. And there was evening and there was morning, the sixth day. Thus the heavens and the earth were *completed* (2), and all their hosts. By the seventh day God *completed* (3) His work which He had *done* (4), and He rested on the seventh day from all His work which He had *done* (5). Then God blessed the seventh day and sanctified it, because in it He rested from all His work which God had *created* (6) and *made* (7)" (Genesis 1:31-2:3).

Seven times this brief passage reminds us that Creation was a finished work. It means that when God "rested," He stopped what He was doing, because He had completed His task. *The point is that God had omitted or overlooked nothing.* There was no part that did not function in perfect harmony with all the others. "God saw all that He had made, and behold, it was very good."

Sign of a Perfect Provision

An illustration can serve to clarify the importance of this point. Try to imagine for a moment that Adam, when first created, might have sprung to his feet and said, "Lord, don't You need me to help You with something?"

At this the Creator would have smiled and replied, "No, Adam, the work is done."

"But there must be something I can do. Maybe I could paint some decorations on the butterfly's wings."

"No, the butterfly's wings already have their colors."

"H'mm, well . . . maybe I could teach the birds to sing."

"No, they already know how to sing much better than you could ever instruct them."

"What if I would check the air to see if it has the right amount of oxygen? You know that a little too much or not enough is dangerous. Maybe I could help You calibrate it."

"No, I already took care of that, too."

"But Lord, there must something I can do."

"Yes, in fact, there is."

"What is it, Lord?"

"I want you to rest."

"Rest! But how can I rest when I haven't done any work?"

"I want you to trust Me, Adam. You need to believe that, in fact, the work is done, that I really have made a complete and perfect provision for all your needs."

And that is the meaning of the rest on the seventh day. If the Creator had brought human beings to life at the beginning of the week and had asked us to help out in some way, or at least had requested our opinion, we could take some credit, couldn't we? But He didn't. Our rest on the seventh day was from the beginning, is now, and always will be a celebration of God's work and not ours. Like Adam, we rest to show that we accept this reality, that we trust in God's perfect provision for our well-being and fulfillment. It means that we repose confidently in His hands, trusting in His wisdom, plan, and provision for our lives.

An Act of Worship

Through Sabbath observance, we concede to God His position as Creator and accept ours as creatures. Thus, in a deep and meaningful sense, our rest on the seventh day is an act of worship.

In nearly every false religion, including false Christianity, worship is a matter of *doing*. Only the Bible instructs us to worship through leaving off our own doing, laying aside our effort and struggles, and ceasing our labor so as to rest in the serene confidence that the work on our behalf is all done.[2] Ironic, isn't it, that some people accuse anyone who observes the Sabbath of believing in salvation by works when, in fact, it means just the opposite?

Our rest on the Sabbath not only symbolizes our trust relationship with God—it promotes and deepens it, becoming a part of its reality. By resting we declare that we find assurance, and therefore peace, in God's love. The Sabbath affirms, and at the same time confirms, the relationship between God and His creation.

A Commandment of Mercy

Do you have any idea how many people feel desperate and frustrated with life's responsibilities and problems? We hurry and worry, but there is never "enough time." All of us feel burdened with the need to make a living, keep up our home, improve our relationships, educate our children, care for our health, get a degree, pay bills, and pursue a career. These and thousands of other tasks constantly clamor for our attention. The problem is that we are finite, and life never stops demanding more and more. When the famous empire builder Cecil Rhodes lay dying, he supposedly muttered, "So little done—so much to do." Countless people today echo his frustration.

In the midst of the onrushing fury of events and the strident demands of a life that, like the mouth of the grave, never cries "Enough!" the great Creator-God offers us the Sabbath. "Six days you shall labor," the commandment states (Exodus 20:9). "This is your allotted time. Work, struggle, and give it your best. But all this has a limit—the Sabbath. In it you are to rest."

The fourth commandment requires us to work, but it does not say: "Work until you fall exhausted." Neither does it tell us to keep toiling until the work is done—that you can rest only when you finish.

The Sabbath is a parable of life because it portrays the reality that we will come to the end of our days and draw our last breath still thinking of more that we would like to do—if we only had the time. It teaches us to do what we can in our allotted time, and then rest. From it we learn to measure our achievement not by the standard of our own perfection but that of God's love.

Jesus reminded people in His day that the Sabbath was made *for* humanity (Mark 2:27). A gift provided by God Himself for our benefit and protection, it is a harbor, a shelter from the interminable storm, an oasis in which the weary traveler can find restoration and renewal before again taking up the struggles of life.

The Sabbath in a Broken World

" 'Indeed,' has God said. 'You shall not eat the fruit from any tree of the garden?' "

It must have seemed like an innocent question.

And the woman, not realizing that she was being set up, answered: "From the fruit of the trees of the garden we may eat; but from the fruit of the tree which is in the middle of the garden, God has said, 'You shall not eat from it or touch it, or you will die.' "

"You surely shall not die!" replied the enemy. "For God knows that in the day you eat from it your eyes will be opened, and you will be like God, knowing good and evil" (Genesis 3:1-5). *Here is something that God doesn't want you to know. He is withholding information and understanding that would be for your benefit.*

The Sabbath was a message of faith: "Trust Me. Accept that I really have made a perfect provision for all your needs." The enemy claimed precisely the opposite: "It is not true that God has made a perfect provision. Something is lacking. You need to separate yourselves from His plan, choose your own way, and fend for yourselves." By accepting his insinuations, Adam and Eve joined the enemy in his attitude of distrust and in his disobedience.

Their action brought in the need for an additional provision, a plan by which God could rescue human beings from their confusion and restore them to a relationship of faith, trust, and obedience.

Another Friday, Another Day of Rest

It was on a Friday that God completed His work and rested from the finished task of Creation. And it was also on a Friday that Jesus concluded the work of redemption. And as He bowed his head and died, he said, "It is finished!" (John 19:30).

After that, the disciples had just enough time to remove His body from the cross and lay it in Joseph's new tomb. As they hastened away, the sun was setting, and Scripture says, "The Sabbath was about to begin" (Luke 23:54).

Then, for the second time, the Savior rested on the seventh day from a finished work.

The Sabbath, created to commemorate God's provision for a perfect world, then took on an additional meaning. From that day forward it would also symbolize His provision for a world in sin—His plan to redeem and heal and restore us to a relationship of faith and trust in Him.

"There remains a Sabbath rest for the people of God. For the one who has entered His [God's] rest has himself also rested from his works, as God did from His" (Hebrews 4:9, 10).[3] The Sabbath rest now means that we accept that Christ really has achieved our salvation on the cross of Calvary. And because of the Savior's finished work, the Christian can "rest from his works," that is, from the frustrating and hopeless effort to earn salvation through personal good deeds. We can simply accept by faith that when Jesus said "It is finished," it really was, and that He had achieved a salvation full and unlimited for "whoever believes" (John 3:16).

Entering Into This Rest

Many times it seems as if the second law of thermodynamics seeks to impose itself on my life, and that the principle of disorder is going to win. I have even thought that the experience of that stormy night on the journey to Livingston was destined to be a permanent reality in my existence.

I suspect the apostle Paul might have felt something like this when he confessed: "I am not practicing what I would like to do, but I am doing the very thing I hate. . . . The good that I want, I do not do, but I practice the very evil that I do not want. . . . For I joyfully concur with the law of God in the inner man, but I see a different law in the members of my body, waging war against the law of my mind and making me a prisoner of the law of sin which is in my members (Romans 7:15-23).

With total honesty the great apostle admits that he is a perfectly normal human being and that spiritual storms are a reality in his life just as they are for the rest of us. It is an experience that every human being convinced of a need for change and improvement, yet finding themselves locked in mortal combat with old habits and passions, can understand and appreciate.

Are we condemned always to flounder in the midst of a relentless storm? No, in the same passage, the apostle tells us where to find the harbor: "Thanks be to God," he exclaims (verse 25). "There is now no condemnation for those who are in Christ Jesus. For the law of the Spirit of life in Christ Jesus has set you free from the law of sin and of death" (Romans 8:1, 2).

Adam accepted that God really had made a perfect provision in His finished work of Creation, and he showed his acceptance by resting on the Sabbath. Christians who keep the Sabbath join him in celebrating the goodness and loving provision of God in the Creation and also in the plan of redemption.

By withdrawing from the furious pace of our habitual activities, by stepping out from under the pressure of life during the Sabbath hours, we remind ourselves that the world doesn't revolve around us, that the sun doesn't rise in the morning and that flowers don't bloom at our command, and that Creation can get along perfectly well without any help at all from us. Our physical rest on the Sabbath celebrates both God's marvelous provision for us in the physical world and His plan to save us and restore us to complete restoration of fellowship with Himself through Jesus Christ.

Our trust relationship with God and experience of living faith is symbolized and deepened when we rest on the seventh day. Reflecting "the peace of God, which surpasses all comprehension" (Philippians 4:7), it is the rest, the freedom from condemnation, enjoyed by all "who are in Christ Jesus" (Romans 8:1).

No wonder Karl Barth observed: "The Sabbath commandment explains all the other commandments, or all the other forms of the one commandment. It is thus to be placed at the head."[4]

Does It Matter Which Day We Keep?

Some people have noticed that *Sabbath* means "rest." So they reason that the main thing is just to rest. Does it matter what day we keep as long as we rest on one day a week? To reason this way is to lose sight of what it is that we are celebrating. Our rest on the seventh day commemorates and acknowledges God's victory over chaos and disorder. It expresses our faith in His finished work and, in His perfect provision for all our needs, our acceptance of His gift of salvation and eternal life. Any change in the plan would also mean that we are assuming the right to alter what God has ordered in one of His Ten Commandments and substitute something of our own devising in its place.

Such was the reasoning of Cain, who believed that it was OK to offer fruits and vegetables instead of the lamb that God had asked them to bring. The lamb showed faith in the coming Redeemer. It meant that he accepted God's gift and His perfect provision for his salvation. But by bringing only fruits and vegetables, Cain attempted to give something to God, to pay his own way and appease God's wrath against sin with something of his own production. In the same way, our rest on the seventh day (Saturday) shows that we accept God's loving provision for all our needs, including His gift of salvation.

God did not work for three days, then take a break on Wednesday to rest up before going on to finish the job. Neither did He hold a celebration on the first day (Sunday) before starting to work. Rather, He rested on the seventh day to commemorate a finished task, and He has ordered us to do the same. It is not left to our discretion to substitute another day as a day of rest in the place of what He has ordered.

Don't Miss Out

Maybe you are wondering what to do about all this. I urge you not to hesitate. Accept the practice of Sabbath observance as a precious gift from God. With joyful and confident steps, make plans to enter into this beautiful experience. "Let us fear if, while a promise remains of entering His rest, any one of you may seem to have come short of it" (Hebrews 4:1).

Lord, what a wonderful plan You have made in offering me the gift of fellowship with Yourself through Sabbath observance! I do want to accept this gift, and I thank and praise You for it. In a practical way, here's how I can begin to do this:

_____

_____

_____

As an aid, I have made arrangements for you to recieve, at no cost or obligation, a copy of Ellen White's brief devotional book Steps to Christ. If you live in the United States or Canada, ask for your free copy by calling 1-800-467-6302. To ask for the book online, go to www.ellenwhitetruth.com and click on "free resources."

---

[1] I make no apology for dealing with the early chapters of Genesis as serious history, but I do understand the misgivings of some who think differently. Such individuals believe that these Bible stories do not represent real events. They see them, rather, as didactic tools or teaching messages. In either case, it is clear that these chapters are foundational to comprehending the message of the entire Bible.

[2] Ironic, isn't it, that some people accuse anyone who observes the Sabbath as believing in salvation by works when, in fact, it means just the opposite?

[3] Not long ago I heard a man asserting that all the Ten Commandments are repeated and upheld in the New Testament except the fourth (the one that refers to the Sabbath). I wondered if perhaps he was repeating what he had heard someone else say without actually investigating the matter in the Bible for himself.

[4] Karl Barth, *Church Dogmatics* (Edinburg: T. & T. Clark, 1975), Vol. III, part 4, p. 53.

Chapter 19

Who Is on Your List?

"*Yo me debo a Cuba.*" There it was, an inspirational sign that caught my eye not far from the airport in Havana. It meant: "I owe myself to Cuba."

And I thought: *What a great slogan!* It really is. Whoever painted it there on the wall wanted to encourage people to be aware of and think about their moral debt—something we all need to consider more than we usually do.

During World War II the pilots of the Royal Air Force engaged in life-and-death combat with the German aviators who flew across the English Channel every day to drop their bombs on London. Known as Battle of Britain, it was one of the deadliest struggles ever waged. But the terrible sacrifice of those brave men succeeded in its purpose. There can be no doubt that they saved Britain and changed the course of the war.

The unforgettable words of Winston Churchill memorialized their heroism: "Never was so much owed by so many to so few."[1]

Your List

Have you taken time to think lately about *your* moral debts? If you were to make up a list, who would be at the top?

Most of us are grateful to the heroes that have left their mark on history, but when we really think of the people who grab our heart at its deepest spot, who have done the most for us personally, we are far more likely to remember someone who is not famous at all—our parents, for example, or maybe a teacher who believed in us, a friend who was there for us, somebody on the job who showed us the ropes when we started or covered for us when we made a mistake, an individual who cheered us on and encouraged us when we needed it most.

The apostle Paul, too, talks about moral obligations. "I am a debtor," he says in Romans 1:14, NKJV. Let's think about it for a minute and try to help him with his list. He might appreciate some suggestions as to whom he should include.

First of all, we remember that Paul was a Roman citizen. He must have been grateful to the people who established the empire and its famous system of justice. More than once it saved him from being brutalized and probably killed (see Acts 16:37-40; 22:25-29).

Next, we recall that Paul was born in Tarsus. A provincial capital with markets, broad streets, and a forum, it also had a waterworks, a gymnasium, and a large stadium. The apostle was well aware of all this. With a sense of justifiable pride, he once said: "I am . . . [from] Tarsus in Cilicia, a citizen of no insignificant city" (Acts 21:39).

Paul must have been grateful as well for the religious principles and rich traditions of the Jewish people. He probably studied at the *yeshiva,* or rabbinical school, of Tarsus before transferring to "sit at the feet" of Gamaliel in Jerusalem (see Acts 22:3). Even today history remembers Gamaliel as one of the greatest rabbis of all time. And Paul was his student! If anyone were to figure in his list of moral indebtedness, we would expect to find Gamaliel there.

And what could we say about Paul's great friend Barnabas, who believed in him when no one else did (see Acts 9:27; 11:25), or the elders of the church at Antioch who commissioned him and sent him on his first missionary journey (see Acts 22:28)?

I hope you appreciate the help that we're giving you here, Paul. Just a few hints as to the people you might want to include on your list of moral indebtedness.

Paul's Strange Answer

But Paul doesn't seem to hear us. For some reason his list is a lot shorter than ours, and yet it is also a lot longer. Here it is: "I am a debtor both to Greeks and to barbarians, both to wise and to unwise" (Romans 1:14, NKJV).

Wait a minute. What did the Greeks ever do for you, Paul? Not much, I would think. And the barbarians? Even less. And what did you get from the wise and the unwise? The answer is, of course: nothing at all.

When Paul talks here about his moral debt, he is trying to tell the Christians at Rome why he has his great burden to visit them. He says he wishes to go there for the same reason that has impelled him to be on the march ever since that day he met Jesus on the Damascus road. The apostle longs to see them because he has received something so wonderful, so beautiful, that he doesn't want them or anyone else to miss out on it. He feels honor-bound to share it with them.

Parable of Judgment

Jesus spoke about the final judgment as a time when He will focus on what we have done for others. He will say to those who are saved:

"I was hungry,
>   and you gave Me something to eat;
I was thirsty,
>   and you gave Me something to drink;
I was a stranger,
>   and you invited Me in;
naked,
>   and you clothed Me;
I was sick,
>   and you visited Me;
I was in prison,
>   and you came to Me."
—Matthew 25:35, 36.

The people hearing His words of approval are shocked. They don't re-call doing such things for Jesus. But He explains: "To the extent that you did it to one of these brothers of Mine, even the least of them, you did it to Me" (verse 40).

This clarifies how a Christian sees the matter of moral indebtedness.

Why should we be kind, helpful, and loving to other people? It is not based on what they have done for us, or whether they deserve it. We are to be kind even to the "least"—the lowest, the most undeserving person on the planet. Again, why? Because of what Jesus has done for us. No moral debt can ever compare with the one that we owe to Jesus. It is the basis of all human relations, the reason behind what we do for others and how we treat them.

Do you have eyes that can look out and see the world? Can you hear when someone speaks? Is there a functioning brain behind your eyebrows that allows you to process the information you take in? Are you ambulatory—physically able to get up and move around? Can you interact and converse with people? What do you know that not everyone does? What have you experienced that they haven't? Every one of these things is a precious gift, and every one of them makes us debtors. And immeasurably far beyond any of them is the gospel and the gift of hope and peace and eternal life that we have through Jesus Christ.

That Makes All the Difference

Some people—and even some Christians—believe that the Christian's life is very similar to that of people who don't know God or love Him. And at first glance the idea seems logical. After all, people who don't know or care about God get up in the morning and put on their clothes. They go to work or wherever their responsibility takes them, have friends, play, joke, love, and laugh. Maybe they are interested in politics or not, but they are concerned about the world around them, and they try to live as best they can under the particular set of circumstances that life has handed them.

Is there any one of these things that doesn't describe how Christians live their lives as well? Of course not.

So what's the difference? Is it just the 2 percent or less of their total time that Christians spend reading the Bible and in similar activities?

The truth is that the Christian life is different totally—100 percent so. What makes it so? It is the principle of responsibility and accountability that we call stewardship. The apostle Paul puts it this way: "Whether, then, you eat or drink or whatever you do, do all to the glory of God" (1 Corinthians 10:31). When Christians get up in the morning the first thing they think about is their heavenly Father, and they talk with Him. They know that the way they dress can help people learn about the God who is a lover of order and beauty. They regard food and drink as a way of ministering to His beautiful gift of their physical bodies. A healthy, attractive body is a powerful witness to His love, and a long life and good health make it possible for them to give a wider and more productive service. In addition, a clear mind will help them understand Him better and enable them to have a better relationship with Him. All this leads them to take good care of their health.

Whatever their work or profession, they see it as a ministry, a way of serving, lifting, and helping other people and contributing to their happiness and well-being. Furthermore, they choose their recreational activities and dedicate their time to things that foster in themselves a spirit of unselfishness, bring honor to their Lord, and strengthen their relationship with Him and with others. And they value money and other material things as a way to help others and advance the knowledge of God in the world.

Most of all, they find joy, peace of mind, wholeness, and mental health in their relationship with God. Their life in God is so fulfilling and joyful that they are brimming over with an eager desire for other people to know about it too. Thus they believe that keeping silent would be the worst kind of selfishness. But their witnessing for God is not just something they do at certain specific times and places while the rest of the time they are off duty. Everything they do, and every aspect of their lives, can help other people know about God.[2] At the same time, they are always ready to speak a word "in due season" (Proverbs 15:23, KJV) on behalf of Jesus.

As I said, even some Christians haven't gotten this message. They haven't caught on, which is why they carry the same burdens as the people who don't know God or love Him do. As a result, they have the same frustrations, run the same rat race, and find themselves trying to compete on the same level, always hoping somehow to catch up. Determined not to miss out on any physical or material advantage, they race along frantically, with never enough time for reflection, for self-improvement or for strengthening family ties, and none at all for spiritual growth or for sharing, helping, and reaching out to others. It is hard to imagine anything sadder than that.

It is the principle of stewardship that makes all the difference. Can you think of anything more essential for being a happy and successful Christian?

One Sabbath afternoon my family and I went for a drive in the countryside not far from our home in northern Mexico. We found a road that we had never seen before and decided to find out where it would take us. Before long we were wending our way between hills and meadows. On one side was a rocky stream, and bougainvilleas and wildflowers bloomed everywhere. As we continued, the local houses became fewer and the road narrower and considerably rougher. After a time in which we had seen no houses at all, we passed by a high wall on the right of the road. Another 200 yards or so we found the way ahead blocked by a wire gate, so we stopped and got out to look around.

A moment later a man appeared walking rapidly toward us from the direction that we had just come. Because he carried a machete, I wondered briefly about his intentions, but he greeted us in a friendly way and seemed eager to chat. He explained that he was the caretaker of the property that we had just passed, and didn't get many visitors. Pretty soon he said: "Would you like to see the property?"

Of course we would. So he went back and opened the enormous gate. There we saw an amazing mansion surrounded by flowers, fountains, and beautiful statues. The lawn was manicured like a Persian carpet, and everywhere there was beauty and order.

"You seem to be alone," I observed. "Are you expecting the owners soon?"

"I'm always expecting them," he replied.

"What do you mean?"

"Well, they don't get here very often, but I'm ready when they do."

"Where do they live?"

"They have places in Monterrey, in Guadalajara, in Mexico City, and who knows where else."

"So you never know when they are going to show up?"

"No, the first thing I hear is the chukka-chukka of their helicopter, and here they are. But it doesn't matter. They know they can count on me."

And I thought: *What a tremendous lesson in stewardship.* I'm not sure if the man was aware of what the Bible says about the subject, but he knows a lot about responsibility and faithfulness. And that's the main requirement of a good steward (1 Corinthians 4:2).[3]

Some of the things I hold in trust are

Simply Put

Some ways in which I can use these things to pay the debt that I owe, because of Jesus, "both to Greeks and to barbarians, both to wise and unwise":

_____

_____

_____

---

[1] Speech to the House of Commons on Aug. 20, 1940.

[2] Or drive them away.

[3] For a powerful story about stewardship, read "The Rich Family in Our Church," by Eddie Ogan, http://www.new-life.net/favrt030.htm .

Chapter 20

Get off the Column

You have probably heard of Simeon Stylites. He's the fellow who lived on the top of a column in Asia Minor. By the time he died in the year 459, he had remained up there for 37 years.

Not many people today admire him. But before we write him off as a fanatic or demented, we need to realize that Simeon was a man who wanted very much to be holy. And holiness is not a bad thing to desire. The Bible says that God has called us to holiness (1 Thessalonians 4:7). It also says that we are to perfect holiness in the fear of the Lord (2 Corinthians 7:1), and that without holiness none of us will see God (Hebrews 12:14).

Simeon knew the texts very well, and he believed them. One day when he was 13 he wandered into a meeting at which someone was reading the Beatitudes (Matthew 5:3-11). As he listened, an intense longing to be like God overwhelmed him. He didn't just think, *Hey, that would be nice.* Rather, the desire to be holy was so powerful that it was stronger than everything else in his mind. In tears he said to the people who were reading: "That's it! That's what I want. How can I be pure in heart?"

In our own day everything that surrounds us, even the air we breathe, is touched by the selfish, pleasure-seeking values of existentialism. Millions of people find themselves influenced by this philosophy even though they may never have heard of Søren Kierkegaard, the man who started it all. That's the way it was in the fifth century when Simeon Stylites lived, except that the sheeplike people in his day had been swayed by the philosopher Plato, who taught that body and soul are enemies and that if one is strong, the other will be weak. It meant that whatever harms or weakens the body will make you a better Christian. So it became popular to whip yourself, to go without sleep, and to fast. Sex has to do with the body, so even between married people it was a sign of weakness, and celibacy was an essential step on the way to sainthood.

Simeon figured that the best place to get away from all this was 50 feet in the air, so up he went. The body demands food, so he fasted with a vengeance. For long periods he ate only once a week.

Too bad he didn't study the idea carefully in the Bible. He might have learned that body and soul are not enemies, but inseparable friends. To the contrary of what Simeon and most people in his day believed, what is good for the body is good for the soul, and vice versa.

Two puzzling passages of Scripture help us understand this. I mean, of course, that they seem "puzzling" at first glance, but they are actually clear. One of them is Exodus 15:26: "If you will give earnest heed to the voice of the Lord your God, and do what is right in His sight, and give ear to His commandments, and keep all His statutes, I will put none of the diseases on you which I have put on the Egyptians; for I, the Lord, am your healer."

Notice that the "if" part of the verse is talking about holiness—just what Simeon wanted. But the consequence part does not mention holiness at all—it refers to health. The message is: If you do these things—if you do what is right, if you keep the commandments, [1] etc.—you will be healthy.

The other puzzling passage is Leviticus 11. Here we find a list of rules for healthful eating. Again, the surprise comes in the consequence section at the end of the chapter. It does not state that if you obey these rules you will live longer, you will have fewer diseases, or anything of the sort. Rather, it declares: "Thus you shall be holy, for I am holy" (Leviticus 11:45).

Notice the message of the two passages taken together: The first says that keeping the laws of holiness will make you healthy. The second says that obeying the laws of health will make you holy.

Here's another text that illustrates the same principle. It says that the Gentiles might live in the midst of unsanitary conditions, but God's people were to bury their filth (Deuteronomy 23:12, 13). Why? "Since the Lord your God walks in the midst of your camp . . . therefore your camp must be holy" (verse 14). Again, we hear the theme that you need to obey health laws if you want to be holy. [2]

Today we find more interest in health than in any time in history. Organic and natural foods are widely available. Gyms and fitness centers abound, and people are buying exercise equipment to the tune of the billions of dollars every year.

It would be hard to fault such a trend. There's nothing wrong with wanting to be healthy, to look and feel better and to live longer. But a lot of people apparently haven't noticed the intimate connection between lifestyle and spirituality. The other day a young man who is an active and enthusiastic Christian was pouring catsup on his Big Mac with cheese and fries when a friend tried to spoil it for him. Looking very solemn, the friend said: "Do you realize that you are about to ingest 54 grams of artery-clogging fat?"[3]

To which he replied, "Hey, who wants to live to be 100 anyway? The important thing is to be ready when it's your time to go."

Another was togged out in a sweatsuit ready for a workout when someone said to her, "Go ahead. That's OK. I'd rather use my time to read the Bible and pray."

Simeon Stylites thought that anything he could do to weaken his body would make him a better Christian. But the Bible message is that just the opposite is true. Good health is an important aid to having a clear mind and a heart that is in tune with God. And that is the most important reason for taking care of our health.

Beyond Health

Of course, the principle that we are talking about here goes far beyond the matter of health, and applies to the whole range of lifestyle issues: How am I going to spend my leisure time? Who will be my close friends? What will I do with my money? What will I listen to, watch, and read? How will I dress, and what will I do for entertainment? The important thing to ask is what effect all such things will have on my relationship with God, my spirituality and values. Will a particular activity, friendship, or decision make me more noble and caring, less self-centered, more sensitive to the rights and needs of others? Will I be more inclined to seek God and spend time with Him in His Word, more aware of His presence all around, more apt to think of Him and be in communion with Him as I go about my daily activities?

The apostle Peter urges the believers "to abstain from fleshly lusts." Why? Because they "war against the soul" (1 Peter 2:11). In case you hadn't noticed, we really are engaged in a conflict. And there's nothing easy or guaranteed about winning. In Galatians 5 the apostle Paul gives a list of things that he calls the "deeds of the flesh" (verse 19). They include enmity, strife, jealousy, outbursts of anger, envying, drunkenness, carousing, and more (verses 20, 21). What does he say is wrong with these things? "For the flesh sets its desire against the Spirit, and the Spirit against the flesh; for these are in opposition to one another, so that you may not do the things that you please" (verse 17). "I forewarn you, just as I have forewarned you, that those who practice such things shall not inherit the kingdom of God" (verse 21).

Such things are bad and will keep us from inheriting eternal life, not because they make God angry at us. It's not that when God sees us coming, He looks at His checklist, and if we have done anything on the list He's going to slam the door in our faces. The problem is the damage such things do to our spiritual life. They will keep us out of heaven because they weaken us in the struggle against evil, destroying our love for eternal values and our sense of holiness and awe in the presence of God.

Transmitting a Message

Another important principle to guide our choices in the matter of lifestyle and Christian behavior is to recall that our conduct is visible—people around us will observe it. Inevitably it transmits a message about who we are and what we believe. What will people who know very little about God learn about Him from observing the way that we dress and how we behave? What will they discover about our faith and values?[4]

Getting Ready for Heaven

It is common today to talk about culture shock. It refers to the discomfort that people experience when they find themselves surrounded by an unfamiliar culture. Suddenly they feel insecure, not at all sure what is expected of them. Put off balance, they may become irritated when people in the new environment behave in ways that seem strange to them. It is a "fish out of water" sensation that is not at all pleasant.

Christian lifestyle and standards of behavior have a lot to do with getting us ready for the culture of heaven. It will be a land in which people live lives of peace and order, in which they don't deceive or take advantage of others, are not governed by pride, and don't do things that destroy their bodies or minds. They honor their Creator above all and express their love for Him by deeds of loving service to one another. Not only is it heaven's lifestyle, it is the behavior that the Bible prescribes for us here and now—the essential preparation for transferring to that happy realm. The people that God will take to heaven will not experience culture shock when they get there, because they have accustomed themselves to the life of heaven here and now.

Making the Change

Benjamin Franklin had a good idea. He wanted to improve himself, so one day he sat down and compiled a list of changes that he intended to make in his life. Then, methodical as always, he organized a careful plan for achieving everything on his list.

What would you think of applying Franklin's idea to the standards of a Christian lifestyle? We could make out a checklist of good behavior that we want to achieve and the things that we intend to avoid. Then set to work until we have a perfect record.

The apostle Paul tells us that was precisely the kind of religion he grew up with. He and his neighbors had a checklist of holy behavior that was very long indeed.

But Paul came to see such an approach as a "ministry of death." Why? How could a sincere attempt to obey God have such a negative result?

Because it made religion into a rulebook and reduced it to a matter of "letters engraved on stones" (2 Corinthians 3:7). Paul contrasted it with the "new covenant," a term he took from the prophecy of Jeremiah 31:31-33. The core of this approach is incredibly simple. It says: "I will be their God, and they shall be My people" (verse 33).

What it means is that true religion focuses not on rules but on a relationship. And it finds its center not in ourselves and our behavior but in God and His everlasting love.

Under this plan the standards of Christian behavior have an altogether different function. Rather than being a ladder that we laboriously ascend, hoping one day to climb high enough to get into heaven, Christian standards become as God intended them to be, holy principles designed to help us avoid endless suffering and foolish mistakes.

Under the new covenant the way we keep these standards is also different, because the covenant includes a promise: "I will put My law within them and on their heart I will write it" (verse 33).

Good conduct—obedience—that comes only from knowing what is right will be superficial and partial at best. But a heart renewed by the Holy Spirit will be able to offer obedience as a genuine and unselfish expression of love and gratitude to God.

And that is the invitation I leave with you: to enter without delay into that covenant of peace, that relationship of love. Here is God's promise to all who respond. I hope that you will consider it carefully and make it your own:

"I will sprinkle clean water on you, and you will be clean. ... Moreover, I will give you a new heart and put a new spirit within you; and I will remove the heart of stone from your flesh and give you a heart of flesh. I will put My Spirit within you and cause you to walk in My statutes, and you will be careful to observe My ordinances" (Ezekiel 36:25-27).

Would you like to record here a few words expressing your response to God's invitation?

---

[1] Theologians point out that holiness includes more than obedience to the commandments. They are right, of course, but obedience is an essential part, and it is the aspect that Simeon Stylites and people of his day focused on almost exclusively.

[2] Similarly, the Gentiles might consume the flesh of an animal that died of itself, but God's people must not eat it. Why? Because "you are a holy people to the Lord your God" (Deuteronomy 14:2).

[3] Nutritional information reported on the McDonald's Web site: http://www.mcdonalds.com/usa/eat/nutrition_info.html.

[4] Just as our verbal language changes from one place to another, so does the cultural language. In most of Asia, for example, people do not wear shoes in church. They invariably leave them at the door. In Latin America where I live, removing one's shoes in church would be shockingly disrespectful. The principle of respect and reverence is invariable. The way that we express it may change from one culture to another.

Chapter 21

A Good Marriage

If you were married to my wife—and I am very glad you are not—you would know from personal experience what it is to have a really great marriage. We recently celebrated 45 years of walking side by side, and I can assure you that with every passing year it gets better and that we love each other more.

Nevertheless, for some reason that I can't quite explain, Ruth Ann seems to enjoy the following story: It seems that an elderly couple were celebrating their golden anniversary in the company of friends and family. Because they were well known in the community, a reporter from the local paper interviewed them.

"In all those years did you ever think about divorce?" he asked the silver-haired woman. "Did it ever cross your mind?"

"Divorce!" She seemed shocked by the idea. "Oh, no, never! . . . not divorce—murder, yes!"

Now, if you want to know why Ruth Ann likes that story, you'll have to ask her. I'm not quite sure.

But what do you think? Could there actually be a relationship in which you sometimes get more than a little ticked off by something that your spouse does, and yet it's a good marriage and you love each other deeply and forever?

What is a "good marriage"? How would you describe it? Here are some points that I find in the Bible on this:

1. A good marriage is one that has a lot of forgiveness. Maybe that's not what you expected me to say. But you have to start with the premise that we're all pretty normal. And that means that sometimes we do offend.

The Bible says that love "does not take into account a wrong suffered." In other words, it doesn't keep a list. It doesn't hang on to grudges and make an issue out of hurt feelings (1 Corinthians 13:5).

Most of the couples that I know whose marriage is in trouble do have a list, and it's a long one. Well, at one time I would have been right there standing in line to toss a stone at such people for being so unforgiving.

But life has a way of teaching us some unexpected lessons, and one day someone did something that left me writhing. It damaged and hurt and affected me in many ways.

What surprised me most about the experience was what I learned about myself. A cold iceberg of unforgiveness filled my soul. If you had asked me about it even a year after that ... well, never mind. I've learned to be ashamed of it now, but it took a long time.

It's not hard to talk about forgiveness when it's someone else who was hurt. No problem. Just write out a prescription and hand it to them. Tell them to get over it.

Unfortunately, it's not always that easy.

Forgiveness Really Is Possible

So how *can* we forgive? I don't know any way except the one that Jesus gave us.

One terrible day the religious leaders came to Him dragging a woman that they then threw down at His feet like a dirty rag.

In loud tones they told Jesus they had caught her sinning—"in the very act" (John 8:4).

Remember what He told them?

"It's true," He said; "she is a sinner. No doubt about that. Now tell me about yourselves. What are you?" His actual words were: "He who is without sin among you, let him be the first to throw a stone at her" (verse 7).

If you can't see any reason that you should forgive someone, just call to mind how much God has forgiven you. Ask yourself how it is that you have any hope at all of salvation and eternal life. "Just as the Lord forgave you, so also should you" (Colossians 3:13).

True heart-forgiveness comes only when we are deeply aware of the depths of the forgiveness that we have ourselves received. When we see ourselves as forgiven sinners, our haughty arrogance against the people who have hurt us will melt away, and we will begin to see them as fellow travelers in life, individuals who are beset by the power of an evil nature, just as we are. Only then can compassion really begin to take the place of hatred, and true forgiveness start to flow. There is no other way.

2. A good marriage is one in which the partners make a conscious effort to notice and focus on the good and positive traits they see in each other.

This principle is a corollary of the first, because such an attitude is the opposite of unforgiveness. It is a decision to celebrate beauty and virtue, to enjoy the flowers and not worry so much about the thorns. Above all, it means that we will focus on happy incidents and good traits. Doing this is the best way to keep that first love alive and healthy.

Most of us have plenty of unlovely, ornery traits. It doesn't take any special genius or skill to discover them. And if we choose to focus on those things, it won't be long before they fill our whole horizon. "He did . . ." "She said . . ." "I felt like . . ." We can continually recall and complain about them. The more we do so, the more we are sure to feel justified in our anger and resentment.

The apostle Paul has a better plan. He says:

"Whatever is true,
   whatever is honorable,
    whatever is right,
     whatever is pure,
      whatever is lovely,
       whatever is of good repute,
  if there is any excellence
   and if anything worthy of praise,
dwell on these things."

—Philippians 4:8

The key word here is "dwell." Where do you choose to let your mind spend most of its time?[1]

This has to be a permanent attitude, because after confetti gets swept up, after the wedding gifts have been stowed away, reality sets in, and it's "welcome to the rest of your life." That's when you get to see me the first thing in the morning when my hair is straggling. Sometimes I have bad breath, and it gets on your nerves when I belch and that I never remember to put my shoes in the closet.

The rose-tinted vision we had of our partner will definitely disappear. But if we have made a conscious decision to emphasize the positive and look for the good, the storybook view will be replaced by one that is more realistic, more mature, and a whole lot better.[2]

3. A good marriage is ruled by faithfulness and steadfast love.[3] The Bible constantly compares mature married love to the way that God cares about His children. An eloquent Hebrew word expresses this idea: *hesed.*

"The lovingkindness *[hesed]* of the Lord
    is from everlasting to everlasting
    on those who fear Him."
            —Psalm 103:17

"The mountains may be removed and the hills may shake,
    But My lovingkindness *[hesed]* will not be removed from you,
        and My covenant of peace will not be shaken."
            —Isaiah 54:10

Hesed becomes *agape* in the Septuagint[4] and the New Testament. It is the kind of love that Paul says husbands are to shower on their wives:

"Husbands, *love* your wives,
    just as Christ also *loved* the church
    and gave Himself up for her."
            —Ephesians 5:25

He explains what he means by referring to the creation of woman from that part of a man's body that is closest to his heart. When Adam saw his wife for the first time, he said:

" 'This is now bone of my bones,
    and flesh of my flesh.'. . .
    For this cause
    a man shall leave his father and his mother,
    and shall cleave to his wife;
    and they shall become one flesh."
            —Genesis 2:23, 24

The Greek philosophers of Paul's day laid heavy emphasis on individuality. They considered each human being an island, entire and complete in itself. According to the Greek view of marriage, my wife is herself and I am myself. Thus I can stand apart from her and be irritated by her weaknesses. I can submit her to my judgment and pass sentence on her.

But if I have understood—and am experiencing—the biblical concept of marriage, standing apart is impossible, because marriage converts the two into one flesh. Thus I cannot condemn my spouse or ridicule her because of her weaknesses. If we are one flesh, they are no longer hers alone—they are also my weaknesses, too. So I cannot stand apart from her and treat her as a separate person. Nor can I scorn her or cast her off, because she is part of my own body. Instead, I must feel her wounds, I must share the frustration and pain of her failures, I must experience her sense of loss and confusion. By the same token, I can rejoice in her victories, because they, too, are mine (see 1 Corinthians 9:22; 2 Corinthians 11:29).

Paul is thinking precisely of this when he continues:
"So husbands ought also to love their own wives
    as their own bodies.
He who loves his own wife loves himself;
for no one ever hated his own flesh,
but nourishes and cherishes it,
just as Christ also does the church,
because we are members of His body."
                    —Ephesians 5:28-30

Here is the meaning of God's *hesed* love for us. We see it in the caring involvement of Christ with the church and of the husband and wife with each other.

Another key word to understand the Bible concept of a good marriage is *yada*, "know." The Greeks understood knowledge to be based on information, objective inalterable facts outside and separate from us. It is "apprehension of ultimate reality."

But in the Bible, knowledge is not only informational but relational; it is not only intellectual but experiential.[5] What this means is that one cannot really know something and remain uninvolved with it. Knowledge demands relationship, concern, and participation in what one knows. There is no such thing as truly "objective" knowledge. Thus it should not surprise us to find that the Bible applies the word *yada* to the marriage relation (see Genesis 4:1).[6]

The Bible teaches that human beings are indivisible. Body, soul, and spirit are legitimate concepts, but it is impossible to defend the Greek idea that they are distinct entities that can be isolated and each go its separate way. They are parts of an inseparable whole. In the same way, the marriage relation is a total intimacy of mind, body, and spirit ruled by *hesed* love.[7]

4. A good marriage is a sanctuary. We noticed that God established a covenant with His people in ancient times that clarified their relationship with Him and defined them as separate and distinct from all other people groups.

Marriage, too, is a covenant, a commitment by the partners to transcend and stand apart from similar relationships. In this way marriage achieves and defines its holiness. It is holy matrimony because it is a sanctuary, a holy ground on which only the partners may tread. Jesus made it clear that the exclusiveness demanded by the seventh commandment embraces even our thoughts (Matthew 5:27, 28).

The transcendence of the marriage relationship also requires the partners to rise above or stand apart from the confused moral values of popular culture. Those who follow the biblical command to "abstain from sexual immorality" thereby place themselves in sharp contrast with the "Gentiles who do not know God" (see 1 Thessalonians 4:3-5). By abstaining "from fleshly lusts which war against the soul," the marriage partners become "aliens and strangers" on the earth (1 Peter 2:11).

As a sanctuary, marriage is a safe harbor in which the couple finds security in each other. They know they are accepted and loved and understood. This too parallels the Christian's relationship with Christ.

In doing these things, a good marriage not only reflects and symbolizes the believer's relationship with Christ, but also strengthens and deepens the relationship. It is a foretaste of the day of Christ's return when He will fulfill the covenant and we see Him face to face.

"There the redeemed shall know, even as also they are known. The loves and sympathies which God Himself has planted in the soul shall there find truest and sweetest exercise. The pure communion with holy beings, the harmonious social life with the blessed angels and with the faithful ones of all ages who have washed their robes and made them white in the blood of the Lamb, the sacred ties that bind together 'the whole family in heaven and earth'—these help to constitute the happiness of the redeemed" (Ellen G. White, *The Great Controversy*, p. 676).

What ideas or thoughts do you find especially encouraging as you look forward to that day?

_____

_____

_____

---

[1] Don't forget that Paul was writing from prison.

[2] See William Wordsworth, "She Was a Phantom of Delight."

[3] In a way, you could say I'm repeating myself here, because this one is a summary of the first two.

[4] The Septuagint is a translation of the Old Testament into Greek.

[5] Knowledge "connotes experience rather than contemplation or ecstasy" (George E. Ladd, *A Theology of the New Testament* [Grand Rapids: William B. Eerdmans Pub. Co., 1974] p. 261).

[6] We see the biblical understanding of knowledge as relationship in the application of the word "know" in Scripture to sexual intercourse, as in Genesis 4:1: "Now Adam knew his wife Eve, and she conceived and bore Cain" (NRSV). The expression is not a euphemism. Rather, it is applied in the most essential sense of the Hebrew idiom—that is, knowledge as relationship, involvement, and intimacy.

[7] The contrast between the biblical concept of marriage and the ideas of Greek philosophy is further discussed in Loron Wade, "Marriage and Covenant: Reflections on the Theology of Marriage," *Journal of the Adventist Theological Society*, 13, no. 2 (Autumn 2002): 73-93.

Chapter 22

King of the Mountain

I don't know if you have ever played "king of the mountain," but you would have if you went to the school I did. It always started when one of the older boys—usually it was Carl Johnson or one of his brothers—would jump on a box and announce, "Who's king of the mountain?" That was a signal for the rest of us to run over and try to push him off so that we could climb up and yell, "I'm the king now." Such encounters tended to be fairly short, because within about 45 seconds all of us would be wrestling around in a huge pile on the floor.[1]

I hadn't remembered the old game for many years, but the other day as I was reading through Daniel 7 the thought "king of the mountain" came to mind.

First the chapter presents Babylon, the lion, who struts around as if to say: "I'm the greatest. My kingdom is going to last forever" (see verse 4). "That's what you think!" growls Persia, the bear, and it comes rushing in to push Babylon out of the way so that it can take over (verse 5). After that, Greece and Rome each take a turn (verses 6, 7). The last and loudest is the little horn, who sprouts from the head of Rome. It goes far beyond the others, getting into such a frenzy that it actually thinks it can be a rival to God and so tries to eliminate everyone who doesn't happen to agree (verses 8, 21, 25).

Now, as I say, this was the animals' version of "king of the mountain." But you can be sure that Daniel didn't feel amused as he watched. He knew about the cruelty of the Babylonian "lion" from personal experience. He must have been about 17 or 18 when Nebuchadnezzar carried him off to Babylon as a captive. After that Judah suffered two more invasions. Before it all ended, thousands of people had perished, and the whole country had turned into a wasteland.

By the time he had this vision, Daniel had been praying about the situation for nearly 60 years, but I am not sure that he felt happy or relieved by what he saw, because it must have been clear to him that the solution was still a long way off. Of course, there was good news, too. When the power struggle finally ceased, the peace would last forever.

Here's the part of the prophecy that tells us the solution:

"I kept looking until thrones were set up, and the Ancient of Days took His seat;

His vesture was like white snow and the hair of His head like pure wool.

His throne was ablaze with flames, its wheels were a burning fire.

A river of fire was flowing and coming out from before Him;

thousands upon thousands were attending Him, and

myriads upon myriads were standing before Him;

the court sat, and the books were opened."

—Daniel 7:9, 10

The message is that God Himself is going to intervene. But He is not going to fight the evil empires by sending in the army. Nor will He combat violence with violence, because evil cannot be stopped by more evil.[2] Instead, He will set up a court of inquiry. Remember the point they are struggling over: Who is the real king? And what this prophecy tells us is that the issue is going to be settled, not on the battlefield, but in a courtroom. God is going to establish an investigative session that will make it clear to everyone who is the winner.

As soon as Daniel saw that the vision was a scene of judgment, he must have thought about Yom Kippur (sometimes called the Day of Atonement), because for the Jewish people Yom Kippur was, and still is, judgment day.[3]

And the next part of the vision made the connection even clearer. It says that after "the court sat, and the books were opened," a "Son of Man," that is, a human being, entered the glorious courtroom (verse 13). And Daniel would have remembered that on Yom Kippur—and only on Yom Kippur—a human being did enter the symbolic throne room known as the Most Holy Place in the sanctuary.

But What About the Little Horn?

In this case, however, if the judgment scene in Daniel 7 represents the cosmic Day of Atonement, it raises a fundamental question. The first part of the vision is about the power struggle of the little horn and the beasts. Every one of them at one time or another persecuted God's people and fought against the truth. The question is: How could the judgment symbolized by Yom Kippur solve this problem? How could it set things straight and avenge the suffering of God's people?

At first glance you would have to say that it couldn't, because on the ancient Day of Atonement the evil nations that surrounded Israel did not assemble for trial at the sanctuary. Only God's people underwent judgment.[4] So, then, how could the judgment solve the problem of the evil empires? This is clearly its intention, because the text says: "The court will sit for judgment, and his [the little horn's] dominion will be taken away, annihilated and destroyed forever" (verse 26).

What Happened on Yom Kippur?

On the ancient Day of Atonement everyone in Israel passed in judgment before God, but the people didn't have to stand in line and then go into the sanctuary to be examined one by one. Instead, they all entered together in the person of a single human being—the high priest. We could say that the high priest was their proxy, or stand-in. He went in not only for the people, but *as* the people. The high priest was their representative in court, but not like modern lawyers who argue and plead, trying to convince the judge that their clients are innocent. Rather, he took the people's place, having assumed their identity, and with it their guilt.

I emphasize this point because it is a key to understanding what is happening in Daniel 7. Notice that the Son of Man does not sit down as a judge. He enters after the court is already seated and after the opening of the record books. Daniel says: "He came up to the Ancient of Days and was presented before Him" (verse 13). So He was escorted in, and rather than taking a seat, He stood before the throne.

Why was the "Son of Man" high priest treated like a prisoner before the bar? Because, as the people's substitute, He was counted as a sinner—for our sake He went into court as a defendant, as if He Himself were on trial.

The good news—in fact, it's the best news that could ever be told—is that the Son of Man does not go in empty-handed. He enters having already paid the price for sin. By a blood sacrifice—His death on the cross—He has obtained a full pardon for the sins that He bears.

We discuss justification by faith. The Yom Kippur ceremony stands at the very heart of it. And we talk about the gospel. The word "gospel" means good news, and what news could be better than this—that Jesus Christ, having taken our place on the cross, has earned the right to assume our place in the judgment (Hebrews 9:11, 12)?

How Does This Relate to the Problem of the Evil Empires?

Once when some people doubted His authority, Jesus said: "The Son of Man has authority on earth to forgive sins" (Matthew 9:6). The little horn, representing the state-church of the Middle Ages, laid claim to such power, boasting that it had the right to forgive sins. In doing so, it was claiming ultimate power—that is, sanctuary power (see Daniel 8:11, 12). In this it went far beyond the claims of any of its power-grabbing predecessors. By dealing with sin in the judgment, Jesus answers this bold claim and shows who is the real king.

The evil empires weren't accused and placed on trial. There was no need to bring them into judgment, because their cases were never really in doubt. The issue to be resolved is not whether they are evil. *Rather, it is: Who is the real king?* And the sentence pronounced on the Son of Man in the judgment is the perfect answer.

Here it is: "And to Him [the Son of Man] was given dominion, glory and a kingdom, that all the peoples, nations and men of every language might serve Him. His dominion is an everlasting dominion which will not pass away; and His kingdom is one which will not be destroyed" (Daniel 7:14).

The divine court does not summon the little horn and his friends and judge them at this time, but it does take care of the problem they represent. Jesus told a story that explains how this works. He said there was "a nobleman" who "went to a distant country to receive a kingdom for himself, and then return. . . . But his citizens hated him and sent a delegation after him, saying, 'We do not want this man to reign over us.' When he returned, after receiving the kingdom," he said: "'these enemies of mine, who did not want

me to reign over them, bring them here and slay them in my presence'"
(Luke 19:12-15, 27, NIV).

The "nobleman," of course, was Jesus Himself, who went to a "distant
country" when He returned to heaven. The prophecy of Daniel 7 shows us
how He "receives a kingdom for himself." He obtains it through the judgment. After the Son of Man has gained His kingdom, the same cloudy char-
iot that took Him in to the judgment will carry Him to the earth to claim
the fruits of His victory (Mark 13:26; 14:62). Then He will say: "These enemies of mine—the lion, the bear, the little horn, and all the rest—bring
them here and slay them in My presence."

When Jesus enters the sanctuary and gets the victory, He is declared the
real king—not of some childish mountain or empire, of course, but King of
the universe and King of the ages, for He is "King of kings, and Lord of
lords" (Revelation 19:16). And His "kingdom . . . will crush and put an end
to all these kingdoms, but it will itself endure forever" (Daniel 2:44).

When this takes place, only one step remains in the great sanctuary
drama. The next verse of the prophecy says: "Then the sovereignty, the dominion and the greatness of all the kingdoms under the whole heaven will
be given to the people of the saints of the Highest One" (Daniel 7:27).

But wait! This is almost word for word the same sentence that the cosmic
court passed on the Son of Man in the divine courtroom, the judgment we
read about in verse 14. Yes, of course it is. Remember that He went into the
judgment as the people, taking their place. Therefore, the victory He obtained was for them, and the sentence imposed on Him then passed to them.

Praise God! Because the very last words of the prophecy remind us once
again that the real King will be forever: "His kingdom will be an everlasting
kingdom, and all the dominions will serve and obey Him" (verse 27).[5]

*We have considered the judgment in the heavenly sanctuary. Is there any aspect
of this study that seems especially important to you? Would you like to write a few
words about it?*

_____

_____

[1] My opinion is that this is not exactly the most intelligent game ever invented. But then you've got to take into account that I'm not 14 years old anymore either. That may have something to do with it.

[2] See also Romans 12:19-21 and Matthew 5:38-48. When do you think the Israelis and the Palestinians are going to figure this out?

[3] The following is from a contemporary Jewish writer: "Yom Kippur is probably the most important holiday of the Jewish year. . . . [There are] 'books' in which God inscribes all our names. On Yom Kippur the judgment entered in these books is sealed. This day is, essentially, your last appeal, your last chance to change the judgment, to demonstrate your repentance and make amends" ("Judaism 101" www.jewfaq.org/holiday4/htm, accessed Aug. 26, 2000). From ancient times the rabbis understood that the judgment of Yom Kippur was a reflection of what went on in the sanctuary of heaven (Talmud, Yoma 7:2; see also Jacob Milgrom, *The Anchor Bible: Leviticus 1-16* [New York: Doubleday, 1991], pp. 1016, 1017).

[4] Leviticus 16:16: "He [the high priest] shall make atonement . . . because of the impurities of the sons of Israel."

[5] For more on this, see Loron Wade, "Son of Man Comes to the Judgment in Daniel 7:13," *Journal of the Adventist Theological Society* 11, no. 1 (Spring 2000); http://www.atsjats.org/publication.php?pub_id=121&journal=1&cmd=view&hash=.

Chapter 23

Jonah's Mistake

Jonah was the prodigal son of the Old Testament. One day, instead of going out to work in the field that his Father had assigned him—that is, to Nineveh, where he was supposed to warn people that their sins had "come up before" God (Jonah 1:2)—he took off, heading instead for Tarshish, about as far a country as you could find in those days.

Like the prodigal that Jesus told about, Jonah went through a terrible crisis, after which he decided to return home. He had just gotten back and was breathing a really big sigh of relief when God summoned him again and said: "OK, now it's time to go do what I asked you to do in the first place. The people in Nineveh still need to know about the danger they are in."

If we were to make an educated guess as to why Jonah was so reluctant to leave on God's errand, it would be fairly easy. The people of Nineveh (the Assyrians) took pride in their reputation for cruelty. They bragged about it, even creating monuments carved with horrifying pictures of the tortures they inflicted on their captives.

But the fact is that we don't have to guess about why Jonah didn't want to go, because he himself tells us the reason. His explanation came just after he achieved a phenomenal success. The Bible says that when the people of Nineveh heard Jonah's message they "believed in God; and they called a fast and put on sackcloth from the greatest to the least of them" (Jonah 3:5).

And then? Well, then "God relented concerning the calamity which He had declared He would bring upon them. And He did not do it" (verse 10).

It was at this point that Jonah protested. "Was not this what I said while I was still in my own country? Therefore in order to forestall this I fled to Tarshish, for I knew that You are a gracious and compassionate God, slow to anger and abundant in lovingkindness, and one who relents concerning calamity" (Jonah 4:2). What an amazing inversion of values! Jonah ran off to Tarshish not because of the cruelty of the Assyrians, but because of the mercy of God! More than 120,000 people would have died if God had remained inflexible, but that apparently didn't bother Jonah at all. What worried him was his reputation as a prophet. What will people think? I told everyone that Nineveh would be burned up, and look! It hasn't happened.

Never Mind About the Loan

When I was 6 years old, my mother took me with her to visit some friends who had recently purchased a new house. They had taken out a 15-year mortgage to pay for it, and I remember the adults laughing about how the bank was never going to get its money on that one. Why? Well, just imagine! Fifteen years! Jesus would come back a *long* time before that.

Before you criticize these people for laughing, let me put the incident into context. D-Day had taken place just a few months earlier. The newspapers carried horrifying pictures of starving people from the concentration camps. Rumors circulated about gas chambers and about a bomb that could level entire cities in a flash. And they said that if we didn't get it first, Hitler would. No one knew for sure how things would turn out.

People who studied Bible prophecy about the second coming of Christ in that context had no doubt at all that the event was about to happen. Didn't Jesus say that just before He returned there would be "wars and rumors of war" (Matthew 24:6, 7)? Didn't He emphasize that that "iniquity" (verse 12, KJV) would abound and the "love of many [would] grow cold" (verse 12, NKJV)? Wasn't there another prophecy about "difficult times" just before the end (2 Timothy 3:1)? Every one of those things sounded like what we were reading in the papers or hearing on Gabriel Heatter's nightly broadcasts on the radio.

Prophetic Embarrassment

I am writing this more than six decades later. Should I feel embarrassed for those people because they expected Jesus immediately? Was it because they didn't know how to read the signs of the times?

If we want to measure prophetic embarrassment in those terms, we will need to go back further. That year—1944—marked a full century of announcing Jesus' soon return by the people whose very name comes from that belief. An "adventist" is someone who believes in the return, or "Second Advent," of Jesus to the earth. For 100 years they had been saying: "He is coming soon!"

But that's not all. We would need to go back still further. The apostle Paul thought Jesus would arrive in his lifetime. He expected to be "alive and remain," and to be "caught up . . . in the clouds to meet the Lord in the air" (1 Thessalonians 4:15, 17). Furthermore, the book of Hebrews assures us: "In a very little while, He who is coming will come, and will not delay" (Hebrews 10:37). So it seems that we would need to be embarrassed for those first-century Christians as well, because they too expected Jesus in their time.

Well, the apostle Peter tells us that way back then some people were already trying to get those who believed in the Second Coming to feel embarrassed about it. They demanded: "So what's happened to the promise of his Coming? Our ancestors are dead and buried, and everything's going on just as it has from the first day of creation. Nothing's changed" (2 Peter 3:3, 4, Message).

It's good to know that the Bible does have an answer.

He Is Coming Soon . . . Isn't He?

Jesus' disciples once asked Him: "What will be the sign of Your coming, and of the end of the world?" (Matthew 24:3).

Notice carefully His reply, especially the part I have placed in italics: "You will be hearing of wars and rumors of wars. See that you are not frightened, for those things must take place, *but that is not yet the end*" (verses 6-8).

The Crimean War didn't mean that Jesus was about to return in 1856, although a lot of people at that time thought it did. World War I didn't indicate that He would come back in 1918. Neither did World War II, the Korean War, or the Vietnam War guarantee that He would appear during them. These things will happen, Jesus told His disciples. There will be wars and rumors of war, but don't get alarmed, because "the end is not yet."

And He goes on: "For nation will rise against nation, and kingdom against kingdom, and in various places there will be famines and earthquakes. But *all these things are merely the beginning of birth pangs*" (verses 7, 8).

Jesus here warns us against sensationalism. He doesn't want us to rush out and announce that the sky is falling every time an acorn hits us on the head.[1]

Does it mean that we don't have a clue as to when Jesus will return? No, not at all. Rather, He wants us not to consider any one specific earthquake, war, or famine as the definitive sign. Aristotle said a long time ago: "One swallow doesn't make a summer."[2] The appearance of a single migratory bird is not a safe sign to know that the season has arrived. We can, however, observe a whole set of signs: the snow melting, the return of many kinds of birds, the lengthening days. All these things, taken together, are reliable evidence that summer is indeed approaching. In the same way, by studying general trends rather than isolated events, we really can know that the time of Christ's return is near.

When I was a teenager, a friend and I explored some uranium mine dumps in the mountains near Gunnison, Colorado. A lot more venturesome than wise, we tried to drive his 1948 Ford across the narrow-gauge railway tracks that ran through the area. With a noisy clatter, the little car high-centered on the rails and could not move forward or back.

Our biggest worry was the possibility of a train coming. So we got down on our hands and knees and put our ears to the track. It would be a lot more dramatic if I could tell you that we heard a faint hum and clacking sound in the rails that kept getting louder and louder. That pretty soon we could see a plume of smoke in the distance and hear the whistle. Next that the train appeared around the curve and rushed on until, with a shriek and a screech, a deafening noise of steam and clattering machinery, it crashed into the little car and sent nuts and bolts and car parts flying in all directions.

What we actually heard was nothing at all, and without much drama we found a long board and pried the car loose, but the illustration of what might have happened can still serve the purpose.

The very first sermon I ever preached was on the nearness of the Second Coming. I still think it was pretty convincing. In that sermon of 50 years ago I mentioned some signs—things that were happening right then—that convinced us the event was near.

The signs of the Second Coming that we talked about in 1959 were more like a faint hum in the rails compared to the loud roar that we are hearing today.

I'll mention a few specific trends that I think we should keep an eye on:

A worldwide breakdown in standards of moral conduct (2 Timothy 3:1-5; Matthew 24:12). In 1949 Ingrid Bergman was one of the brightest and highest paid stars in Hollywood. Then the news came out that she was having a baby with film director Roberto Rossellini. For a while it seemed as if the world had turned upside down. A prominent legislator denounced Bergman on the floor of the U.S. Senate as "a horrible example of womanhood and a powerful influence for evil." The Senate then proceeded to declare her a persona non grata to the United States. Can you imagine anything like that happening today? When Paul Newman died in 2008, most reports of his death referred to his 50-year marriage to actress Joanne Woodward as almost unheard-of in the film industry today.

And this decline in moral standards appears not only in Hollywood but also on Main Street and around the world. In 2005 the U.S. Census Bureau reported 4.85 million cohabiting couples—people living together in a sexual relationship without being married, an increase of more than 1,000 percent since 1960. In Japan a study undertaken a number of years ago found that less than 3 percent of women between 25 and 29 were cohabiting. A more recent study by the same researcher reported that couples born in the 1970s—approximately the same age group as the previous study—now have a cohabitation rate of 53.9 percent.[3] Statistics from around the world confirm that the trend is widespread and still growing.

Another symptom of the shift in moral standards is the explosion of STDs (sexually transmitted diseases). During the 1960s the main diseases transmitted by sexual contact were syphilis and gonorrhea, and many believed them to be rapidly disappearing because of the development of antibiotics. Today medical science has identified more than 20 widespread types of STDs, with an average of 15 million new cases reported each year in the United States alone.[4] Several of them are virus-based diseases such as AIDS, for which there still exists no known cure.

At least 45 million people are infected with HIV, the virus that causes AIDS. According to the U.S. Centers for Disease Control and Prevention, AIDS is now the leading cause of death among 25- to 44-year-olds in the United States, although by far the largest number of people infected by the disease live in developing countries, especially in sub-Saharan Africa, where it is wiping out a large portion of the population. An estimated 650,000 children have lost a parent to AIDS in Zambia, and almost 20 percent of adults are HIV-positive. A report in 2002 stated that at least 130,000 children in that country are also infected.

A sharp rise in the frequency and power of natural disasters (Matthew 24:7; Luke 21:25, 26). "If it seems like disasters are getting more common, it's because they are," wrote Amanda Ripley in *Time* magazine. "The number of flood and storm disasters has gone up 7.4 percent every year in recent decades," according to the Britain's Centre for Research on the Epidemiology of Disasters. "Between 2000 and 2007 the growth was even faster, with an average annual rate of increase of 8.4 percent."[5]

Sea temperatures have risen significantly during the past 30 years. Hurricanes and typhoons, fueled by the warm, moist air, have become more frequent and more ferocious. Cloudbursts have increased because, as the atmosphere warms, it can hold more moisture. One of the most damaging storm effects is the enormous amount of rain dumped on inland areas.

The number of earthquakes measuring 4.0 or more on the Richter scale—the really big ones—has grown from 3,680 in 1970 to 15,770 in 2005, with the greatest increase occurring since 2000 (statistics from the U.S. Geological Survey).

Meanwhile, tsunamis, mudslides, avalanches, tornadoes, and volcanic eruptions have been breaking all previous records for their violence and disastrous effects.

A rise in supranationalism (Revelation 13:11-17). This is the political doctrine that above the authority of individual nations there is a higher authority that can call the leaders or citizens of any given nation to account.

The idea has been present at least since the Nuremberg trials at the end of World War II when a group of leading nations put the leaders of the Third Reich on trial and punished them for "crimes against humanity." The 1994 genocide in Rwanda brought a sense of guilt to many world leaders: "Why didn't we do something?" It has resulted in more energetic military interventions in places like Kosovo and in internationally supervised trials such as that of Slobodan Milosevic in the Hague.

On October 30, 2008, a federal jury in Florida convicted Charles Taylor, Jr., of torture and other atrocities he committed in Liberia during his father's regime as president of the country. The trial took place under a 1990s law that allows people to be tried in the United States for certain crimes committed in their own countries.

For now, such efforts may be seen as benevolent, but they present a worrisome trend. It is not hard to see that supranationalism—if it advances a bit more—can make it possible for a limited cadre of world leaders to control the lives of millions of people in every country of the world.

The ease with which civil rights can be compromised (Revelation 13:11-17). During times of crisis, fundamental principles established over centuries of often-bloody struggles can instantly evaporate.

September 11, 2001, is the most famous (or infamous) date in recent history. Within 48 hours after the attack on the World Trade Center more than 3,000 people in the United States found themselves under arrest because of suspicion of supporting terrorism. The authorities held them incommunicado, without being charged or tried, and with no right to counsel.

One of the oldest and most fundamental of all civil rights, dating back at least to 1215 and the Magna Charta, is the principle of habeas corpus. It means that people cannot be arrested and held indefinitely without being charged. In addition, it includes the right to a fair and speedy trial. But because of what happened on September 11 the U.S. government totally disregarded the principle, and it was also trampled on with respect to the people held at the prison camp in Guantánamo, Cuba.

Nobody would question the need to deal with those who have engaged in acts of terror. But it is not hard to see that detaining people and holding them indefinitely without trial and without the right of self-defense puts us all in danger.

Some experts believe that the next terror strike is not a matter of if but of when. The question is: When it happens, how many more fundamental rights will disappear?

Amazing growth in the influence and political power of religion in the public square (Revelation 13:1-8, 11-17). In February of 1798 General Louis Berthier marched his army into Rome and occupied the city under orders from the French Directorate. He ordered Pope Pius VI to appear before him. Berthier asked the pope if he was willing to renounce his temporal power and concern himself only with the souls of the faithful. When Pius refused, the general placed him under arrest and declared his temporal power at an end anyway. The French rationalists did not seek to bring an end to the Catholic religion or the Papacy. They were not anti-catholic in the sense of favoring a different religion. Rather, they wanted to end *the political power of the Papacy and its incursion into the affairs of state.*

Rationalistic thinkers of the nineteenth century took the idea a step further when Friedrich Nietzsche proclaimed: "God is dead."[6] He meant by this that the *idea* of God was over and that an age of reason had replaced the age of religion. Nietzsche and friends believed that in this new era religion of any kind was a thing of the past and could no longer influence politics or anything else.

No doubt they would be astounded to learn that today religion is a stronger influence than ever both in the public square and in the lives of millions of people. It is the tinder of conflicts that are sowing terror, hatred, and cruelty in many countries around the world. As a result it has brought suffering and death to hundreds of thousands in places such as Ireland, the Balkans, India, Pakistan, Lebanon, Israel, Afghanistan, Darfur, and Iraq.

At the same time the tireless diplomacy of John Paul II successfully restored the Papacy to a position of political influence that it has not enjoyed since the Middle Ages. A cover story on the June 24, 2001, *Time* magazine entitled "The Holy Alliance" described how cooperation between the pope and American president Ronald Reagan helped bring down the Communist regime in Poland, a step that was the beginning of the end for the iron curtain.

Nearly every Western nation today sends an ambassador to the Vatican, a tiny enclave with approximately 800 citizens. It is a frank recognition of the pope's status as a full-fledged player in the geopolitical arena and that what the French liberals tried to achieve in 1798 has now been amazingly reversed.

What the late pope accomplished in this area was also reflected at his funeral, held on April 8, 2001. It was the single largest gathering of heads of state in history. Four kings, five queens, and at least 70 presidents and prime ministers, plus 14 leaders of other religions attended. Probably one could also consider it the largest single gathering of Christianity, with numbers estimated in excess of 4 million mourners in Rome while countless millions watched the proceedings on television in every country of the world.[7]

How is all of this going to play out over the new few years? Stay tuned. Any one event, in and of itself, may not be significant. We can, however, follow those trends that appear to be preparing us for the moment that God will add the final link to the long, long chain of events foretold in Bible prophecy.

"He Is Coming Soon"

As I said, I have been preaching the second coming of Christ for 50 years, always saying that it is going to take place soon. So should I feel embarrassed because I've been announcing it for so long and yet it still hasn't happened? If I do, I am right in there with Jonah—more worried about my reputation as a prophet than about the salvation of the lost. While those 50 years have gone by, millions more have learned to trust in Jesus and have found peace and a new life in Him. I can rejoice in that with all my heart.

God didn't tell Jonah to worry if the punishment of Nineveh got delayed. What He commanded him to do was to go out fearlessly and preach the message. And that's what the Lord expects us to do today. He wants us to tell people before it's too late that He is holding them accountable for their conduct and that they need to repent and get ready to meet Him in peace.

And if the Lord, in His mercy, continues to delay a little longer while still more people can hear the message, that's His decision. In fact, that was Peter's answer to the "scoffers," the "mockers" who were laughing at the message of the Second Coming in his day:

"God isn't late with his promise as some measure lateness," he wrote. "He is restraining himself on account of you, holding back the End because he doesn't want anyone lost. He's giving everyone space and time to change. But when the Day of God's Judgment does come, it will be unannounced, like a thief. The sky will collapse with a thunderous bang, everything disintegrating in a huge conflagration, earth and all its works exposed to the scrutiny of Judgment.

"Since everything here today might well be gone tomorrow, do you see how essential it is to live a holy life? Daily expect the Day of God, eager for its arrival" (2 Peter 3:9-12, Message).

That's what we need to do: to "live a holy life" and be ready to meet Him in peace. We also must go forth boldly and share the good news. So don't hesitate, but say it loud and clear: "He is coming soon!"

In response to what the Bible says about the Second Coming, I believe that God wants me to

_____

_____

_____

---

[1] An allusion to the children's story about Chicken Little. See one version at http://www.geocities.com/mjloundy/.

[2] Attributed.

[3] By M. Iwasawa at the National Institute of Population and Social Security Research.

[4] Shepherd Smith and Joe S. McIlhaney, M.D., "Statement of Dissent on the Surgeon General's Call to Action to Promote Sexual Health and Responsible Sexual Behavior," issued by the Medical Institute of Sexual Health (Austin, Tex.: June 28, 2001) and American Social Health Association (Triangle Park, N.C.), "STD Statistics," at http://www.ashastd.org/stdfaqs/statistics.html.

[5] Sept. 3, 2008.

[6] *Thus Spoke Zarathustra*. Deutsch: *Also sprach Zarathustra,* 1883-1885.

[7] See also Daniel Burke, "A Catholic Wind in the White House," http://www.washingtonpost.com/wp-dyn/content/article/2008/04/11/AR2008041103327_pf.html . Notice also the conversion of former prime minister Tony Blair to the Catholic faith (http://www.guardian.co.uk/politics/2007/jun/22/uk.religion1 and many other evidences of this notable trend.

Chapter 24

The Beginning of Life Eternal

In a strange and unusual kingdom far away, the king once sent his soldiers to arrest a man and put him in jail.

"Why are you doing this?" he demanded as the soldiers began to torture him.

"We don't know," they replied. "It's the king's orders."

All day the horror continued, and all that night. The man screamed, cried, and pleaded. Again and again he asked why they were torturing him. But the answer was always the same. The torture never ended. The only things the poor man could hear were the screams of other prisoners also undergoing torture, and no one ever gave any explanation or reason for what was happening. The man soon stopped pleading for mercy and begged the soldiers to let him die, but that, too, was denied. Days turned into months, and months to years. Years and years went by, and the torment never stopped.

Finally, one day, instead of torturing the man, the soldiers told him to get ready to go with them.

"Now what?" the man asked.

"The king is sending for you. He has decided that the time has come to convene a judgment and determine if you are guilty."

"I never imagined there could be such monstrous injustice," the prisoner protested.

"Quiet!" they said. "You're just confirming your guilt."

The soldiers brought the man to an enormous hall containing a great white throne. A lot of other people were there too. To his amazement, the prisoner recognized one of his former neighbors. The neighbor had put on a little weight, but otherwise he looked good. In fact, he appeared a lot younger than the last time they had met, and he now wore a white robe. In spite of this, the neighbor trembled, and an expression of terror contorted his face.

"What's going on? What are you doing here?" the prisoner questioned his former neighbor.

"Didn't they tell you?" the neighbor replied. "Judgment day has come. The king is going to decide if we are innocent or guilty."

"It looks to me as if you're in pretty good shape. Why are you so afraid?"

"Well," the neighbor said, "a little while after the soldiers took you away, they came for me, too. Naturally I was worried because we had heard rumors about what had happened to you, but instead they took me to the king's palace garden and gave me a beautiful mansion that the king said that he had built especially for me. A fountain and a river flowed through the center. Birds and flowers were everywhere, and the streets were paved with pure gold. I could hear singing and beautiful music all day long. Nothing but loving words from everyone. Day after day for all these years my happiness has only increased."

"'Happiness? So why are you terrified?"

"Why shouldn't I be terrified? It's the end of the age. After all these years the king is going to decide my eternal destiny. You know that I never really loved him. So what if I don't get approved? I could end up like you. In fact, we could even trade places."

Step and Misstep

My tale seeks to illustrate the absurd situation into which some good people have gotten themselves. I'm not talking about the hapless individuals in the story, but about people who believe that something like this is really possible, and that God Himself could be involved in it.

How did such a confused state of affairs come about? It resulted from listening to two very different drummers and trying to march to the beat of both at the same time—an effort that has them stumbling and tripping over themselves because of the obvious theological contradiction.

The first drummer such people hear is Scripture. The Bible confirms that at the end of the age the dead "small and great" will be resurrected— they will come back to life—and stand before a "great white throne" to hear their sentence in the judgment (Matthew 25:31-36; Romans 14:10;

2 Corinthians 5:10; 2 Timothy 4:1; Revelation 20:11, 12, etc.).[1] It also says that both those who love God and those who don't will receive their rewards after the resurrection (John 5:28, 29). Speaking of the patriarchs Abraham, Isaac, and Jacob, Jesus stated that if it were not for the resurrection, these faithful men of God would have no part with God or eternal life (Matthew 22:31, 32). So it is obvious that before that event takes place they are not in heaven. In the last chapter of the Bible Jesus Himself makes it clear that people will receive their reward at the time of the Second Coming: "Behold, I am coming quickly, and My reward is with Me, to render to every man according to what he has done" (Revelation 22:12).

Notice the order of events in the following prophecy from the apostle Paul:

1. *The Second Coming:* "For the Lord Himself will descend from heaven with a shout, with the voice of the archangel, and with the trumpet of God."
2. *The Resurrection:* "And the dead in Christ will rise first."
3. *The Ascension:* "Then we who are alive and remain will be caught up together with them [with the resurrected ones] in the clouds to meet the Lord in the air."
4. *Eternal Life:* "And so we shall always be with the Lord."—1 Thessalonians 4:16, 17.

The apostle states categorically that he is telling them this "by the Word of the Lord" (verse 15). It is something that he had received by divine revelation.

He further declares that his purpose in sharing the information is to comfort those whose loved ones have died (verse 18). If he had believed that their loved ones, as disembodied spirits, were already living in heaven with Jesus, he certainly would have said so. Instead he refers to them as "asleep" (verse 13).

They are asleep, but when Jesus returns He will summon them, and His voice will wake them up. It is after the resurrection that they will "always be with the Lord"—not before then. And that, says Paul, is the Christian's hope and comfort.

Solomon wrote: "The living know that they will die, but the dead do not know anything" (Ecclesiastes 9:5). One night a thief broke the lock on the back door of our house and entered. He made his way into the bedroom where a guest was sleeping. The guest had placed his trousers over the back of a chair. The thief removed the man's billfold from his pants pocket and left as quietly has he had arrived. Now, which of the following alternatives do you think is true? At the instant this happened the sleeping man (a) started to weep and cry because his money and vital documents were gone or (b) he continued to sleep peacefully. Of course—the answer is that he slept on just has peacefully as before.

The World Health Organization reports that 13,700 children die every day from causes related to malnutrition. The United Nations High Commissioner for Refugees has found that 20 million people have either fled their homes or are living under extremely insecure conditions. And, speaking of children—how many do you think sleep every night on the streets in the great urban centers of the world, with nothing more than the cold pavement for a bed? No one knows the exact number, but UNICEF believes it may be as many as 100 million, and it is growing rapidly because the AIDS epidemic is killing so many parents in Africa and other regions. What if the popular idea regarding the dead were true? What if all the good people were already in heaven? If they were, some of them would be praising God while others would be weeping bitterly and maybe even cursing Him as they see what is happening to their loved ones. Heaven would not be paradise for the latter, and I would think not for anybody else, either. I am profoundly thankful to God for the clear teaching of the Bible that the dead are asleep and that they "know nothing" about what is happening here.

At the end of time God will halt sin and suffering. "According to His promise we are looking for new heavens and a new earth, in which righteousness dwells" (2 Peter 3:13). And only then will God "wipe away every tear from their eyes; and there will no longer be any death; there will no longer be any mourning, or crying, or pain; the first things have passed away" (Revelation 21:4).

The Other Drummer

The Bible witness on this subject is clear. What is it, then, that has confused people? The second "drummer" who has influenced popular thinking is Plato and other Greek philosophers of his time.[2] Greek philosophy taught that the human essence—the real person—is an entity that they called the *psyche,* a word sometimes translated "spirit." It claimed that the *psyche* is eternal in both directions—it has always existed and always will. When a human is conceived, a *psyche,* unfortunately, gets trapped and imprisoned for a time in a physical body, but one happy day it will be released and will then be free again from time, space, and matter.

As we study religious history, it is clear that the early church struggled against the influence of Platonistic thinking. And yet it seemed (as sometimes happens today) that when church leaders shut the front door against the idea, it came creeping in the back, and when church closed the back door, it swept in through the windows. Through the years more and more Christians adopted the belief and tried to blend it with the teachings of the Bible—an impossible task, of course.

In the end, most Christians came to accept the platonic *psyche* as the equivalent of the "soul." And people began to believe that the soul escapes from the body at death and immediately goes to receive its eternal reward.

Escape From Absurdity

In 1958 theologian Oscar Cullmann published a little volume called *Immortality of the Soul or Resurrection of the Dead?* that has had a crucial influence in waking up people to the error. Cullmann opens his book with a powerful example: he compares the death of Socrates, who was calm and composed at the prospect of liberating his soul from the confines of its material prison, his body; with the death of Christ, who suffered terrible anguish. Jesus saw death, not as a good thing, but as an evil to be overcome.

Death entered the world as an enemy (1 Corinthians 15:26). It is the "wages of sin" (Romans 6:23; see also Genesis 2:17). "Through one man sin entered into the world, and death through sin, and so death spread to all men, because all sinned" (Romans 5:12).

The theologian N.T. Wright made the following observations during a lecture at Emory University: "The resurrection of the body—it's a totally strange doctrine to many devout Christians who really do think that the name of the game is to get their soul into a disembodied place called heaven. And when they say, 'I believe in the resurrection of the body,' in the creed, they think, 'but I don't really mean that; we actually know it's the immortality of the soul.' *Well, that's just being fooled by the incipient Platonism of much Western culture.*"[3]

Some Results of This False Belief

The writings of Cullmann and others have brought a great change in the thinking of many people about this subject, including serious theologians.[4] In the public mind, however, Platonistic teaching about disembodied spirits appears to be stronger than ever. Popular journals carry a steady stream of articles promoting the idea that dead people are really still alive, and books on the subject regularly appear on the best seller lists. Frequent television specials also feature this philosophy. The Omni Channel on cable TV promotes it. Feature films such as Disney's *Lion King* and *Brother Bear* echo it, as do the incredibly popular Harry Potter and Lord of the Rings series and many others. One well-known promoter has been Raymond Moody, whose book *Life After Life* has sold millions of copies.

We find countless variations on this theme—something, it seems, to suit every taste. There are ghosts and apparitions, haunted houses, and séances in darkened chambers for those who prefer the more traditional kind of communication with the dead. Reincarnationists and New Age groups appeal to the younger, more *avant garde* types.

I heard an inspirational talk by a well-known pastor who explained how he had transformed a congregation of 60 or so members into a mega church that thousands attend every Sunday. He explained that one of his strategies was to organize people into small groups to converse with those who have graduated and learn from their wisdom.

At the end, he asked if anyone had any questions, and my hand went up. "I'm not sure what you meant by the expression, 'those who have graduated,'" I said. "Perhaps you could clarify."

From the expression on his face, it seemed as if my question had seriously annoyed him. Nevertheless, he answered courteously: "Graduated? People commonly say, 'those who have died,' but we know, of course, that death is nothing more than 'graduation' to a higher sphere."

So at this popular church in middle-class suburbia the members were meeting in small groups to converse with the dead. It appears there really is something for every taste in this matter.

The warning of Scripture against such practices is clear: "When they say to you, 'Consult the mediums and the spiritists who whisper and mutter,' should not a people consult their God? Should they consult the dead on behalf of the living?" (Isaiah 8:19; see also Leviticus 20:27; Deuteronomy 18:10-12). Such practices may appear harmless, but they are not, because Satan makes use of all false religious beliefs and practices for carrying out his plans (1 Corinthians 10:20; 2 Corinthians 11:14). People who believe they are talking with the dead may be conversing with their imagination— or they may be speaking with demons. In either case it is dangerous and forbidden in Scripture.

Until Then

We need to notice that by dying, Jesus conquered death for us. He died the death that we deserve. His death was horrifying because He suffered a sinner's death, the one that is "the wages of sin" (Romans 6:23). But because Jesus experienced this death, we don't have to. That is why we can say that by dying, He conquered death. And because He did, we can go to sleep confidently, resting in faith and in the knowledge that the next time we open our eyes, we will see Him face to face. He took away the "sting"—that is, the "bitterness"—of death for us (1 Corinthians 15:55). As a result, Paul could refer to his own death as going to be "with the Lord" (2 Corinthians 5:8), because he thought of it as resting in the arms of Jesus.

The dead in Christ are "absent from the body" (verse 8), but they are not absent from the Lord. They are with Him in the same sense that they were with Him before they were born. Before we were born, we were not living in another sphere of existence as conscious spirits—that would be Platonism—but we existed in the heart and mind of God, who loved us from all eternity and always will (Ephesians 1:3-6; Jeremiah 31:3). In this same way, we continue to exist and be with Him after death and while waiting for the resurrection.[5]

All those who are in Christ Jesus *have* eternal life (John 3:36; 6:47; 1 John 5:12). The verses don't say that they "will have" eternal life—they possess it now. Those who have died in Christ have it, too, just as much as those who live in Him. His love for them is no less than when they were alive, and that is their infallible assurance and security.

"He who eats My flesh and drinks My blood has eternal life, and I will raise him up on the last day" (John 6:54).

"Christ became one flesh with us, in order that we might become one spirit with Him. It is by virtue of this union that we are to come forth from the grave—not merely as a manifestation of the power of Christ, but because, through faith, His life has become ours. Those who see Christ in His true character, and receive Him into the heart, have everlasting life. It is through the Spirit that Christ dwells in us; and the Spirit of God, received into the heart by faith, is the beginning of the life eternal" (Ellen G. White, *The Desire of Ages*, p. 388).

Thank You, Lord, for dying the death that I deserve. Thank You for Your gift of eternal life here and now. I want to accept it so that whether I live until Your coming or sleep for a while in the grave, I can live with You forever.

My affirmation

---

[1] The final judgment is affirmed, as well, in the Apostles' Creed, which states that Jesus Christ "shall come to judge the living and the dead." The following chapter will discuss the details and sequence of events.

[2] Notably Pythagoras, Heracletus, and Aristotle.

[3] http://highergroundonline.wordpress.com/2008/07/28/the-wright-view-of-resurrection/. Wright's lecture series is also available in audio and video. Further information on the intermediate state of the dead is available at http://www.indisputable.org/?topic=the_dead.

[4] I asked Carl F. M. Henry, considered by many the dean of evangelical theologians, his opinion about the ideas of Oscar Cullmann. He said: "Cullmann is right, of course." Henry may have thought that I would be upset by this, because he immediately added: "But of course, that doesn't mean our loved ones are not with the Lord."

[5] Some cite Jesus' words to the thief on the cross to support the idea that people receive their reward immediately after they die. It is important to note, however, that the original Greek had no punctuation marks. Did Jesus say "Truly I say to you, today you will be with Me in Paradise" or "Truly I say to you today, you will be with Me in Paradise"? Either reading is acceptable on the basis of the Greek. The second is preferable because it is in harmony with what the rest of Scripture teaches about this subject.

Chapter 25

To Know the Truth

It's late at night as we walk with a police officer through a dangerous part of the city. Suddenly, about a half block ahead of us, a man races desperately out of an alley. Close behind him another man follows with a knife raised in the air. He is obviously gaining on the first one, but just as he is about to reach him, the first man pulls out a pistol. He turns and fires point-blank into the face of his pursuer, killing him instantly.

By this time you and I have taken cover in a doorway, but our policeman friend runs forward. Peeking around the corner, we see him pull out his service pistol and fire at the first man, the one who had just shot and killed the other. Reeling under the impact of the high-caliber bullet, the man tries to lift his gun, but before he can get off a round, the officer blasts away again and again, and this man, too, falls to the ground.

A moment later the police officer returns to where we cower in the doorway. Wiping the pistol carefully with his handkerchief, he returns it to its holster. "Well, that was a good one," he says, smiling with satisfaction. "The more of these people we can get off the streets, the better. Shall we continue our little stroll?"

In some parts of the world today such a scene would not really be that unlikely. Vigilante or extrajudicial justice done without due process, retribution based only on the decision of someone who thought it needed to be done, is not at all uncommon.

A friend of mine was kidnapped by a group of urban guerrillas. He escaped alive—something that seldom happens—because one of the young men in the group decided to turn against the others and help him. Within a week the young man was dead—murdered, not by the other guerrillas, but by the police while in their custody. They knew the boy was a kidnapper, and that was enough.

What is wrong with extrajudicial justice? The most obvious answer is that it can lead to gross injustice. Human justice is never perfect, but it is almost always better when it follows due process. An essential safeguard is accountability, because justice needs to be able to validate itself. It has to be transparent and open to public scrutiny. And there has to be an option for judicial review, an appeals system that can consider the decisions of the lower courts, thus in a sense passing judgment on their decisions.

Justice and Beyond

We learn from the Bible that God doesn't believe in extrajudicial justice either. In His amazing humility He has made Himself open to our scrutiny. The principle of divine transparency is fundamental to understanding the message of Scripture, the plan of salvation, and end-time events.

Jesus Himself was part of God's self-revelation (John 1:18; 18:37), a message that included His life of service and His submission and obedience. His passion was the culmination of His effort. The scourging, the nails, the agony and shame sought to bring home to our dull senses the pain that sin has brought to God from its very inception. He designed the cross to teach us His willingness to absorb the blows that we deserved, to stand in our place and pay the debt that we owed (Isaiah 53:5, 6; 2 Corinthians 5:21). It took something that terrible to rip the callus of indifference from our minds and help us understand.

Jesus' suffering on our behalf did not begin and did not end at Calvary. He was the Lamb slain from the foundation of the world (Revelation 13:8). Here is the great "mystery of Christ, which in other generations was not made known to the sons of men, ... [but] has now been revealed to His holy apostles and prophets in the Spirit" (Ephesians 3:4, 5; cf. Romans 16:25).

Romans 3:24-26 declares that God put Jesus on public display to demonstrate His own righteousness.

Why would God want or need to "demonstrate His [own] righteousness"? Verse 25 tells us the answer: "Because in the forbearance of God He passed over the sins previously committed." He wanted to make it clear fully and forever that when He forgave our sins, He did so without setting aside any principle of the law. He saved us in a way that allowed Him to be both "just and the justifier of the one who has faith in Jesus" (verse 26).

God has given time for the mystery of iniquity to play itself out so that the entire universe can see the result and natural consequences of rebellion. When the time is right and when the revelation is complete, He will step forward and bring things to a conclusion. Then He will conduct the most absolute of all the exercises in transparency—He will hold a court of inquiry that will fully open the record so that all can see the justice of His dealing with every human being.

What's Going to Happen, and Why It's Important

The principle of divine transparency is vital for understanding the series of events described in Bible prophecy with regard to the judgment and the end of time.

The following diagram (p. 195) brings together the end-time events portrayed in Revelation 19-21 and many other parts of the Bible. You may want to take a minute to study it. Then we will offer a few comments as to its meaning.

Maybe the diagram impresses you as being somewhat complicated. People are going up, coming down, dying, being resurrected and judged. After the Second Coming, 1,000 years pass by before things finally get wrapped up.

It is reasonable to ask: Why such a series of events? And how is it relevant to us?

God Wants Us to Know

The reason and relevance of this series of events is clear when we consider the principle of divine transparency. It can help us understand that God doesn't just mow the sinners down and get it over with—and why He didn't do it a long time ago. He certainly could have saved Himself a lot of trouble if He had.

1. *The judgment begins before the Second Coming.* Those raised to eternal life when Jesus returns are called "the dead in Christ" (1 Thessalonians 4:15, 16). The expression shows that even before their resurrection they already belong to Christ. That means they have already been judged.[1]

Why does the judgment need to have a pre-Advent phase? The prophet

ONE THOUSAND YEARS

At the Second Coming

End of 1000 Years

D U R I N G   T H E   1 0 0 0   Y E A R S

Redeemed Judge
Rev. 20:4; 1 Cor. 6:2, 3; Dan. 7:22

Eternal Life

In Heaven

On Earth
Satan is "bound" Rev. 21:1-3

1. The Holy City descends Rev. 21:2
2. The wicked resurrected Rev. 20:5
3. The wicked judged Rev. 20:11
4. Fire from God consumes the wicked and the Earth. Rev. 20:9; Mal. 4:1

Second resurrection

Eternal Death for the lost

Living Righteous
Transformed and taken to Heaven.
1 Thes. 4:16, 17

Living Wicked
Die. Rev. 19:2; 2 Thes. 2:8

First resurrection

Dead Righteous
Resurrected and taken to Heaven
1 Thes. 4:16

Dead Wicked
Remain dead. Rev. 20:5

Daniel, in vision, saw God, the "Ancient of Days," seated on His throne to judge. "Thousands upon thousands were attending Him, and myriads upon myriads were standing before Him" (Daniel 7:10).

The angels have been intimately involved in the lives of God's people. "Are they not all ministering spirits, sent forth to minister for them who shall be heirs of salvation?" (Hebrews 1:14, KJV; see also Genesis 24:7; Exodus 23:20; Matthew 18:10). They have encouraged and sought to motivate us (Genesis 19:16; 28:12). At times they have intervened to protect (Psalm 91:11; Daniel 6:22), rebuke (Numbers 22:22-32), or even punish (Isaiah 37:36).

Also the angels have heard Satan's accusations as he denounced God's people as sinners, claiming that the Lord was unjust if He saved them (Zechariah 3:1, 2; Revelation 12:10). The judgment serves to confirm God's justice and fairness in dealing with each individual.

Furthermore, the redeemed will be neighbors of these heavenly beings. Before raising them to life and taking them to heaven, God will show that the human beings are safe to save and that their presence in heaven would not endanger the peace and safety of that beautiful place. Therefore, He calls the angels as witnesses and observers as He opens the record books and reviews each case.

At the Second Coming, Jesus will reveal the result of the first phase of the judgment. "When the Son of Man comes in His glory, and all the angels with Him, then He will sit on His glorious throne. All the nations will be gathered before Him; and He will separate them from one another, as the shepherd separates the sheep from the goats; and He will put the sheep on His right, and the goats on the left" (Matthew 25:31-33).

Because this is a parable, we must be cautious about using it to establish doctrine, but this much is clear: the judge is not deciding the cases at that time. Why? Because he begins the judgment by putting the sheep (the saved) at His right hand and the goats (the lost) on His left. Then He tells each group their sentence. So it seems clear that the examination of the individual cases has already taken place.

2. *The judgment continues during the period that follows the Second Coming.* From studying the closing verses of Revelation 19 and other prophecies we find that many of God's enemies will destroy each other in the Battle of Armageddon. And what will happen to the others, those who survive the battle? Revelation 19:21 tells us: "And the rest were killed with the sword which came from the mouth of" Jesus at His second coming. The "sword" represents the Word of God (Ephesians 6:17)—that's why it appears to emerge from His mouth. It symbolizes divine energy and power. "The word of God is living and active and sharper than any two-edged sword" (Hebrews 4:12; cf. 11:3). "By the word of the Lord the heavens were made, and by the breath of His mouth all their host" (Psalm 33:6; see also 2 Peter 3:5). This same "Word" that God once employed to create He will one day unleash to punish and destroy (2 Peter 3:5-7; see also 2 Thessalonians 2:8). It is the "sword" that will destroy those of God's enemies still alive at the time of the Second Coming.

And what about God's children? At the Second Advent, when the Lord Jesus appears in the clouds of heaven with His holy angels (Matthew 25:31), He will rescue His people. They will be "caught up . . . to meet the Lord in the air" (1 Thessalonians 4:14-17). Then He will take them to live in the places that He Himself has gone to prepare for them (John 14:2, 3).

The redeemed are blessed (greatly favored by God) because they will be always with the Lord (1 Thessalonians 4:17; John 14:3), and because "the second death has no power" over them (Revelation 20:6). The second death is the eternal punishment for sin, but because they are already justified and sanctified they now enjoy eternal security in God. "And I saw thrones, and they sat upon them, and judgment was given to them. . . . They will be priests of God and of Christ and reign with Him for a thousand years" (verse 6).

The priestly reign of God's people as they take part in the judgment during the 1,000 years is the final and complete fulfillment of the covenant that He made with His people at Sinai. The redeemed are now fully kings and priests. It is also the fulfillment of the promise that Jesus made to His disciples: "Truly I say to you, that you who have followed Me, in the regeneration, when the Son of Man will sit on His glorious throne, you also shall sit upon twelve thrones, judging the twelve tribes of Israel" (Matthew 19:28). His promise is to "you who have followed me," so it is not only for the 12 apostles. Paul also spoke of this time: "Or do you not know that the saints will judge the world? . . . Do you not know that we will judge angels?" (1 Corinthians 6:2, 3; see also Revelation 3:21).

Why does the judgment continue during the millennium? After the heavenly court has decided each case, is there really a need for more judgment? It is obvious that it does not convene to determine the eternal destiny of anyone. So what is its purpose?

Human beings often have a mistaken idea as to who is right with God (1 Samuel 14:1-3; Romans 14:10-12). Among the lost will be many who were known and loved by the redeemed. Many of their cases will seem like a great mystery. "How is it possible," the saved will ask, "that this person, who was always so good and sincere, is not here with us?" In order to answer their questions and resolve any possible doubt, the Lord has established this phase of the judgment.

And that is why it is necessary to have a period of delay between the Second Coming and the final consummation. Before the definitive destruction of the wicked, God wants to reveal to the redeemed the perfect justice of His dealing with those who have chosen to be lost.

3. *The final phase of the judgment comes at the end of the 1,000 years.* "Then I saw a great white throne and Him who sat upon it, from whose presence earth and heaven fled away, and no place was found for them. And I saw the dead, the great and the small, standing before the throne, and books were opened; . . . and the dead were judged from the things which were written in the books, according to their deeds" (Revelation 20:11, 12).

The people arrayed before the throne at the close of the millennium are called "the dead" because they were dead during the 1,000 years. They have just been brought back to life in the second resurrection (verse 5).

Those who trusted in the shed blood of Jesus on their behalf had Him as their substitute on the cross and in the judgment (cf. chapter 24). But those awaiting final judgment at the end of the 1,000 years have no substitute. They stand before the God with nothing but the record of "the things which were written in the books, according to their deeds" (verse 12).

Every Knee

"For we will all stand before the judgment seat of God," the apostle Paul declares (Romans 14:10). And in support of his assertion he cites Isaiah 45:23: "For it is written, 'As I live, says the Lord, every knee shall bow to Me, and every tongue shall give praise to God'" (verse 11). That is both the result of the judgment and its purpose. It will cause every knee to bow and every tongue to give Him praise. In the first phase of the judgment the angels bowed and praised God for His perfect justice and mercy. During the millennium the redeemed humans did the same thing. After that, only one group has yet to acknowledge the perfect love and justice of God—the lost themselves. And this explains why even they will be raised one last time to appear before the tribunal. As the books open, the lost will review the mercy of God in dealing with them, the opportunities they had to know and obey the truth, the times the Holy Spirit spoke to their hearts convicting them of sin and righteousness and judgment to come (John 16:8), and yet they rejected it (Ephesians 4:30).

Even the people who did not have access to the Bible will be judged for the knowledge they did have. "The basic reality of God is plain enough. Open your eyes and there it is! By taking a long and thoughtful look at what God has created, people have always been able to see what their eyes as such can't see: eternal power, for instance, and the mystery of his divine being. So nobody has a good excuse" (Romans 1:19, 20, Message).

The blind poet Milton asked: "Doth God exact day-labour, light denied?"[2] The obvious answer is no. But we would have to ask: Is there anyone who has no light, no opportunity at all to know the truth about God? Nature alone may not be a sufficient guide, but the Holy Spirit speaks to everyone, giving at least some knowledge of the principles of righteousness and truth. "When Gentiles who do not have the Law do instinctively the things of the Law, these, not having the Law, are a law to themselves, in that they show the work of the Law written in their hearts [by the Spirit], their conscience bearing witness and their thoughts alternately accusing or else defending them" (Romans 2:14, 15).

So even those who have no access to the light of God's Word have the testimony of nature and the witness of His Spirit. "Great gifts mean great responsibilities; greater gifts, greater responsibilities" (Luke 12:48, Message). No one is without at least some gifts and some degree of responsibility before God.[3]

The last phase of judgment presents the perfect love and the perfect justice of God with overwhelming power. It is then that the words of Scripture have their complete and final fulfillment: "Every knee [absolutely and totally every knee] shall bow to Me, and every tongue shall give praise to God" (Roman 14:11).

Time	Who are judged	For benefit of	Verdict
Before the Second Coming	All who have professed faith in Jesus' sacrifice	Angels and other unfallen beings	God is just
During the 1,000 years	The lost	Redeemed	God is just
At the end of the 1,000 years	The lost	The lost	God is just

Here is a chart that will help clarify the three phases of the judgment as seen through the principle of divine transparency:

The third confession, in which even God's enemies acknowledge His justice, is not the result of a true conversion or change of heart, because soon after they have confessed God's justice, they will attack His people. "And they came up on the broad plain of the earth and surrounded the camp of the saints and the beloved city" (Revelation 20:9). After this final evidence of their irrevocable attitude of rebellion, the record says: "Fire came down from God out of heaven and devoured them" (verse 9, RSV).

Here is the fulfillment of the prophecy of Malachi: " 'For behold, the day is coming, burning like a furnace; and all the arrogant and every evildoer will be chaff; and the day that is coming will set them ablaze,' says the Lord of hosts, 'so that it will leave them neither root nor branch' " (Malachi 4:1). And of Peter: "But the day of the Lord will come like a thief, in which the heavens will pass away with a roar and the elements will be destroyed with intense heat, and the earth and its works will be burned up" (2 Peter 3:10).

"Be Diligent"

Then Peter asks us the most solemn question anyone could ever raise: "Since all these things are to be destroyed in this way, what sort of people ought you to be in holy conduct and godliness, looking for and hastening the coming of the day of God, on account of which the heavens will be destroyed by burning, and the elements will melt with intense heat! But according to His promise we are looking for new heavens and a new earth, in which righteousness dwells. Therefore, beloved, since you look for these things, be diligent to be found by Him in peace, spotless and blameless" (verses 11-14).

Think about the amazing effort that God has made to get His message across. Consider His sacrifice, which goes far beyond our comprehension. Contemplate the tremendous alternatives that He has set before us in His Word: on the one hand, eternal life in the company of Jesus and the angels and the redeemed of all ages; on the other, fire from God out of heaven, followed by eternal death.[4] With tenderness and infinite love He continues to invite everyone.

Don't look to the right or the left. It's you He's calling today. Ask yourself with the apostle: "How can we expect to escape punishment if we refuse this tremendous gift of salvation?" (Hebrews 2:3, Clear Word).

As you continue to respond each day to the call of God, He will bless you with more than you can imagine or hope. Why not record a few words expressing your acceptance and gratitude for this gift?

_____

_____

_____

---

[1] Scripture contains more evidence about the judgment previous to the Second Coming. See, for example, John 5:28, 29. See also chapter 24 about the sanctuary.

[2] John Milton, "On His Blindness" (c. 1670).

[3] Some may point to individuals born without enough mental capacity to make a rational decision. It is good to know that we can leave such cases in the hands of God, who is merciful and just.

[4] Some readers will recall having been told that the lost will burn forever, an idea based on Revelation 14:9-11: "If anyone worships the beast and his image, and receives a mark on his forehead or on his hand, he also will drink of the wine of the wrath of God, which is mixed in full strength in the cup of His anger; and he will be tormented with fire and brimstone in the presence of the holy angels and in the presence of the Lamb. And the smoke of their torment goes up forever and ever; and they have no rest day and night, those who worship the beast and his image, and whoever receives the mark of his name."

It is an allusion to a prophecy of Isaiah regarding the Edomites, who were enemies of God's people at that time: "For the Lord has a day of vengeance, a year of recompense for the cause of Zion. Its streams shall be turned into pitch, and its loose earth into brimstone, And its land shall become burning pitch. It shall not be quenched night or day; its smoke shall go up forever" (Isaiah 34:8-10). The Lord did punish the Edomites, but their land, which corresponds approximately to the present kingdom of Jordan, did not burn literally, and it is not still burning with fire and brimstone today. This graphic, vivid language is typical of apocalyptic prophecy, and it is symbolic rather than literal.

Chapter 26

Eternity Will Not Be Long Enough

During the last few days of my father's life he was comatose most of the time. We would talk and pray with him, but received no response. On Saturday our son Jonathan came from Grand Rapids, but Dad gave no sign that he was aware. The next morning, however, he opened his eyes and looked at me.

"How are you feeling, Father?" I asked him.

"Fine."

"You don't have any pain?"

"No," he replied. That seemed like a miracle, because he had bone cancer. The doctor had prescribed morphine, but he had never used it.

"Would you like some water?" He took a few sips.

"Did you know Jonathan was here yesterday?"

"Yes."

We talked a bit more. Then I said: "You know what the really good news is?"

He looked at me questioningly.

"Very soon we're going to see Jesus and be with Him forever," I said.

He smiled and nodded. A moment later he closed his eyes and slipped away again. That afternoon he died.

Maybe you remember that beautiful song:

"I'm homesick for heaven, seems I cannot wait.

Yearning to enter Zion's pearly gates.

Where never a heartache, never a care,

I long for my home over there."

Now more than ever!

Eternity Won't Be Long Enough

What a wonderful day that will be! Don't you agree?

Think of the glad reunions! Who are some of the people that you will look for when you first get to heaven? What will it be like when you can give them a hug! There will be tears, praise, and lots of thank-yous, won't there?

After our first family reunion, I'm going to look for Mrs. Shaftner, the fourth-grade teacher I loved and admired so much. And Victor Johnson. He was a music educator who taught us far more than notes and scales. Grace and Gene Thomsen were young teachers at Campion Academy who opened their hearts to a homesick kid. I owe them a lot. Thad Collins believed in me at a time I very much needed it . . . Well, the list would be much too long to give it all here. I owe so much to so many. Who are some of the people who would be on *your* list?

A tradition declares that our heavenly crown will have a star for every soul we have brought to Christ. If so, I'll be on the crown of more than one person, I think. And just imagine the crown of somebody such as the apostle Paul or the prophet Daniel. Maybe we will want to look for our sunglasses before we go to say hello to them.

We will tell Daniel how much his example of faithfulness blessed us, how his prophecies increased our faith as we saw the way they were fulfilled. Surely we will explain to him how his book of the Bible helped us to understand God and His mercy and wisdom. Then we will notice a quiet woman standing nearby, and Daniel will say, "Folks, I want you to meet this beautiful woman. She is my mother." Then we will look again and notice that her crown has as many stars as his—plus one more.

Think of the stories! We know from the Bible only a few highlights about some of the great heroes such as David, Elijah, Esther, Daniel, and Paul. Imagine how many more wonderful stories they can relate to us about things that happened during their long lives of faith! John the revelator saw the redeemed, and he said they were "a great multitude which no one could count" (Revelation 7:9). That gives us an idea of how many wonderful stories of grace and salvation there are. Every one of those people will have a thrilling testimony to share about God's love and care and personal blessings.

Some amazing stories about ourselves we won't know until we get there. Then the angels will recount the times they intervened to save and protect us. We'll realize that a lot of those times we weren't even aware of the danger.

Think of the questions! What would you like to ask some of the Bible characters if you could talk to them in person?

Methuselah, describe to us about growing up as Enoch's son. What was it like to have a father who walked so closely with God that finally the Lord took him?

Noah, what thoughts went through your mind when the sky grew dark and you heard those first raindrops?

Jochebed, tell about the years that Moses was growing up. What went through your mind every evening, when you knew you were one day closer to the time he would go to live as the son of Pharaoh's daughter? Did you have any idea of how God would use him in the coming years?

Moses, how did you keep from getting discouraged when the people were so perverse and ungrateful? How could you still love them and ask God to take your name out the book of life if they couldn't be saved?

Manoah, what was it like going to Samson's wedding and trying to act cheerful when your heart was breaking? Did you ask yourself: Where have I failed? What did I do wrong?

David, your songs have inspired and comforted us so many times. Thank you for opening your heart the way that you did. Maybe you still remember the tunes, the melodies, you composed for them? Could you sing some of them for us, please?

Paul, you wrote a few things not easy to understand. Even Peter recognized this (2 Peter 3:16). People have argued about some of them for centuries. Now, if you've got the time, we would like to ask you just a few questions . . .

Some of the questions we will want to ask there won't be easy. "Lord, You allowed some of Your most faithful servants to suffer and die under painful and tragic circumstances. Where were You then? Where were the angels that You said would keep us from even stubbing our toes" (see Psalm 91:11, 12)?

Don't worry. Jesus didn't get upset with Mary and Martha when they raised the issue after their brother died (John 11:21). So it will be OK for us to ask it of Him, too.

"Then much will be revealed in explanation of matters upon which God now keeps silence. ... The ways of Providence will be made clear; the mysteries of grace through Christ will be unfolded. That which the mind cannot now grasp, which is hard to be understood, will be explained. We shall see order in that which has seemed unexplainable; wisdom in everything withheld; goodness and gracious mercy in everything imparted. Truth will be unfolded to the mind, free from obscurity, in a single line, and its brightness will be endurable. The heart will be made to sing for joy. Controversies will be forever ended, and all difficulties will be solved" (*The Seventh-day Adventist Bible Commentary,* vol. 6, p. 1091).

Think of the opportunities for study and research! I'm sure some will have questions that have never occurred to me. What will the physicists want to know? And the historians? Imagine taking a class in biochemistry from the One who invented it. And the guided tours that will be part of Astronomy 101.

But a lot of things will not be instantly plain even when we hear the answer. Even though our minds will no longer be clouded by sin, it will still take a while to grasp and assimilate some aspects of truth. And each new revelation will open doors that invite us to enter avenues of further inquiry and research.

Theologians, scientists, and others who have spent their entire lives studying the deep things of God and His creation will no doubt have a head start on the rest of us. But all of us will be pretty much at the primary level when it comes to learning the really deep things that He will show us.

A lot of good people there will need to refocus because they dedicated their lives to areas of service no longer needed—those who worked in law enforcement, for example. The locksmiths, the undertakers, and the investment bankers will also have to shift their emphasis. But many of them have done their particular work because they have a natural gift for helping and serving others. They will still find plenty to do there. Maybe the health-care people can retrain as health educators and researchers. I'm pretty sure that even the farmers and gardeners will need to relearn the methods of agriculture in such a different setting.

Don't ever worry about what you will find to do in heaven! Eternity will not be long enough to exhaust all the possibilities for learning and exploring all the areas of interest that will open up to our undimmed view.

Think of meeting Jesus! Of course, the first and last, the best of all, is that we will see Jesus. We will bow at His feet. With our eyes filled with tears we will look at those scars. Instead of diminishing over time, our gratitude, our admiration and praise, will continue to grow as we learn more and more about the plan of salvation. "In the ages to come [God will] show the surpassing riches of His grace" (Ephesians 2:7). "Oh, the depth of the riches both of the wisdom and knowledge of God! How unsearchable are His judgments and unfathomable His ways!" (Romans 11:33).

"In this life we can only begin to understand the wonderful theme of redemption. With our finite comprehension we may consider most earnestly the shame and the glory, the life and the death, the justice and the mercy, that meet in the cross; yet with the utmost stretch of our mental powers we fail to grasp its full significance. The length and the breadth, the depth and the height, of redeeming love are but dimly comprehended. The plan of redemption will not be fully understood, even when the ransomed see as they are seen and know as they are known; but through the eternal ages, new truth will continually unfold to the wondering and delighted mind" (Ellen G. White, *God's Amazing Grace,* p. 98).

Eternity will not be long enough to fully explore all the riches of God's grace. We will continually discover more and more of His infinite wisdom and the love that He has displayed on our behalf. Neither will it not be long enough to fully thank and praise Him.

What else do you think about as you look forward to that day? What beauties will you want to enjoy, what deep and loving relationships will you want to develop, what areas of study and understanding come to mind? What skills in the arts and what areas of creativity would you like to expand? Think of the absolute ideal, the very best you can possibly imagine. Heaven will be a *lot* better than that.

"When Time Shall Be No More"

A well-known Christian song tells of "when the trumpet of the Lord shall sound, and time shall be no more." Some people take this as an accurate description of our situation in the future life. Eternity, they say, will not be an infinite extension of time, but a timeless state of existence. We will be like God, who, they believe, is also timeless. But we need to ask if such a view reflects sound biblical interpretation or ideas drawn from Greek philosophy. Those who hold such a concept may not have considered the fact that neither space nor matter can exist without time. Plato built his philosophy of idealism on the belief that ideas or concepts exist without reference to time, space, or matter. This, he held, is the true reality, whereas matter and space only appear to exist. But a careful study of Scripture offers no support for such a belief, which ends up spiritualizing, mythologizing, and, in fact, destroying all concrete reality, especially with regard to the future life.

Tale of Two Cities

The book of Revelation depicts two women. An angel who said to John, "Come here, I will show you . . ." introduced both of them. Then, both times, the angel carried the prophet away in spirit and showed him a woman who was also a city.

In the first case, the angel took John to a wilderness and revealed to him an evil woman "with whom the kings of the earth [have] committed acts of immorality, and those who dwell on the earth were made drunk with the wine of her immorality" (Revelation 17:1, 2). As the city of Babylon (verse 5), she represented false religion supported and enforced by civil authorities—the "kings of the earth." The "wine" symbolizes her teaching that confuses people's brains like an intoxicating drink.

Next an angel took John to a "great and high mountain" (Revelation 21:10) and showed him a pure woman who was "a bride adorned for her husband" (verse 2), the wife of the Lamb. She is also a city, the New Jerusalem, and John sees her "coming down out of heaven from God, having the glory of God. Her brilliance was like a very costly stone, as a stone of crystal-clear jasper" (Revelation 21:10, 11).

Just as the evil woman represents the enemies of God and their false teaching, the pure woman, the Lamb's bride, portrays His church, His people, and the truth they uphold.

Does this mean that what we read about the New Jerusalem in the book of Revelation is nothing more than symbolic language?

Our heavenly homeland is a real place—it is concrete and not to be lost in the mists of someone's imagination, but the description we have of it may not be entirely literal, because the reality it represents is beyond anything that we know at present. For example, John saw a record book opened in heaven. He viewed it as a papyrus scroll. Why? Because that was the kind of book that John knew and could relate to. If God had shown him a computer, it would have been meaningless to him. Was the papyrus scroll literal? Do the angels sit there writing with a quill pen? Of course not. Does it represent something that is real? Certainly. The fundamental truth is that God has a system of recordkeeping. We don't know, and we don't need to know, exactly how it works. The way that God preserves His records is as far beyond computers as computers are beyond parchment scrolls and quill pens. But we can be sure that it is real.

And behind this fundamental truth about God's recordkeeping there looms one that is far more important: God is holding us accountable for what we do and say. It might be interesting to know more details about how the system works. But that is secondary to the fundamental truth of our responsibility before God. And if we really want to know more about the record system and more, we can soon find out, because before long Jesus will come to take us home. Until then, we must be content to say what the Bible reveals about it, and leave it at that. "The secret things belong to the Lord our God, but the things revealed belong to us and to our sons forever, that we may observe all the words of this law" (Deuteronomy 29:29).

Lessons for Life Here and Now

As our example illustrates, it would be a mistake to focus on the literal description of the future life if we fail to see spiritual truths that are far more important. For example, ancient cities had high walls, as the one in the book of Revelation does, but they had as few gates as possible, because every gate was a weak spot in the city's defenses. But the New Jerusalem has 12 gates (Revelation 21:12). Furthermore, we read that its gates never close by day, and there is no night there (Revelation 21:25; 22:5). What does this tell us? Remember that the city represents the Lamb's bride, His people.

John saw "a river of the water of life, clear as crystal, coming from the throne of God and of the Lamb" (Revelation 22:1) What does this reveal?

"On either side of the river was the tree of life, bearing twelve kinds of fruit, yielding its fruit every month; and the leaves of the tree were for the healing of the nations" (verse 2). All who receive the Word of God into their hearts can know here and now what it means to eat the leaves of the tree of life and drink of that life-giving water. A current of spiritual life will refresh their souls as they believe and practice the Word. The weak and timid become strong and their faith unshakable. The water of life that comes to strengthen and refresh their souls flows through them and goes out to gladden the hearts of all around (see John 7:38).

"As through Jesus we enter into rest, heaven begins here. We respond to His invitation, Come, learn of Me, and in thus coming we begin the life eternal. Heaven is a ceaseless approaching to God through Christ. The longer we are in the heaven of bliss, the more and still more of glory will be opened to us; and the more we know of God, the more intense will be our happiness. As we walk with Jesus in this life, we may be filled with His love, satisfied with His presence. All that human nature can bear, we may receive here. But what is this compared with the hereafter? There 'are they before the throne of God, and serve him day and night in his temple: and he that sitteth on the throne shall dwell among them. They shall hunger no more, neither thirst any more; neither shall the sun light on them, nor any heat. For the Lamb which is in the midst of the throne shall feed them, and shall lead them unto living fountains of waters: and God shall wipe away all tears from their eyes'" (Ellen G. White, *The Desire of Ages,* pp. 331, 332).

Nothing in the present life can compare with the wonderful privilege of walking with God here and now. Moses understood this. That's why he "refused to be called the son of Pharaoh's daughter, choosing rather to endure ill-treatment with the people of God" (Hebrews 11:24, 25). He knew that even "the reproach of Christ [was] greater riches than the treasures of Egypt" (verse 26).

The apostle Paul also put on the scales all the wealth, the degrees, academic honors, and family ties, all the positions of influence and prestige that he had once valued so highly. And he found their value to be nothing, and less than nothing. They were "rubbish" compared with the glorious privilege of knowing Jesus and of fellowship with Him in a life of service (Philippians 3:7-10).

These individuals knew, as every child of God can, that "as we walk with Jesus in this life, we may be filled with His love, satisfied with His presence."

And yet the question still remains: "But what is this compared with the hereafter?" If walking with God in this life and the peace that He gives us here and now already surpass "all comprehension" (Philippians 4:7), what will it be like to walk with Him there, where we will see Him face to face (1 Corinthians 13:12), where no one will ever say, "I am sick" (Isaiah 33:24), and where "the wolf will dwell with the lamb, and the leopard will lie down with the young goat, . . . and a little boy will lead them" (Isaiah 11:6).

Why Wait?

All of this calls for a response on our part, doesn't it? If we were talking about some far-off, future event, it might make sense to say: *That's nice, but I still have plenty of time to decide.* But what He is offering us is fellowship right here and right now. Why would you want to wait even one more day to begin to enjoy it?

Maybe you are already committed to God. Perhaps everyone who knows you thinks of you as a Christian, but you know your own heart, and the Spirit has brought you under conviction that you are far from enjoying that beautiful communion as you could be. If that is the case, why wait any longer? Step forward and make it your own. Allow the fullness of His love to warm your soul. Don't deprive yourself even for another minute of that wonderful experience.

On the other hand, maybe you have never made a public commitment to serve God. Think about how your life could be different if you did. What do you have to lose and what do you have to gain by such a decision? Please do consider carefully the alternatives. Remember the incredible effort that God has made to make them plain to us. Yes, I know you have received blessings already, but they are only an appetizer—a few drops in comparison to what our Father has in store for you as you commit your life to Him.

"As it is written:
'No eye has seen,
   no ear has heard,
  no mind has conceived,
   what God has prepared
    for those who love him'"
      — Corinthians 2:9, NIV

He wants you to do something more than just say "That's nice." Because if that's all you do, you know what will happen: the pressures of life will take over, and the conviction you have from the Holy Spirit will fade. The only way this can be of any definite and lasting value will be if you express your decision in a concrete way. In many cases this will imply baptism. And it will certainly call for church fellowship and a public visible commitment to a life of faith.

Do it your own way, and say it in your own words, because it's your heart and your life, and the Spirit speaks to each of us individually according to our needs. But before you put this book down, I hope you will compose a short statement of commitment. And at the end, add a few words about your intentions and how you plan to follow up on your decision in a practical way. God will receive you into His arms and bless you more than you can imagine as you do this.

_____

_____

_____

_____

_____

_____

Appendix

Fundamental Belief 1—The Holy Scriptures:

The Holy Scriptures, Old and New Testaments, are the written Word of God, given by divine inspiration through holy men of God who spoke and wrote as they were moved by the Holy Spirit. In this Word, God has committed to man the knowledge necessary for salvation. The Holy Scriptures are the infallible revelation of His will. They are the standard of character, the test of experience, the authoritative revealer of doctrines, and the trustworthy record of God's acts in history. (2 Peter 1:20, 21; 2 Timothy 3:16, 17; Psalm 19:105; Proverbs 30:5, 6; Isaiah 8:20; John 17:17; 1 Thessalonians 2:13; Hebrews 4:12.)

Fundamental Belief 2—The Trinity:

There is one God: Father, Son, and Holy Spirit, a unity of three coeternal Persons. God is immortal, all-powerful, all-knowing, above all, and ever present. He is infinite and beyond human comprehension, yet known through His self-revelation. He is forever worthy of worship, adoration, and service by the whole creation. (Deuteronomy 6:4; Matthew 28:19; 2 Corinthians 13:14; Ephesians 4:4-6; 1 Peter 1:2; 1 Timothy 1:17; Revelation 14:7.)

Fundamental Belief 3—The Father:

God the eternal Father is the Creator, Source, Sustainer, and Sovereign of all creation. He is just and holy, merciful and gracious, slow to anger, and abounding in steadfast love and faithfulness. The qualities and powers exhibited in the Son and the Holy Spirit are also revelations of the Father. (Genesis 1:1; Revelation 4:11; 1 Corinthians 15:28; John 3:16; 1 John 4:8; 1 Timothy 1:17; Exodus 34:6, 7; John 14:9.)

Fundamental Belief 4—The Son:

God the eternal Son became incarnate in Jesus Christ. Through Him all things were created, the character of God is revealed, the salvation of humanity is accomplished, and the world is judged. Forever truly God, He became also truly man, Jesus the Christ. He was conceived of the Holy Spirit and born of the virgin Mary. He lived and experienced temptation as a human being, but perfectly exemplified the righteousness and love of God. By His miracles He manifested God's power and was attested as God's promised Messiah. He suffered and died voluntarily on the cross for our sins and in our place, was raised from the dead, and ascended to minister in the heavenly sanctuary in our behalf. He will come again in glory for the final deliverance of His people and the restoration of all things. (John 1:1-3, 14; Colossians 1:15-19; John 10:30; 14:9; Romans 6:23; 2 Corinthians 5:17-19; John 5:22; Luke 1:35; Philippians 2:5-11; Hebrews 2:9-18; 1 Corinthians 15:3, 4; Hebrews 8:1, 2; John 14:13.)

Fundamental Belief 5—The Holy Spirit:

God the eternal Spirit was active with the Father and the Son in Creation, incarnation, and redemption. He inspired the writers of Scripture. He filled Christ's life with power. He draws and convicts human beings; and those who respond He renews and transforms into the image of God. Sent by the Father and the Son to be always with His children, He extends spiritual gifts to the church, empowers it to bear witness to Christ, and in harmony with the Scriptures leads it into all truth. (Genesis 1:1, 2; Luke 1:35; 4:18; Acts 10:38; 2 Peter 1:21; 2 Corinthians 3:18; Ephesians 4:11, 12; Acts 1:8; John 14:16-18, 26; 15:26, 27; 16:7-13.)

Fundamental Belief 6—Creation:

God is Creator of all things, and has revealed in Scripture the authentic account of His creative activity. In six days the Lord made "the heaven and the earth" and all living things upon the earth, and rested on the seventh day of that first week. Thus He established the Sabbath as a perpetual memorial of His completed creative work. The first man and woman were made in the image of God as the crowning work of Creation, given dominion over the world, and charged with responsibility to care for it. When the world was finished it was "very good," declaring the glory of God. (Genesis 1; 2; Exodus 20:8-11; Psalm 19:1-6; 33:6, 9; 104; Hebrews 11:3.)

Fundamental Belief 7—The Nature of Man:

Man and woman were made in the image of God with individuality, the power and freedom to think and to do. Though created free beings, each is an indivisible unity of body, mind, and spirit, dependent upon God for life and breath and all else. When our first parents disobeyed God, they denied their dependence upon Him and fell from their high position under God. The image of God in them was marred and they became subject to death. Their descendants share this fallen nature and its consequences. They are born with weaknesses and tendencies to evil. But God in Christ reconciled the world to Himself and by His Spirit restores in penitent mortals the image of their Maker. Created for the glory of God, they are called to love Him and one another, and to care for their environment. (Genesis 1:26-28; 2:7; Psalm 8:4-8; Acts 17:24-28; Genesis 3; Psalm 51:5; Romans 5:12-17; 2 Corinthians 5:19, 20; Psalm 51:10; 1 John 4:7, 8, 11, 20; Genesis 2:15.)

Fundamental Belief 8—The Great Controversy:

All humanity is now involved in a great controversy between Christ and Satan regarding the character of God, His law, and His sovereignty over the universe. This conflict originated in heaven when a created being, endowed with freedom of choice, in self-exaltation became Satan, God's adversary, and led into rebellion a portion of the angels. He introduced the spirit of rebellion into this world when he led Adam and Eve into sin. This human sin resulted in the distortion of the image of God in humanity, the disordering of the created world, and its eventual devastation at the time of the worldwide flood. Observed by the whole creation, this world became the arena of the universal conflict, out of which the God of love will ultimately be vindicated. To assist His people in this controversy, Christ sends the Holy Spirit and the loyal angels to guide, protect, and sustain them in the way of salvation. (Revelation 12:4-9; Isaiah 14:12-14; Ezekiel 28:12-18; Genesis 3; Romans 1:19-32; 5:12-21; 8:19-22; Genesis 6-8; 2 Peter 3:6; 1 Corinthians 4:9; Hebrews 1:14.)

Fundamental Belief 9—The Life, Death, and Resurrection of Christ:

In Christ's life of perfect obedience to God's will, His suffering, death, and resurrection, God provided the only means of atonement for human sin, so that those who by faith accept this atonement may have eternal life, and the whole creation may better understand the infinite and holy love of the Creator. This perfect atonement vindicates the righteousness of God's law and the graciousness of His character; for it both condemns our sin and provides for our forgiveness. The death of Christ is substitutionary and expiatory, reconciling and transforming. The resurrection of Christ proclaims God's triumph over the forces of evil, and for those who accept the atonement assures their final victory over sin and death. It declares the Lordship of Jesus Christ, before whom every knee in heaven and on earth will bow. (John 3:16; Isaiah 53; 1 Peter 2:21, 22; 1 Corinthians 15:3, 4, 20-22; 2 Corinthians 5:14, 15, 19-21; Romans 1:4; 3:25; 4:25; 8:3, 4; 1 John 2:2; 4:10; Colossians 2:15; Philippians 2:6-11.)

Fundamental Belief 10—The Experience of Salvation:

In infinite love and mercy God made Christ, who knew no sin, to be sin for us, so that in Him we might be made the righteousness of God. Led by the Holy Spirit we sense our need, acknowledge our sinfulness, repent of our transgressions, and exercise faith in Jesus as Lord and Christ, as Substitute and Example. This faith which receives salvation comes through the divine power of the Word and is the gift of God's grace. Through Christ we are justified, adopted as God's sons and daughters, and delivered from the lordship of sin. Through the Spirit we are born again and sanctified; the Spirit renews our minds, writes God's law of love in our hearts, and we are given the power to live a holy life. Abiding in Him we become partakers of the divine nature and have the assurance of salvation now and in the judgment. (2 Corinthians 5:17-21; John 3:16; Galatians 1:4; 4:4-7; Titus 3:3-7; John 16:8; Galatians 3:13, 14; 1 Peter 2:21, 22; Romans 10:17; Luke 17:5; Mark 9:23, 24; Ephesians 2:5-10; Romans 3:21-26; Colossians 1:13, 14; Romans 8:14-17; Galatians 3:26; John 3:3-8; 1 Peter 1:23; Romans 12:2; Hebrews 8:7-12; Ezekiel 36:25-27; 2 Peter 1:3, 4; Romans 8:1-4; 5:6-10.)

Fundamental Belief 11—Growing in Christ:

By His death on the cross Jesus triumphed over the forces of evil. He who subjugated the demonic spirits during His earthly ministry has broken their power and made certain their ultimate doom. Jesus' victory gives us victory over the evil forces that still seek to control us, as we walk with Him in peace, joy, and assurance of His love. Now the Holy Spirit dwells within us and empowers us. Continually committed to Jesus as our Savior and Lord, we are set free from the burden of our past deeds. No longer do we live in the darkness, fear of evil powers, ignorance, and meaninglessness of our former way of life. In this new freedom in Jesus, we are called to grow into the likeness of His character, communing with Him daily in prayer, feeding on His Word, meditating on it and on His providence, singing His praises, gathering together for worship, and participating in the mission of the church. As we give ourselves in loving service to those around us and in witnessing to His salvation, His constant presence with us through the Spirit transforms every moment and every task into a spiritual experience. (Psalm 1:1, 2; 23:4; 77:11, 12; Colossians 1:13, 14; 2:6, 14, 15; Luke 10:17-20; Ephesians 5:19, 20; 6:12-18; 1 Thessalonians 5:23; 2 Peter 2:9; 3:18; 2 Corinthians 3:17, 18; Philippians 3:7-14; 1 Thessalonians 5:16-18; Matthew 20:25-28; John 20:21; Galatians 5:22-25; Romans 8:38, 39; 1 John 4:4; Hebrews 10:25.)

Fundamental Belief 12—The Church:

The church is the community of believers who confess Jesus Christ as Lord and Savior. In continuity with the people of God in Old Testament times, we are called out from the world; and we join together for worship, for fellowship, for instruction in the Word, for the celebration of the Lord's Supper, for service to all mankind, and for the worldwide proclamation of the gospel. The church derives its authority from Christ, who is the incarnate Word, and from the Scriptures, which are the written Word. The church is God's family; adopted by Him as children, its members live on the basis of the new covenant. The church is the body of Christ, a community of faith of which Christ Himself is the Head. The church is the bride for whom Christ died that He might sanctify and cleanse her. At His return in triumph, He will present her to Himself a glorious church, the faithful of all the ages, the purchase of His blood, not having spot or wrinkle, but holy and without blemish. (Genesis 12:3; Acts 7:38; Ephesians

4:11-15; 3:8-11; Matthew 28:19, 20; 16:13-20; 18:18; Ephesians 2:19-22; 1:22, 23; 5:23-27; Colossians 1:17, 18.)

Fundamental Belief 13—The Remnant and Its Mission:

The universal church is composed of all who truly believe in Christ, but in the last days, a time of widespread apostasy, a remnant has been called out to keep the commandments of God and the faith of Jesus. This remnant announces the arrival of the judgment hour, proclaims salvation through Christ, and heralds the approach of His second advent. This proclamation is symbolized by the three angels of Revelation 14; it coincides with the work of judgment in heaven and results in a work of repentance and reform on earth. Every believer is called to have a personal part in this worldwide witness. (Revelation 12:17; 14:6-12; 18:1-4; 2 Corinthians 5:10; Jude 3, 14; 1 Peter 1:16-19; 2 Peter 3:10-14; Revelation 21:1-14.)

Fundamental Belief 14—Unity in the Body of Christ:

The church is one body with many members, called from every nation, kindred, tongue, and people. In Christ we are a new creation; distinctions of race, culture, learning, and nationality, and differences between high and low, rich and poor, male and female, must not be divisive among us. We are all equal in Christ, who by one Spirit has bonded us into one fellowship with Him and with one another; we are to serve and be served without partiality or reservation. Through the revelation of Jesus Christ in the Scriptures we share the same faith and hope, and reach out in one witness to all. This unity has its source in the oneness of the triune God, who has adopted us as His children. (Romans 12:4, 5; 1 Corinthians 12:12-14; Matthew 28:19, 20; Psalm 133:1; 2 Corinthians 5:16, 17; Acts 17:26, 27; Galatians 3:27, 29; Colossians 3:10-15; Ephesians 4:14-16; 4:1-6; John 17:20-23.)

Fundamental Belief 15—Baptism:

By baptism we confess our faith in the death and resurrection of Jesus Christ, and testify of our death to sin and of our purpose to walk in newness of life. Thus we acknowledge Christ as Lord and Savior, become His people, and are received as members by His church. Baptism is a symbol of our union with Christ, the forgiveness of our sins, and our reception of the Holy Spirit.

It is by immersion in water and is contingent on an affirmation of faith in Jesus and evidence of repentance of sin. It follows instruction in the Holy Scriptures and acceptance of their teachings. (Romans 6:6; Colossians 2:12, 13; Acts 16:30-33; 22:16; 2:38; Matthew 28:19, 20.)

Fundamental Belief 16—The Lord's Supper (Communion):

The Lord's Supper is a participation in the emblems of the body and blood of Jesus as an expression of faith in Him, our Lord and Savior. In this experience of communion Christ is present to meet and strengthen His people. As we partake, we joyfully proclaim the Lord's death until He comes again. Preparation for the Supper includes self-examination, repentance, and confession. The Master ordained the service of foot washing to signify renewed cleansing, to express a willingness to serve one another in Christlike humility, and to unite our hearts in love. The communion service is open to all believing Christians. (1 Corinthians 10:16, 17; 11:23-30; Matthew 26:17-30; Revelation 3:20; John 6:48-63; 13:1-17.)

Fundamental Belief 17—Spiritual Gifts:

God bestows upon all members of His church in every age spiritual gifts which each member is to employ in loving ministry for the common good of the church and of humanity. Given by the agency of the Holy Spirit, who apportions to each member as He wills, the gifts provide all abilities and ministries needed by the church to fulfill its divinely ordained functions. According to the Scriptures, these gifts include such ministries as faith, healing, prophecy, teaching, administration, reconciliation, compassion, and self-sacrificing service and charity for the help and encouragement of people. Some members are called of God and endowed by the Spirit for functions recognized by the church in pastoral, evangelistic, apostolic, and teaching ministries particularly needed to equip the members for service, to build up the church to spiritual ministry, and to foster unity of the faith and knowledge of God. When members employ these spiritual gifts as faithful stewards of God's varied grace, the church is protected from the destructive influence of false doctrine, grows with a growth that is from God, and is built up in faith and love. (Romans 12:4-8; 1 Corinthians 12:9-11, 27, 28; Ephesians 4:8, 11-16; Acts 6:1-7; 1 Timothy 3:1-13; 1 Peter 4:10, 11.)

Fundamental Belief 18—The Gift of Prophecy:

One of the gifts of the Holy Spirit is prophecy. This gift is an identifying mark of the remnant church and was manifested in the ministry of Ellen G. White. As the Lord's messenger, her writings are a continuing and authoritative source of truth which provide for the church comfort, guidance, instruction, and correction. They also make clear that the Bible is the standard by which all teaching and experience must be tested. (Joel 2:28, 29; Acts 2:14-21; Hebrews 1:1-3; Revelation 12:17; 19:10.)

Fundamental Belief 19—The Law of God:

The great principles of God's law are embodied in the Ten Commandments and exemplified in the life of Christ. They express God's love, will, and purposes concerning human conduct and relationships and are binding upon all people in every age. These precepts are the basis of God's covenant with His people and the standard in God's judgment. Through the agency of the Holy Spirit they point out sin and awaken a sense of need for a Savior. Salvation is all of grace and not of works, but its fruitage is obedience to the Commandments. This obedience develops Christian character and results in a sense of well-being. It is an evidence of our love for the Lord and our concern for our fellow men. The obedience of faith demonstrates the power of Christ to transform lives, and therefore strengthens Christian witness. (Exodus 20:1-17; Psalm 40:7, 8; Matthew 22:36-40; Deuteronomy 28:1-14; Matthew 5:17-20; Hebrews 8:8-10; John 15:7-10; Ephesians 2:8-10; 1 John 5:3; Romans 8:3, 4; Psalm 19:7-14.)

Fundamental Belief 20—The Sabbath:

The beneficent Creator, after the six days of Creation, rested on the seventh day and instituted the Sabbath for all people as a memorial of Creation. The fourth commandment of God's unchangeable law requires the observance of this seventh-day Sabbath as the day of rest, worship, and ministry in harmony with the teaching and practice of Jesus, the Lord of the Sabbath. The Sabbath is a day of delightful communion with God and one another. It is a symbol of our redemption in Christ, a sign of our sanctification, a token of our allegiance, and a foretaste of our eternal future in God's kingdom. The Sabbath is God's perpetual sign of His eternal covenant between

Him and His people. Joyful observance of this holy time from evening to evening, sunset to sunset, is a celebration of God's creative and redemptive acts. (Genesis 2:1-3; Exodus 20:1-11; Luke 4:16; Isaiah 56:5, 6; 58:13, 14; Matthew 12:1-12; Exodus 31:13-17; Ezekiel 20:12, 20; Deuteronomy 5:12-15; Hebrews 4:1-11; Leviticus 23:32; Mark 1:32.)

Fundamental Belief 21—Stewardship:

We are God's stewards, entrusted by Him with time and opportunities, abilities and possessions, and the blessings of the earth and its resources. We are responsible to Him for their proper use. We acknowledge God's ownership by faithful service to Him and our fellow men, and by returning tithes and giving offerings for the proclamation of His gospel and the support and growth of His church. Stewardship is a privilege given to us by God for nurture in love and the victory over selfishness and covetousness. The steward rejoices in the blessings that come to others as a result of his faithfulness. (Genesis 1:26-28; 2:15; 1 Chronicles 29:14; Haggai 1:3-11; Malachi 3:8-12; 1 Corinthians 9:9-14; Matthew 23:23; 2 Corinthians 8:1-15; Romans 15:26, 27.)

Fundamental Belief 22—Christian Behavior:

We are called to be a godly people who think, feel, and act in harmony with the principles of heaven. For the Spirit to re-create in us the character of our Lord we involve ourselves only in those things which will produce Christlike purity, health, and joy in our lives. This means that our amusement and entertainment should meet the highest standards of Christian taste and beauty. While recognizing cultural differences, our dress is to be simple, modest, and neat, befitting those whose true beauty does not consist of outward adornment but in the imperishable ornament of a gentle and quiet spirit. It also means that because our bodies are the temples of the Holy Spirit, we are to care for them intelligently. Along with adequate exercise and rest, we are to adopt the most healthful diet possible and abstain from the unclean foods identified in the Scriptures. Since alcoholic beverages, tobacco, and the irresponsible use of drugs and narcotics are harmful to our bodies, we are to abstain from them as well. Instead, we are to engage in whatever brings our thoughts and bodies into the discipline of Christ, who desires our wholesomeness, joy, and goodness. (Romans 12:1, 2; 1 John 2:6; Ephesians 5:1-21; Philippians 4:8; 2 Corinthians 10:5; 6:14-7:1; 1 Peter 3:1-4; 1 Corinthians 6:19, 20; 10:31; Leviticus 11:1-47; 3 John 2.)

Fundamental Belief 23—Marriage and the Family:

Marriage was divinely established in Eden and affirmed by Jesus to be a lifelong union between a man and a woman in loving companionship. For the Christian a marriage commitment is to God as well as to the spouse, and should be entered into only between partners who share a common faith. Mutual love, honor, respect, and responsibility are the fabric of this relationship, which is to reflect the love, sanctity, closeness, and permanence of the relationship between Christ and His church. Regarding divorce, Jesus taught that the person who divorces a spouse, except for fornication, and marries another, commits adultery. Although some family relationships may fall short of the ideal, marriage partners who fully commit themselves to each other in Christ may achieve loving unity through the guidance of the Spirit and the nurture of the church. God blesses the family and intends that its members shall assist each other toward complete maturity. Parents are to bring up their children to love and obey the Lord. By their example and their words they are to teach them that Christ is a loving disciplinarian, ever tender and caring, who wants them to become members of His body, the family of God. Increasing family closeness is one of the earmarks of the final gospel message. (Genesis 2:18-25; Matthew 19:3-9; John 2:1-11; 2 Corinthians 6:14; Ephesians 5:21-33; Matthew 5:31, 32; Mark 10:11, 12; Luke 16:18; 1 Corinthians 7:10, 11; Exodus 20:12; Ephesians 6:1-4; Deuteronomy 6:5-9; Proverbs 22:6; Malachi 4:5, 6.)

Fundamental Belief 24—Christ's Ministry in the Heavenly Sanctuary:

There is a sanctuary in heaven, the true tabernacle which the Lord set up and not man. In it Christ ministers on our behalf, making available to believers the benefits of His atoning sacrifice offered once for all on the cross. He was inaugurated as our great High Priest and began His intercessory ministry at the time of His ascension. In 1844, at the end of the prophetic period of 2300 days, He entered the second and last phase of His atoning ministry. It is a work of investigative judgment which is part of the ultimate disposition of all sin, typified by the cleansing of the ancient Hebrew sanctuary on the Day of Atonement. In that typical service the sanctuary was cleansed with the blood of animal sacrifices, but the heavenly things are purified with the perfect sacrifice of the blood of Jesus. The investigative judgment reveals to heavenly intelligences who among the dead are asleep in Christ and therefore, in Him, are deemed worthy to have part in the first resurrection. It also makes manifest who among the living are abiding in Christ, keeping the commandments of God and the faith of Jesus, and in Him, therefore, are ready for translation into His everlasting kingdom. This judgment vindicates the justice of God in saving those who believe in Jesus. It declares that those who have remained loyal to God shall receive the kingdom. The completion of this ministry of Christ will mark the close of human probation before the Second Advent. (Hebrews 8:1-5; 4:14-16; 9:11-28; 10:19-22; 1:3; 2:16, 17; Daniel 7:9-27; 8:13, 14; 9:24-27; Numbers 14:34; Ezekiel 4:6; Leviticus 16; Revelation 14:6, 7; 20:12; 14:12; 22:12.)

Fundamental Belief 25—The Second Coming of Christ:

The second coming of Christ is the blessed hope of the church, the grand climax of the gospel. The Savior's coming will be literal, personal, visible, and worldwide. When He returns, the righteous dead will be resurrected, and together with the righteous living will be glorified and taken to heaven, but the unrighteous will die. The almost complete fulfillment of most lines of prophecy, together with the present condition of the world, indicates that Christ's coming is imminent. The time of that event has not been revealed, and we are therefore exhorted to be ready at all times. (Titus 2:13; Hebrews 9:28; John 14:1-3; Acts 1:9-11; Matthew 24:14; Revelation 1:7; Matthew 24:43, 44; 1 Thessalonians 4:13-18; 1 Corinthians 15:51-54; 2 Thessalonians 1:7-10; 2:8; Revelation 14:14-20; 19:11-21; Matthew 24; Mark 13; Luke 21; 2 Timothy 3:1-5; 1 Thessalonians 5:1-6.)

Fundamental Belief 26—Death and Resurrection:

The wages of sin is death. But God, who alone is immortal, will grant eternal life to His redeemed. Until that day death is an unconscious state for all people. When Christ, who is our life, appears, the resurrected righteous and the living righteous will be glorified and caught up to meet their Lord. The second resurrection, the resurrection of the unrighteous, will take place a thousand years later. (Romans 6:23; 1 Timothy 6:15, 16; Ecclesiastes 9:5, 6; Psalm 146:3, 4; John 11:11-14; Colossians 3:4; 1 Corinthians 15:51-54; 1 Thessalonians 4:13-17; John 5:28, 29; Revelation 20:1-10.)

Fundamental Belief 27—The Millennium and the End of Sin:

The millennium is the thousand-year reign of Christ with His saints in heaven between the first and second resurrections. During this time the wicked dead will be judged; the earth will be utterly desolate, without living human inhabitants, but occupied by Satan and his angels. At its close Christ with His saints and the Holy City will descend from heaven to earth. The unrighteous dead will then be resurrected, and with Satan and his angels will surround the city; but fire from God will consume them and cleanse the earth. The universe will thus be freed of sin and sinners forever. (Revelation 20; 1 Corinthians 6:2, 3; Jeremiah 4:23-26; Revelation 21:1-5; Malachi 4:1; Ezekiel 28:18, 19.)

Fundamental Belief 28—The New Earth:

On the new earth, in which righteousness dwells, God will provide an eternal home for the redeemed and a perfect environment for everlasting life, love, joy, and learning in His presence. For here God Himself will dwell with His people, and suffering and death will have passed away. The great controversy will be ended, and sin will be no more. All things, animate and inanimate, will declare that God is love; and He shall reign forever. Amen. (2 Peter 3:13; Isaiah 35; 65:17-25; Matthew 5:5; Revelation 21:1-7; 22:1-5; 11:15.)

GLOBAL EVENTS AND
YOUR FUTURE

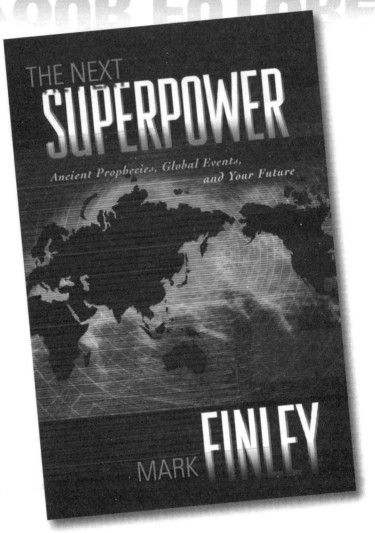

THE NEXT
SUPERPOWER
Ancient Prophecies, Global Events, and Your Future

MARK **FINLEY**

Mark Finley explores ancient prophecies, exposes common misunderstandings about the end-times, and explains related teachings such as the Second Coming, the Sabbath, and the state of the dead—and how it all affects you. 978-0-8280-1918-7. Hardcover.